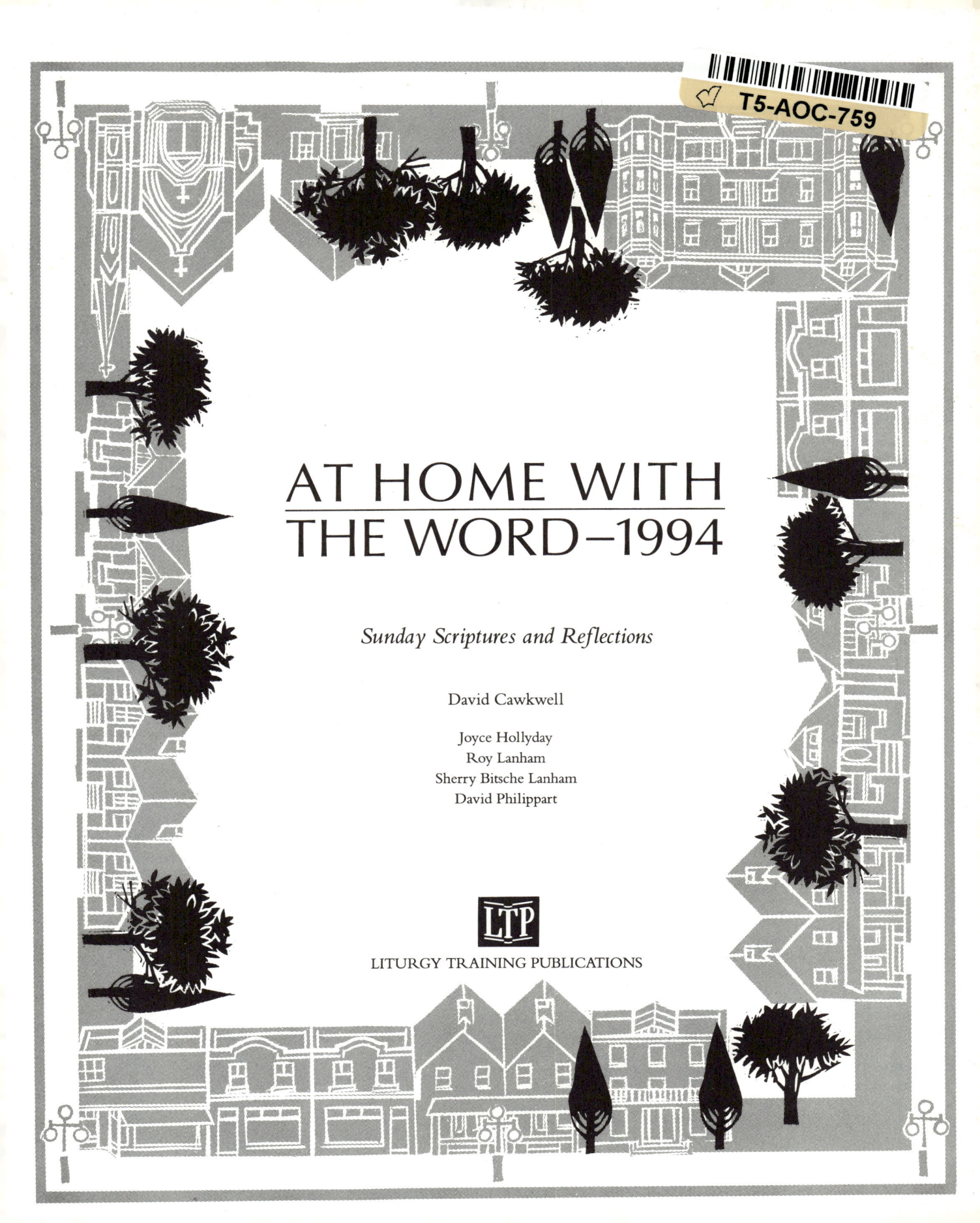

AT HOME WITH THE WORD—1994

Sunday Scriptures and Reflections

David Cawkwell

Joyce Hollyday
Roy Lanham
Sherry Bitsche Lanham
David Philippart

LTP
LITURGY TRAINING PUBLICATIONS

Reprinting from *At Home with the Word 1994*

A parish or an institution may purchase a license to reprint the Reflections (and their discussion questions), Practices of Faith, Hope and Charity, the Prayer of the Season or the holy day boxes from *At Home with the Word 1994*. Please see page 158 for details.

If a parish or institution wishes to reproduce some or all of the scripture texts or prayer texts, a license must be acquired from the copyright owners. (See below.) When writing to copyright owners, state clearly which texts you wish to use, the number of copies to be made, and how often you'll be using the copies. There may be a license fee.

Acknowledgments

The Sunday scripture pericopes contained herein are from the *Revised Standard Version Bible,* copyright © 1946, 1952, 1971 by the Division of Christian Education of the National Council of Churches of Christ in the U.S.A., as emended in the *Lectionary for the Christian People,* copyright © 1988 by Pueblo Publishing Company, Inc. Used with permission. All rights reserved. For information on reprint permission, write: The Liturgical Press, St. John's Abbey, Collegeville MN 56321.

Most Roman Catholic parishes proclaim the Sunday scriptures using the *New American Bible* readings from the *Lectionary for Mass,* copyright © 1970 by the Confraternity of Christian Doctrine. For information on reprint permission, write: Confraternity of Christian Doctrine, 1312 Massachusetts Avenue NW, Washington DC 20005.

The translations of the psalms used herein are copyright © 1986, 1989 and 1990 by the International Committee on English in the Liturgy, Inc. (ICEL); excerpts from the English translation of *The Roman Missal,* copyright © 1973 by ICEL; the English translation of the gospel canticles ("Canticle of Zechariah," "Canticle of Mary" and "Canticle of Simeon") are copyright © 1990 by ICEL; the "Salve Regina" from *A Book of Prayers,* copyright © 1982 by ICEL. Used with permission. All rights reserved. For reprint permission, write: ICEL, 1275 K Street NW, Suite 1202, Washington DC 20005-4097.

The Prayers of the Season were written by Gabe Huck.

The holy day commentaries were written by Peter Mazar.

The art in this book is by Suzanne Novak. Jane Kremsreiter and Jill Smith designed the book. Sheila McLaughlin, Jerry Reedy and Sarah Huck assisted the editor, David Philippart. Typesetting was done by Kari Nicholls; the text is set in Optima and Sabon. The book was printed and bound by Noll Printing, Huntington, Indiana.

At Home with the Word 1994, copyright © 1993, Archdiocese of Chicago: Liturgy Training Publications. All rights reserved.

Printed in the United States of America.

ISBN-0-929650-97-2

Order additional copies of *At Home with the Word 1994* from:
Liturgy Training Publications
1800 North Hermitage Avenue
Chicago IL 60622-1101
1-800-933-1800 (FAX: 1-800-933-7094)

*Receive with meekness the implanted word,
which is able to save your souls.
Be doers of the word,
and not hearers only.*

JAMES 1:21-22

CALENDAR
TABLE OF CONTENTS

- 6 HOW TO USE *AT HOME WITH THE WORD*
- 8 AN INTRODUCTION TO THE GOSPEL OF MARK
- 10 MORNING PRAYER
- 12 EVENING PRAYER
- 14 NIGHT PRAYER
- 16 SUNDAY PRAYER
- 17 FRIDAY PRAYER
- 18 THE ORDER OF MASS

ADVENT PSALM
page 22

- 24 NOVEMBER 28, 1993
  First Sunday of Advent
- 26 DECEMBER 5, 1993
  Second Sunday of Advent
    - ◆ The Immaculate Conception of Mary: December 8
- 29 DECEMBER 12, 1993
  Third Sunday of Advent
- 30 DECEMBER 19, 1993
  Fourth Sunday of Advent

CHRISTMASTIME PSALM
page 32

- 34 DECEMBER 25, 1993
  Christmas
- 36 DECEMBER 26, 1993
  The Holy Family
    - ◆ Mary, the Mother of God: January 1
- 38 JANUARY 2, 1994
  The Epiphany of the Lord
- 40 JANUARY 9, 1994
  The Baptism of the Lord

WINTER PSALM
page 42

- 44 JANUARY 16, 1994
  Second Sunday in Ordinary Time
- 46 JANUARY 23, 1994
  Third Sunday in Ordinary Time
- 48 JANUARY 30, 1994
  Fourth Sunday in Ordinary Time
    - ◆ The Presentation of the Lord: February 2
- 50 FEBRUARY 6, 1994
  Fifth Sunday in Ordinary Time
- 52 FEBRUARY 13, 1994
  Sixth Sunday in Ordinary Time
    - ◆ Ash Wednesday: February 16

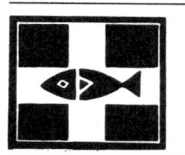

LENT PSALM
page 54

- 56 FEBRUARY 20, 1994
  First Sunday of Lent
- 58 FEBRUARY 27, 1994
  Second Sunday of Lent
- 60 MARCH 6, 1994
  Third Sunday of Lent
- 62 MARCH 13, 1994
  Fourth Sunday of Lent
    - ◆ Joseph, the Husband of Mary: March 19
- 64 MARCH 20, 1994
  Fifth Sunday of Lent
    - ◆ The Annunciation of the Lord: March 25
- 66 MARCH 27, 1994
  Palm Sunday of the Passion of the Lord

TRIDUUM PSALM
page 70

- 72 MARCH 31–APRIL 3, 1994
  The Paschal Triduum
- 84 APRIL 3, 1994
  Easter Sunday

EASTERTIME PSALM
page 86

- 88 APRIL 10, 1994
  Second Sunday of Easter
- 90 APRIL 17, 1994
  Third Sunday of Easter

92 APRIL 24, 1994
Fourth Sunday of Easter

94 MAY 1, 1994
Fifth Sunday of Easter

96 MAY 8, 1994
Sixth Sunday of Easter
- The Ascension of the Lord: (U.S.A.) May 12; (CANADA) May 15

98 MAY 15, 1994
Seventh Sunday of Easter
- Pentecost Vigil: May 21–22

100 MAY 22, 1994
Pentecost

SUMMER PSALM
page 102

104 MAY 29, 1994
The Holy Trinity

106 JUNE 5, 1994
The Body and Blood of Christ
- The Sacred Heart of Jesus: June 10

108 JUNE 12, 1994
Eleventh Sunday in Ordinary Time

110 JUNE 19, 1994
Twelfth Sunday in Ordinary Time
- The Birth of John the Baptist: June 24

112 JUNE 26, 1994
Thirteenth Sunday in Ordinary Time
- Peter and Paul: June 29

114 JULY 3, 1994
Fourteenth Sunday in Ordinary Time

116 JULY 10, 1994
Fifteenth Sunday in Ordinary Time

118 JULY 17, 1994
Sixteenth Sunday in Ordinary Time
- Mary Magdalene: July 22

120 JULY 24, 1994
Seventeenth Sunday in Ordinary Time

122 JULY 31, 1994
Eighteenth Sunday in Ordinary Time
- The Transfiguration of the Lord: August 6

124 AUGUST 7, 1994
Nineteenth Sunday in Ordinary Time

126 AUGUST 14, 1994
Twentieth Sunday in Ordinary Time
- The Assumption of Mary: August 15

128 AUGUST 21, 1994
Twenty-first Sunday in Ordinary Time

130 AUGUST 28, 1994
Twenty-second Sunday in Ordinary Time

132 SEPTEMBER 4, 1994
Twenty-third Sunday in Ordinary Time
- The Birth of Mary: September 8

134 SEPTEMBER 11, 1994
Twenty-fourth Sunday in Ordinary Time
- The Triumph of the Cross: September 14

136 SEPTEMBER 18, 1994
Twenty-fifth Sunday in Ordinary Time

AUTUMN PSALM
page 138

140 SEPTEMBER 25, 1994
Twenty-sixth Sunday in Ordinary Time
- Archangels Michael, Gabriel and Raphael: September 29

142 OCTOBER 2, 1994
Twenty-seventh Sunday in Ordinary Time

144 OCTOBER 9, 1994
Twenty-eighth Sunday in Ordinary Time

146 OCTOBER 16, 1994
Twenty-ninth Sunday in Ordinary Time

148 OCTOBER 23, 1994
Thirtieth Sunday in Ordinary Time

150 OCTOBER 30, 1994
Thirty-first Sunday in Ordinary Time
- All Saints' Day: November 1
- All Souls' Day: November 2

152 NOVEMBER 6, 1994
Thirty-second Sunday in Ordinary Time
- The Dedication of St. John Lateran, the Cathedral of Rome: November 9

154 NOVEMBER 13, 1994
Thirty-third Sunday in Ordinary Time

156 NOVEMBER 20, 1994
The Last Sunday in Ordinary Time: Christ the King
- Thanksgiving Day: (CANADA) October 10; (U.S.A.) November 28

How to Use *At Home with the Word*

This book invites you to be at home with God's word, to live with the Sunday scriptures in order to live by them. The scriptures that we hear proclaimed on Sunday are one of God's answers to our prayer, "Give us this day our daily bread." *At Home with the Word* allows us to return to the Sunday readings throughout the week to be nourished and challenged.

Every week of the year is here, from the first Sunday of Advent in 1993 to the last Sunday of Ordinary Time in 1994. In addition, the scriptures for our great festival, the Paschal Triduum, are included, as well as the scriptures for Christmas Midnight Mass. Each Sunday entry includes eight parts:

NAME AND DATE: It's easy to find any particular Sunday (or feast) by looking up its date or liturgical name in the Calendar/Table of Contents.

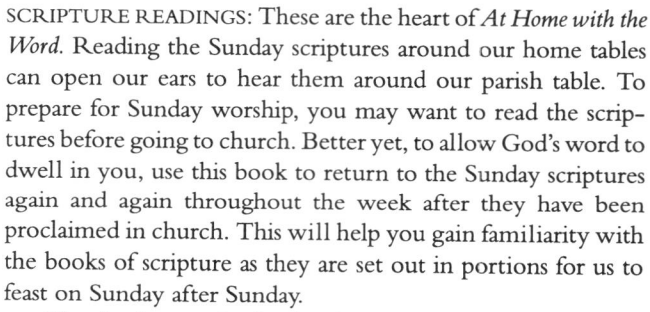

SCRIPTURE READINGS: These are the heart of *At Home with the Word*. Reading the Sunday scriptures around our home tables can open our ears to hear them around our parish table. To prepare for Sunday worship, you may want to read the scriptures before going to church. Better yet, to allow God's word to dwell in you, use this book to return to the Sunday scriptures again and again throughout the week after they have been proclaimed in church. This will help you gain familiarity with the books of scripture as they are set out in portions for us to feast on Sunday after Sunday.

The lectionary is the book of readings in which the scriptures are divided up in an orderly fashion. It is used at Mass. *At Home with the Word* provides the translation of the Sunday readings found in the *Lectionary for the Christian People*, which uses the *Revised Standard Version* (RSV) of the Bible emended for inclusive language.

We use the RSV in *At Home with the Word* so people have an opportunity to read a beautiful translation of scripture with which they may be unfamiliar, especially if their parish uses some other translation such as the *New American Bible* or the *Jerusalem Bible*. Although these two Bible translations have much to recommend them, the RSV is still the most commonly read translation of the scriptures among Christians, and the most commonly used by scriptural scholars.

REFLECTION: Scripture interpreter David Cawkwell asks us to mull over the gospel readings, and there are several ways to do that. We can read the reflections to learn background information and to consider things we've never considered before. We can also keep a journal of thoughts and discoveries, perhaps writing on the blank spaces in this book. Households or small groups can meet weekly to share the readings (or just the gospel) and the reflection. The group can then take on one or both of the discussion questions that follow the reflection. Each person may want to jot down her or his own question for the group to tackle. That's a good way to include children; their questions are often forthright and challenging.

This is Year B, the year of the gospel according to St. Mark. Throughout Ordinary Time we will be reading most often from this gospel. Please see David Cawkwell's Introduction to the Gospel of Mark on page 8.

PRACTICE OF FAITH: Traditions and customs that we practice at home flow out of and lead back into the traditions we practice at church. David Philippart suggests a variety of prayers, rituals and customs to help you practice your faith at home. Having ministered in parishes in Buffalo, New York, he is now an editor at Liturgy Training Publications.

PRACTICE OF HOPE: For 16 years, Joyce Hollyday has lived in inner-city Washington, D.C., as part of Sojourners Community. As the associate editor of *Sojourners* magazine, she has traveled widely. In places of suffering and violence, she has gleaned stories of hope, which she shares here. She currently is writing a book on the lives of biblical and contemporary women, to be published by Westminster/John Knox Press in 1994.

PRACTICE OF CHARITY: The practice of charity begins at home, but can never end there. That's why Sherry and Roy Lanham—campus ministers at Eastern Illinois University in Charleston and new parents—have compiled suggestions for living the law of love at home, at school, at work and at play. From their marriage and their ministry, they offer concrete suggestions for practicing charity.

WEEKDAY READING: Some people may want to read more than the Sunday scriptures. We've listed the chapters of the books of the Bible from which the first readings for daily Mass are taken each week. (Most gospel passages for daily Mass are eventually also read on Sundays.)

FEAST DAYS: The scripture citations and brief explanations of major weekday feasts are included in boxes as they occur throughout the year, unless lengthy Sunday scriptures don't leave room. For example, May 12, Jesus' Ascension, is included in the week of May 8.

At Home with the Word also includes:

MORNING, EVENING AND NIGHT PRAYER: Here are simple patterns of prayer for the home. They're for every day and for all ages. These prayers take five or ten minutes of our time, perhaps, when we are eating, rising or going to sleep. (And that suggests that we keep *At Home with the Word* by our bedsides or on the kitchen table.) These prayers are meant to be repeated every day. Don't be afraid of repetition. After all, that's how we learn. Discipline is involved, but it's the discipline of disciples.

SEASONAL PSALMS AND PRAYERS: Each season of the year is introduced by a special page that includes an acclamation, psalm and short prayer delightfully illustrated by Suzanne Novak. Repeating a single psalm throughout a season is a fine way to learn the psalms by heart. They can be prayed as a grace at mealtime. They also can be used in place of the psalms for morning or evening prayer. These seasonal psalms and prayers are perfect to conclude the reading of the scriptures. The translation used here is the new one prepared over recent years by the International Commission on English in the Liturgy. It's bold and fresh and true to the spirit of the psalms.

SUNDAY AND FRIDAY PSALMS AND PRAYERS: Sunday is our day of feasting, Friday our day of fasting. Both days need extra prayer and acts of discipleship. Here are psalms, a Lord's Day poem by Henry Baker and a prayer for Fridays from the bishops' letter, *The Challenge of Peace*. This letter calls for prayer, fasting and almsgiving every Friday outside Eastertime.

ORDER OF MASS: The Mass is the heart of our heritage of Sunday prayer. Individual acclamations and songs and litanies of Mass also can be used as prayers during the week. For example, the Gloria makes a splendid song to sing at home every Sunday morning. Folks gathered in chapels or nursing homes to celebrate the eucharist—as well as anyone who is trying to become better acquainted with the Mass—will find this section useful. It contains all the texts and acclamations needed by people who watch televised Masses.

An Introduction to the Gospel of Mark

The Gospel of Mark is an eye-opening journey of discovery. Throughout this gospel we are travel companions of Jesus. As we travel, we arrive at a twofold destination: the city of Jerusalem and a trust-filled faith.

The written document that we now call the gospel according to Mark was the first to gather together historical traditions about Jesus and to organize them into a unique and coherent story of faith. This is the only one of the four gospels that tells us—in the first words—that what follows is "gospel." We also hear whose gospel it is: Jesus Christ's and God's. This good news is the living presence of God, embodied in Jesus and described as "the dominion of God." It is no wonder that Mark often uses the word "immediately" to describe events. Jesus proclaims: The time is fulfilled, God is present, change your lives accordingly, this is the truth and this is the good news!

What Mark unfolds for us in this writing is the history of that good news: how it was proclaimed, how some people accepted it, how most people rejected it, how the gospel created a moment of decision for all. Poor people, rich people, the sick, the blind, those in authority, disciples, Jews and Gentiles—none are left untouched by the presence of good news embodied in Jesus. Responses range from the joy of a liberated paralytic to the vengeance of those who crucify him.

MARK BEGINS WITH A PREAMBLE that recalls the ministry of John the Baptist and that links John to the Hebrew prophets. Jesus comes from Nazareth and is baptized and identified for us by a heavenly voice as "the Son of God." The Spirit drives Jesus into the desert of testing. Here the battle with Satan begins.

MARK PORTRAYS OPPOSITION TO THE GOOD NEWS IN TWO WAYS, the visible and the invisible. The visible opposition is those people whose power and authority depend on the captivity of other people. The invisible opposition is called Satan. Both invisible and visible forces lie in wait to bind again those whom Jesus liberates. These forces appear early in the gospel as an essential feature of the meaning Mark gives to his history of good news announced to the world. The murmurings of human opposition are suggested by Mark's mention of John's arrest (1:14) and are vocalized by scribes after they witness Jesus' claim to forgive sins. The forgiveness of sins sets people free from the powers who oppose the dominion of God (2:6).

THE TONE OF JESUS' MINISTRY CHANGES WHEN A PLOT IS MENTIONED (3:6). Disciples are urgently appointed to proclaim good news, sent out by a Jesus reminiscent of Moses, with twelve disciples given authority from on the mountain (3:13). With John the Baptist's death (6:27), the opposition becomes obvious, and Jesus has to face a deputation of scribes and Pharisees from Jerusalem (7:1–2).

Jesus' awareness of this opposition is given expression in the three passion predictions. He is confronted by authorities when he reaches the Temple (11:27–33), where an attempt is made to embroil him in a well-worn dispute between Sadducees and Pharisees, ironically, about resurrection (12:18–27). But it is from within Jesus' own chosen twelve that the opposition is most painful—when the final collusion at his death is perpetrated (14:1–2, 10–11).

MARK'S PORTRAIT OF THE DISCIPLES IS NONE TOO FLATTERING. They frequently misunderstand Jesus, they do or say the wrong things, and they finally desert him. Mark is making a clear point: True discipleship is no soft option. The reign of God and the reign of Satan are opposed, and the authentic disciple, like Jesus, is the one who encounters the often messy results of that opposition.

From the outset of his ministry, Jesus has called for a complete reorientation of life toward the powerful reality of God's presence. This is the seed (4:1–9, 26–32) and the light (4:21–25) that cannot be countered without devastating consequences. The dominion of God is a tremendous power (4:35–41) embodied in Jesus and shared with disciples (6:7–13) so that they too embody the dominion.

The passion is never far away from an authentic disciple. When Mark tells about Jesus sending the disciples with power and authority (6:7–32), between their departure and return Mark gives us the account of John the Baptist's murder (6:14–29). Even those sent out with good news from God will find themselves at the mercy of the unrepentant. John dies because of the fear, jealousy and spiritual blindness of those still held captive by Satan. Proclaiming the gospel of God is rarely welcome, and disciples should expect trouble.

FOR MOST OF THE FIRST NINE CHAPTERS OF MARK THE IDENTITY OF JESUS IS KEPT SECRET. Although the "powerful Jesus"—the healer, the exorcist and the feeder of thousands—amazes everyone, Mark's "secret" suggests to us that a glorious Christ is an incomplete picture of the Son of God. After Peter announces that he knows Jesus' true identity as "the Christ" (8:27), the passion throws its shadow over everything.

Slowly Jesus unveils an aspect of the Christ that is unpalatable, even to his closest followers. This amazing miracle worker must suffer and die! The passion is the inevitable cost of the faithful proclamation of the good news of God's presence. It is the cost of discipleship.

One of Mark's many writing techniques is demonstrated in the section of the gospel that begins with the healing of a nameless blind man (8:22–26) and ends with the blind Bartimaeus receiving his sight and then following Jesus "on the way" (10:46–52). These carefully placed miracles form "brackets"; in between them Mark arranges his story of the gradual revealing of the suffering Son of God. Mark suggests through this writing technique that a certain kind of seeing is needed, a sight that comes from the presence of God, a kind of gift, a kind of healing. This kind of seeing is called "faith."

CHAPTER 10 OF THE GOSPEL INCLUDES A DOUBLE TRANSITION IN MARK'S STORY. Jesus' public ministry has moved from Galilee and its environs to Jerusalem, and from secrecy about Jesus' identity to public and private revelations of Jesus' true identity. The final revelations about Jesus will come at his trial and on Golgotha.

WHO IS JESUS? Mark opens his gospel document with a clear statement that Jesus is the Son of God (1:1). As the story unfolds, several "titles" are attached to Jesus by a variety of people seeking their answer to the question, "Who is he?" Only one human being in Mark's story ever proclaims Jesus as the Son of God—the centurion at the scene of Jesus' death (15:39), perhaps his executioner, certainly one who witnessed the suffering and death of Jesus. The centurion saw beyond the gory fact of crucifixion to the "blood of the covenant poured out for many" (14:24). The eyes of faith, however new, see the Son of God suffering and dying.

In only two other places in Mark is Jesus identified as the Son of God: at the baptism and the transfiguration, and both are by a voice from heaven. The high priest asks Jesus if he is the Son of the Blessed One (14:61), at which point Jesus utters the name of God—"I am." The embodied reign of God, Jesus, is rejected and condemned. To blind eyes, Jesus is just a common blasphemer deserving of death.

SO JESUS' HISTORICAL JOURNEY COMES TO AN END. The journey of faith awaits a conclusion. We are left with an empty tomb which, in great mystery, silently but eloquently asks us to identify Jesus for ourselves. The young man dressed in white (16:5) provides a link between the Jesus of the gospel narrative and the fearful, not-yet-believing community of disciples. Astonishment, silence and fear grip the women even when faced with the evidence of God's apparent victory in Jesus.

Mark seems to pose a question throughout the gospel, even in the brief account of the discovery of the empty tomb: Is Jesus' suffering and death the execution of a common criminal or the death of the Son of God? Jesus asks the hearer of Mark's gospel the same question he asked Peter: Who do you say that I am?

MORNING PRAYER

This order of prayer may be said when waking, at breakfast, even while showering.

O Lord, open my lips,
and my mouth shall declare your praise.

The Sign of the Cross

You may dip your hand in water while making the sign of the cross:
In the name of the Father
and of the Son
and of the Holy Spirit.

Psalm 63

God, my God, you I crave;
My soul thirsts for you,
my body aches for you,
like a dry and weary land.
Let me gaze on you in your temple—
a vision of strength and glory.

Your love is better than life;
my speech is full of praise.
I give you a lifetime of worship;
my hands lifted in prayer.
I feast at a rich table;
my lips sing out your praise.

On my bed I lie awake;
your memory fills the night.
You have been my help;
I rejoice beneath your wings.
Yes, I cling to you;
your right hand holds me fast.

Let those who want me dead
end up deep in the grave!
They will die by the sword;
their bodies food for jackals.
But let the king find joy in God.
All who swear the truth be praised;
every lying mouth be shut.

*One of the seasonal psalms throughout this book
may be prayed instead of Psalm 63.*

The Canticle of Zechariah

Praise the Lord, the God of Israel,
who shepherds the people and sets them free.

God raises from David's house
a child with power to save.
In ages past God promised,
through the holy prophets,
to save us from enemy hands,
from the grip of all who hate us.

God favored our ancestors
remembering the covenant,
the pledge to Abraham,
our father in faith,
freedom from fear
and from all our enemies,
so we might serve the Lord,
and be holy and just all our days.

Now, child, you are called
prophet of the Most High,
to prepare paths for God
by teaching salvation
through forgiveness of sin.

For our tender-hearted God
comes as dawn from heaven,
light for those shadowed by death,
guide for our feet on the way to peace.

The Lord's Prayer

*You may join hands with others or hold your hands with
palms facing upward while praying the Our Father.*

EVENING PRAYER

This order of prayer may be said before or after supper.

O God, come to my assistance.
O Lord, make haste to help me.

The Lighting of a Candle

A candle may be lit to welcome the evening while saying:
Jesus Christ is the light of the world,
a light no darkness can overcome.

Psalm 141:1–5, 8

Hurry, Lord! I call and call!
Listen! I plead with you.
Let my prayer become incense,
my upraised hands, an evening sacrifice.

Keep watch, Lord,
over my thought and word;
let evil not seduce me
to commit hateful deeds.
Let me never join the wicked
to eat their lavish meals.

The just may correct me,
their rebuke is kindness.
But the unction of the wicked
will never touch my head.
I pray and pray
against their hateful ways.

Lord my God, I turn to you,
in you I find safety.
Do not strip me of life.

*One of the seasonal psalms throughout this book
may be prayed instead of Psalm 121.*

The Canticle of Mary

I acclaim the Lord's greatness;
I delight in my Savior,
who regarded my humble state.
Now see, all people call me blest.

For God, wonderful in power,
has used that strength for me.
Holy is the Lord!
whose mercy embraces the faithful,
one generation to the next.

God's mighty arm
strikes down the proud,
pulls tyrants from thrones,
and lifts up the poor,
so the starving are filled,
and the rich go hungry.

God rescues lowly Israel,
recalling the mercy
promised to our ancestors,
to Abraham's heirs for ever.

Intercession and Lord's Prayer

*At day's end we offer our petitions in Jesus' name.
We make intercession for our church, our world, our
parish, our neighbors, our family and friends and
ourselves. We seal all our prayers with the Our Father.
In conclusion, all may exchange the sign of peace.*

NIGHT PRAYER

This order of prayer may be said before going to sleep.

May Almighty God give us a restful night
and a peaceful death.

Psalm 131

Lord, I am not proud,
holding my head too high,
reaching beyond my grasp.

See for yourself!
I am calm and tranquil
like a weaned child
resting in its mother's arms:
my whole being at rest.

Let Israel rest in the Lord,
now and for ever.

The Canticle of Simeon

Lord, let your servant
now die in peace.
You kept your promise.

With my own eyes
I see the salvation
you prepared for all peoples:

light revealing life to the Gentiles
and glory to Israel your people.

Invocation to Mary

*The final prayer of the day is customarily
to Mother Mary.*

Hail, holy Queen, Mother of mercy,
    our life, our sweetness, and our hope!
To you we cry, the children of Eve;
to you we send up our sighs,
mourning and weeping in this land of exile.
Turn, then, most gracious advocate,
    your eyes of mercy toward us;
lead us home at last
and show us the blessed fruit of your womb,
    Jesus:
O clement, O loving, O sweet Virgin Mary!

The Sign of the Cross

*We end the day the way we began it,
with the sign of the cross:*

May the almighty and merciful Lord,
    the Father and the Son and the Holy Spirit,
bless and keep us. Amen.

Sunday is our weekly feast day, our celebration of creation, liberation and resurrection.

The wedding feast of the Lamb has begun, and his bride is prepared to welcome him.

SUNDAY PRAYER

Psalm 100

Shout joy to the Lord, all earth,
serve the Lord with gladness,
enter God's presence with joy!

Know that the Lord is God,
our maker to whom we belong,
our shepherd, and we the flock.

Enter the temple gates,
the courtyard with thanks and praise;
give thanks and bless God's name.

Indeed the Lord is good,
"God is lasting love!"
faithful from age to age.

Prayer of the Day

On this day, the first of days,
God the Father's name we praise;
who, creation's Lord and Spring,
did the world from darkness bring.

On this day the eternal Son
over death the triumph won.
On this day the Spirit came
with the gift of living flame.

God, the blessed Holy One,
may thy saving work be done;
in this work our souls are free
as we rest this day with thee.

FRIDAY PRAYER

Friday is our weekly fast day, our day of special prayer, fasting and almsgiving.

Lord, by your cross and resurrection
   you have set us free.
You are the savior of the world.

Psalm 51:3–6, 12–13

Have mercy, tender God,
forget that I defied you.
Wash away my sin.
Cleanse me from my guilt.

I know my evil well,
it stares me in the face,
evil done against you
before your very eyes.

Creator, reshape my heart.
God, steady my spirit.
Do not cast me aside
stripped of your holy spirit.

Prayer of the Day

All praise be yours, God our Creator,
as we wait in joyful hope
for the flowering of justice
and the fullness of peace.

All praise for this day, this Friday.
By our weekly fasting and prayer,
cast out the spirit of war, of fear and mistrust,
and make us grow hungry
   for human kindness,
thirsty for solidarity
   with all the people of your dear earth.

May all our prayer, our fasting and our deeds
be done in the name of Jesus. Amen.

The Order of Mass

INTRODUCTORY RITES

Entrance Song

A psalm or hymn may be sung.

Greeting

After the sign of the cross, the presider greets the assembly, and all respond:

And also with you.

Rite of Blessing and Sprinkling Holy Water

On Sundays there may be a blessing and sprinkling of water to remember baptism. Then the penitential rite is omitted.

Penitential Rite

This rite may take many forms. It may include the "I confess" and the "Lord, have mercy":

I confess to almighty God,
and to you, my brothers and sisters,
that I have sinned through my own fault
in my thoughts and in my words,
in what I have done,
and in what I have failed to do;
and I ask blessed Mary, ever virgin,
all the angels and saints,
and you, my brothers and sisters,
to pray for me to the Lord our God.

Lord, have mercy.
Christ, have mercy.
Lord, have mercy.

Gloria

On feast days and on Sundays outside Advent and Lent all sing:

Glory to God in the highest,
and peace to his people on earth.
Lord, God, heavenly King,
almighty God and Father,
    we worship you, we give you thanks,
    we praise you for your glory.

Lord Jesus Christ, only Son of the Father,
Lord God, Lamb of God,
you take away the sins of the world:
> have mercy on us;
you are seated at the right hand of the Father:
> receive our prayer.

For you alone are the Holy One,
you alone are the Lord,
you alone are the Most High,
> Jesus Christ,
> with the Holy Spirit,
> in the glory of God the Father. Amen.

The introductory rites conclude with the opening prayer, to which all respond:

Amen.

LITURGY OF THE WORD

Reading(s)

After each reading the lector says, "The word of the Lord," and all respond:

Thanks be to God.

Then all share a moment of silent reflection.

Psalm

A psalm is sung from the psalter or the lectionary.

Gospel

The proclamation of the gospel is welcomed by singing the Alleluia or, during Lent, some other acclamation of praise.

Before the gospel the proclaimer says, "The Lord be with you," and all respond:

And also with you.

Then the proclaimer says, "A reading from the holy gospel according to N.," and all respond:

Glory to you, Lord.

After the gospel the proclaimer says, "The gospel of the Lord," and all respond:

Praise to you, Lord Jesus Christ.

Homily

After the homily, a moment of silent reflection may be shared.

Profession of Faith

On Sundays and solemnities all say:

We believe in one God,
> the Father, the Almighty,
> maker of heaven and earth,
> of all that is seen and unseen.

We believe in one Lord, Jesus Christ,
> the only Son of God,
> eternally begotten of the Father,
> God from God, Light from Light,
> true God from true God,
> begotten, not made,
>> one in Being with the Father.
> Through him all things were made.
> For us and for our salvation
>> he came down from heaven:
> by the power of the Holy Spirit
>> he was born of the Virgin Mary,
>> and became man.
> For our sake he was crucified
>> under Pontius Pilate;
>> he suffered, died, and was buried.
>> On the third day he rose again
>> in fulfillment of the scriptures;
>> he ascended into heaven and is seated
>> at the right hand of the Father.
> He will come again in glory
>> to judge the living and the dead,
>> and his kingdom will have no end.

We believe in the Holy Spirit, the Lord,
> the giver of life,
who proceeds from the Father and the Son.
With the Father and the Son
> he is worshiped and glorified.
He has spoken through the prophets.

We believe in one holy catholic
    and apostolic Church.
We acknowledge one baptism
    for the forgiveness of sins.
We look for the resurrection of the dead,
    and the life of the world to come.
Amen.

General Intercessions

The liturgy of the word concludes with prayers of petition for our church and our world, to which the assembly may respond:

Lord, have mercy.

or:

Lord, hear our prayer.

LITURGY OF THE EUCHARIST

Preparation of the Altar and the Gifts

Gifts are collected for the poor and the church.

If there is no music or song, prayers may be said aloud to which all respond:

Blessed be God for ever.

The assembly speaks to the presider:

May the Lord accept the sacrifice at your hands
for the praise and glory of his name
for our good and the good of all his Church.

The presider says the prayer over the gifts, and all respond:

Amen.

Eucharistic Prayer

Our great prayer of praise and thanksgiving begins with a dialogue between the presider and the assembly. The presider says, "The Lord be with you," to which all respond:

And also with you.

Then the presider says, "Lift up your hearts," and all respond:

We lift them up to the Lord.

Then the presider says, "Let us give thanks to the Lord our God," and all respond:

It is right to give him thanks and praise.

Then the presider offers the eucharistic prayer of the assembly, and all sing the acclamations:

PREFACE ACCLAMATION

Holy, holy, holy Lord, God of power and might,
heaven and earth are full of your glory.
    Hosanna in the highest.
Blessed is he who comes in the name
    of the Lord.
    Hosanna in the highest.

MEMORIAL ACCLAMATION

Christ has died,
Christ is risen,
Christ will come again.

or:

Dying you destroyed our death,
rising you restored our life.
Lord Jesus, come in glory.

or:

When we eat this bread and drink this cup,
we proclaim your death, Lord Jesus,
until you come in glory.

or:

Lord, by your cross and resurrection
    you have set us free.
You are the Savior of the world.

GREAT AMEN

The eucharistic prayer concludes with all singing:

Amen!

Communion Rite

LORD'S PRAYER

The presider invites the assembly to join in the Lord's Prayer, which concludes with the presider saying, ". . . as we wait in joyful hope for the coming of our Savior, Jesus Christ." Then all say:

For the kingdom, the power and the glory
    are yours,
now and for ever.

SIGN OF PEACE
Following a prayer, the deacon or presider says, "The peace of the Lord be with you always," and all respond:

And also with you.

Then all are invited to exchange a sign of the peace of Christ.

THE BREAKING OF THE BREAD
The holy bread is broken and the holy wine poured in preparation for communion. The following litany is sung throughout this action:

Lamb of God,
you take away the sins of the world:
have mercy on us.

The litany continues:

Lamb of God,
you take away the sins of the world:
grant us peace.

COMMUNION
The presider invites all to share in holy communion, and the assembly says:

Lord, I am not worthy to receive you,
but only say the word and I shall be healed.

The minister of communion says, "The Body of Christ" or "The Blood of Christ," and the communicant responds:

Amen.

A song or psalm is sung during communion.

All share a moment of silent reflection.

The communion rite concludes with a prayer to which all respond:

Amen.

CONCLUDING RITE

Blessing

The presider says, "The Lord be with you," and all respond:

And also with you.

The blessing may take several forms. All respond by saying:

Amen.

Dismissal

The deacon or presider invites all to go in the peace of Christ, and all respond:

Thanks be to God.

Advent

Maranatha!
Come, Lord Jesus!

God owns this planet
and all its riches.
The earth and every creature
belong to God.
God set the land on top of the seas
and anchored it in the deep.

Who is fit to climb God's mountain
and stand in that holy place?
Whoever has integrity:
not chasing shadows,
not living lies.
God will bless them,
their savior will bring justice.
These people long to see the Lord,
they seek the face of Jacob's God.

Stretch toward heaven, you gates.
Open high and wide,
let the glorious sovereign enter.
Who is this splendid ruler?
The Lord of power and might,
the conqueror of chaos.

Stretch toward heaven, you gates.
Open high and wide,
let the glorious sovereign enter.
Who is this splendid ruler?
The Lord of heaven's might,
this splendid ruler is God.

—*Psalm 24*

In the long nights of December,
we call you God of Jacob
because our ancestor Jacob
    wrestled all night long with you
and won your blessing and the name
    Israel.
Remember Jacob
who saw the ladder in the sky
and all your angels going up and down,
Jacob, who was the child
of Rebekah and Isaac,
the husband of Leah and Rachel,
the father of Joseph and Judah
and of all the tribes.
These are the tribes
that climb your mountain,
seek your face.
These are the tribes of Joseph and Mary
with whom we stand and reach up
like high, open gates
that wait for you to enter, God of Jacob,
wait for your gentleness and justice
to save us.

—*Prayer of the Season*

NOVEMBER 28, 1993
FIRST SUNDAY OF ADVENT

READING I   *Isaiah 63:16–17; 64:1–8*

You, O LORD, are father to us,
   our Redeemer from of old is your name.
O LORD, why do you make us err from your ways
   and harden our heart, so that we fear you not?
Return for the sake of your servants,
   the tribes of your heritage.
O that you would rend the heavens and come down,
   that the mountains might quake at your presence—
When you did terrible things which we
      looked not for,
you came down, the mountains quaked
      at your presence.
From of old no one has heard
      or perceived by the ear,
no eye has seen a God besides you,
   who works for those who await you.
You meet those who joyfully work righteousness,
   those who remember you in your ways.
Behold, you were angry, and we sinned;
   in our sins we have been a long time,
      and shall we be saved?
We have all become like one who is unclean,
   and all our righteous deeds are like
      a polluted garment.
We all fade like a leaf,
   and our iniquities, like the wind, take us away.
There is no one that calls upon your name,
   who arises to take hold of you;
for you have hid your face from us,
   and have delivered us into the hand
      of our iniquities.
Yet, O LORD, you are father to us;
   we are the clay, and you are our potter;
   we are all the work of your hand.

[Note: In the New American Bible this reading is Isaiah 63:16–17, 19; 64:2–7. These same verses are numbered slightly differently in the Revised Standard Version Bible used here.]

READING II   *1 Corinthians 1:3–9*

Grace to you and peace from God, our Father, and the Lord Jesus Christ.

I give thanks to God always for you because of the grace of God which was given you in Christ Jesus, that in every way you were enriched in Christ with all speech and all knowledge—even as the testimony to Christ was confirmed among you—so that you are not lacking in any spiritual gift, as you wait for the revealing of our Lord Jesus Christ; who will sustain you to the end, guiltless in the day of our Lord Jesus Christ. God is faithful, by whom you were called into the communion of the Son of God, Jesus Christ our Lord.

GOSPEL   *Mark 13:33–37*

[At that time Jesus said,]

"Take heed, watch; for you do not know when the time will come. It is like someone going on a journey, who leaving home and putting the servants in charge of their work, commands the doorkeeper to be on the watch. Watch therefore—for you do not know when the lord of the house will come, in the evening, or at midnight, or at cockcrow, or in the morning—lest the lord come suddenly and find you asleep. And what I say to you I say to all: Watch."

REFLECTION

In contemporary America we are preoccupied with being "in shape." We want to look good and feel fit. We can apply the same attitude toward Advent, a time to get into shape spiritually. But do we shape up ourselves or dare to allow God to do it? In the first reading, Isaiah says to God, "We are the clay, you are the potter."

The Isaiah reading is part of a longer psalm (63:7—64:12) in which the prophet intercedes for the people. It starts with a reminder of God's graceful action in the past—the Exodus—and concludes with Isaiah begging God's compassion for an out-of-shape people, a ruined Jerusalem and a desecrated Temple. The people are exiles. Only the love of God will put such fractured folk into shape to receive God.

The parable from Mark gives another perspective on being "in shape." For Mark, it means being alert and ready, being watchful. Notice that in the parable there are two roles: The servants have their household chores to do and the door keeper is supposed to watch for the master's return. So it is with us.

We have our chores—nothing less than the mission of Jesus himself. At the same time, we must watch for Jesus' return and be ready to greet him when he comes.

Today's gospel comes from chapter 13 of Mark, a chapter concerned with the end-time. Disciples will be "in shape" for the end times if they do what Jesus expects of them: attend to their mission and watch for his return. So Advent is here. It's time to shape up.

1. Read Isaiah 63:7—64:12, the entire passage from which the first reading comes. Then read Jeremiah 18:1–12 and Romans 9:20–24, where the image of the potter also is used for God. How are you allowing God to mold you and your community this Advent?

2. The second reading says that your community is not lacking the spiritual gifts needed to be in good Christian shape. So how is it using its gifts? How are you excercising yours this Advent?

Practice of FAITH

KEEPING VIGIL. Keeping vigil—staying awake all night or waking up well before dawn to watch for the sunrise and pray—is an ancient Christian tradition. It is a way of practicing the attitude of alertness that today's gospel tells us is necessary. Our greatest and oldest vigil is on Easter Eve, when the church stays up late into the night to baptize. Christmas Midnight Mass, with its time of singing before twelve, is a vigil, too. Being vigilant takes practice, and Advent can be that rehearsal. Take heed and watch for God now. Stay up late at night or rise a bit earlier to sit quietly. Watch how, until December 21, the night grows longer. Concentrate on the Advent wreath candles. Watch how each week, as you light another candle, the light grows stronger. Make your prayer one word, repeated over and over: "Maranatha." This last word of the Bible is addressed to Jesus: "Come."

Practice of HOPE

GIVE THANKS TO GOD ALWAYS. The line forms just after dawn on Saturday mornings, even on winter's most bitterly cold days. It winds toward the vacant lots and boarded-up buildings of 14th Street. Here, in Washington, D.C., powerful hands that shape the world exist in sharp contrast to those that arrive outstretched for a bag of groceries on Saturday mornings at the Sojourners Neighborhood Center.

Inside, as volunteers clasp hands before opening the food line, 69-year-old Mary Glover offers a prayer: "We thank you, Lord, for our lying down last night and our rising up this morning. We thank you that our bed was not our cooling board, and that our bedclothes were not our winding-sheet. We thank you, Lord, for another day to serve you."

Mary Glover is poor by the world's standards but rich in faith. And she offers us the wisdom we need to carry us through another year: Hope flourishes in a grateful heart.

Practice of CHARITY

TAKE HEED, WATCH. As we begin the church year with the promise and certainty of the Lord's coming, we are invited to practice charity in a new way. Our God is a Trinity, a God of relationships who longs to be in a loving relationship with us. This is the root of all charity. Practicing charity means being in right relationships with others. It is not just doing something *for* others that is important, but also how we relate with those in need, aware that we, too, are needy. This year, all suggestions for practicing charity will stress "being with" along with "doing for." So take heed and watch. What you do may lead you into a deeper relationship with God.

Weekday Reading
Isaiah 2:1–5; Romans 10:9–18; Isaiah 25:6–10; 26:1–6; 29:17–24; 30:19–26

DECEMBER 5, 1993
SECOND SUNDAY OF ADVENT

READING I   *Isaiah 40:1–5, 9–11*

Comfort, comfort my people, says your God.
Speak tenderly to Jerusalem,
  and cry to the city
that its warfare is ended,
  that its iniquity is pardoned,
that it has received from the LORD's hand
  double for all its sins.
A voice cries:
"In the wilderness prepare the way of the LORD,
  make straight in the desert a highway for our God.
Every valley shall be lifted up,
  and every mountain and hill be made low;
the uneven ground shall become level,
  and the rough places a plain.
And the glory of the LORD shall be revealed,
  and all flesh shall see it together,
  for the mouth of the LORD has spoken."
Get you up to a high mountain,
  O Zion, herald of good tidings;
lift up your voice with strength,
  O Jerusalem, herald of good tidings,
  lift it up, fear not;
say to the cities of Judah,
  "Behold your God!"
Behold, the Lord GOD comes with might,
  with an arm to rule;
behold, God comes bearing the reward,
  preceded by the recompense.
The LORD will feed the chosen flock like a shepherd;
  God's arms will gather the lambs.
God's bosom will bear them up;
  the LORD will gently lead those that are
  with young.

READING II   *2 Peter 3:8–14*

Do not ignore this one fact, beloved, that with the Lord one day is as a thousand years, and a thousand years as one day. The Lord is not slow concerning the promise as some count slowness, but is forbearing toward you, not wishing that any should perish, but that all should reach repentance. But the day of the Lord will come like a thief, and then the heavens will pass away with a loud noise, and the elements will be dissolved with fire, and the earth and the works that are upon it will be burned up.

Since all these things are thus to be dissolved, what sort of persons ought you to be in lives of holiness and godliness, waiting for and hastening the coming of the day of God, because of which the heavens will be kindled and dissolved, and the elements will melt with fire! But according to God's promise we wait for new heavens and a new earth in which righteousness dwells.

Therefore, beloved, since you wait for these, be zealous to be found by God without spot or blemish, and at peace.

GOSPEL   *Mark 1:1–8*

The beginning of the gospel of Jesus Christ, the Son of God.

As it is written in Isaiah the prophet,

"Behold, I send my messenger before your face,
  who shall prepare your way;
the voice of one crying in the wilderness:
Prepare the way of the Lord,
  make straight the paths of the Lord—"

John the baptizer appeared in the wilderness, preaching a baptism of repentance for the forgiveness of sins. And there went out to him all the country of Judea, and all the people of Jerusalem; and they were baptized by him in the river Jordan, confessing their sins. Now John was clothed with camel's hair, and had a leather belt around his waist, and ate locusts and wild honey. And he preached, saying, "After me comes one who is mightier than I, the thong of whose sandals I am not worthy to stoop down and untie. I have baptized you with water; but the one who is coming will baptize you with the Holy Spirit."

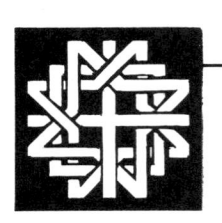

The Immaculate Conception of Mary
Wednesday, December 8, 1993

Genesis 3:9–15, 20   Eve is "the mother of the living."
Ephesians 1:3–6, 11–12   God chose us before the world began.
Luke 1:26–38   I am the servant of the Lord.

Sin means separation from God. We believe Mary was not separated from God even from her conception in her mother's womb. On this Advent feast of Mary, her "yes" undoes Eve's "no." Mary is our new Eve, the mother of the living God.

REFLECTION

Mark wastes no time introducing two major characters of the story he's going to tell us for 29 Sundays of this new year. The very first sentence of this gospel—the good news—identifies for us the person of Jesus. He is also called "Christ," the Greek form of "Messiah," the anointed one. Also, he is Son of God: He lives in unique relationship to the God of Israel.

As Mark tells the story, an air of mystery surrounds the true identity of Jesus. As the story unfolds, the disciples and and others slowly, and sometimes painfully, come to an awareness of Jesus. Their faith in him is built on his words and deeds and finally on his perplexing and ignominious death. In Mark's understanding, the anointed Son of God must suffer and die to complete his mission. Only slowly is the necessity of suffering made clear to those who witness Jesus' words and deeds and are impelled to follow his teachings as disciples.

John the Baptist opens this drama. He appears as the expected herald, identified by Mark and the early church in the writings of Isaiah the prophet. Eight centuries before John, Isaiah himself was called to announce God's coming, to console and reassure a demoralized people that their exile was over, and that God was present in glory and compassion. In that prophetic tradition, John announces the good news of the impending advent of the one who will baptize with the Holy Spirit.

To receive the one who comes, a change of heart, a repentance, is called for. All obstacles that would block Christ's coming into human lives need to be removed. God's highway is to be straight and clear.

1. Many scripture passages describe the coming of God in colorful, dramatic and sometimes curious scenarios (see today's second reading). God's first coming, remembered at Christmas, was as a defenseless child. How does God come into your life and community now? What are the clearest signs of God's presence?

2. Last Sunday's gospel called for a watchful disposition. Today's requires overt action. How have we been watchful since last Sunday? How are we clearing away the obstacles to God's renewed coming in our personal and communal lives?

Practice of **FAITH**

CHAMPION OF THE PEOPLE. The name Nicholas in Greek means "champion of the people." Bishop Nicholas, whose feast is Monday, is the hero of many stories. In most versions, Nicholas goes to great trouble to leave gifts for poor children—even climbing onto the roofs of windowless shacks in order to drop them down the chimney! A darker version of the story says that Nicholas—at great expense and danger—ransomed kidnaped children from slave traders. The traders would murder the children they could not sell.

Many people today continue to champion the rights of children to life and love. They include parents, foster parents, teachers, orphanage employees, social workers, day care attendants, pediatricians and many others. St. Nicholas, pray for them!

Practice of **HOPE**

COMFORT, COMFORT MY PEOPLE. A massive stroke left my favorite college professor, Art Brown, helpless and broken. He pleaded, "Plug up the holes in my brain, please. . . . They're killing me. . . . They're making an awful draft." On a visit, I offered a prayer for him, and after my "Amen," he began the Lord's Prayer; it was the only thing his battered brain remembered from beginning to end. When we finished, he wept and said, "All I have left is faith."

On my next visit, just before Christmas, Art greeted me with a smile, calling his predicament "struggling from tears to cheers." He produced a large piece of white paper, on which he had drawn a small face surrounded by bold red strokes that swept in two large arcs toward the top of the page. At the bottom of the page he had written, "The late Aunt Minnie encased in a lobster claw." He grinned and explained, "Well, I was trying to draw a Christmas angel—but it didn't come out quite right." There is always comfort in sharing a laugh with a friend.

Practice of **CHARITY**

THE UNEVEN GROUND SHALL BECOME LEVEL. This time of year—with all the talk about family, all the pressures of shopping and all the pleasures of exchanging gifts—often makes more acute the huge disparity that exists in our land between rich and poor, between the haves and the have-nots. To respond to this, "adopt" a family this Advent. Don't try to be their Santa Claus; first try to relate to them as friends. Visit them or invite them to visit you to share some simple refreshments. Help with gifts for the children or groceries if that seems proper. You can receive a name of a family from your parish's social justice committee or from your local Salvation Army. It is only as we begin to put a face on poverty that we can begin to deal with it and transform ourselves.

Weekday Reading
Isaiah 35:1–10; Isaiah 40:1–11; Genesis 3:9–20; Isaiah 41:13–20; 48:17–19; Sirach 48:1–4, 9–11

DECEMBER 12, 1993
THIRD SUNDAY OF ADVENT

READING I *Isaiah 61:1–2, 10–11*

The Spirit of the Lord GOD is upon me,
   because the LORD has anointed me
to bring good tidings to the afflicted;
   the LORD has sent me to bind up
      the brokenhearted,
to proclaim liberty to the captives,
   and the opening of the prison to those
      who are bound;
to proclaim the year of the LORD's favor,
   and the day of vengeance of our God;

I will greatly rejoice in the LORD,
   my soul shall exult in my God;
for God has clothed me with the garments
      of salvation,
   and covered me with the robe of righteousness,
as a bridegroom decks himself with a garland,
   and as a bride adorns herself with her jewels.
For as the earth brings forth its shoots,
   and as a garden causes what is sown in it
      to spring up,
so the Lord GOD will cause righteousness and praise
   to spring forth before all the nations.

READING II *1 Thessalonians 5:16–24*

Rejoice always, pray constantly, give thanks in all circumstances; for this is the will of God in Christ Jesus for you. Do not quench the Spirit, do not despise prophesying, but test everything; hold fast what is good, abstain from every form of evil.

May that very God of peace sanctify you wholly; and may your spirit and soul and body be kept sound and blameless at the coming of our Lord Jesus Christ. God who calls you is faithful and will do it.

GOSPEL *John 1:6–8, 19–28*

There was sent by God a person named John. He came for testimony, to bear witness to the light, that all might believe through him. He was not the light, but came to bear witness to the light.

And this is the testimony of John, when the Jewish people sent priests and Levites from Jerusalem to ask him, "Who are you?" John confessed and did not deny, but confessed, "I am not the Christ." And they asked him, "What then? Are you Elijah?" John said, "I am not." "Are you the prophet?" And he answered, "No." They said to him then, "Who are you? Let us have an answer for those who sent us. What do you say about yourself?" John said, "I am the voice of one crying in the wilderness, 'Make straight the way of the Lord,' as the prophet Isaiah said."

Now they had been sent from the Pharisees. They asked him, "Then why are you baptizing, if you are neither the Christ, nor Elijah, nor the prophet?" John answered them, "I baptize with water; but among you stands one whom you do not know, even the one who comes after me, the thong of whose sandal I am not worthy to untie." This took place in Bethany beyond the Jordan, where John was baptizing.

REFLECTION

When the adult Jesus went home to Nazareth, according to St. Luke (4:16–30), he chose the opening lines of today's first reading as a kind of summary of the mission he was about to begin. Through Isaiah's message, a beleaguered exiled people were given hope in God's faithfulness and compassion. God's Spirit empowered the anointed messenger to deliver this good news to a desolate, abandoned people. God's vengeance (verse 2a) is taken, not on the people, but on their misery: They are rescued to proclaim God's righteousness and praise to all nations.

The prophet's mission to the exiles becomes that people's own mission to their world. Clothed in garments of salvation and covered with the robe of righteousness, this messenger-people makes God visible in their words and deeds.

A Christian parallel to Isaiah is John the Baptist. In the fourth gospel, John is quite certain who he is not! He is not the Christ, nor Elijah, nor the prophet reincarnated. But he is a heralding voice crying out—like Isaiah—to an abandoned people about the coming of God.

The Baptist had a mission. Jesus had a mission. That mission was bequeathed to all who call themselves Christians—followers of Christ. They are good news for the world. Their message is proclaimed, their flesh is torn and their blood spilled. But in Jesus that torn flesh becomes food and the spilt blood becomes drink. These link believers to Jesus and sustain them in their faith and their mission. The Gospel of John is very clear on this: The mission of Jesus and of the church is the same.

In John the Baptist's ministry, there is no call to repentance, but a solemn announcement that the light is about to shine and the reality of human lives is about to be made truly visible. People must choose: light or darkness.

1. The first reading is reminiscent of Isaiah's "Servant Songs" (49:1–6; 50:4–11; 52:13—53:12) where an individual's mission becomes that of a whole people, once they have truly heard the message. How do these texts teach us about Christ, the church as a whole, and the individual?

2. What aspects of the Christian mission is Advent clarifying for you and your community? How is God anointing you for the spreading of good news?

Practice of **FAITH**

DIA DE GUADALUPE. Because the feast of Our Lady of Guadalupe falls on a Sunday this year, the readings and prayers of the Mass are for the Third Sunday of Advent instead. Even so, this will not stop Mexicans from remembering a most important event in their history: the day in 1531 when Mary appeared to Juan Diego, leaving an image of herself on his cloak. She appeared as a native Mexican, shining with the light of the moon and the stars and the sun, and wearing the traditional sash around her waist, a sign of pregnancy.

The Third Sunday of Advent is known as Guadete (Rejoice) Sunday, because the word "rejoice" appears in the second reading. Mary's loving care for the poor—the native Mexicans were poor and oppressed by Spanish rulers—is certainly a reason to rejoice today. And in Mexico, people will rise well before dawn—a good Advent practice—to begin the celebration.

Practice of **HOPE**

GOOD TIDINGS TO THE AFFLICTED. The refugees from El Salvador had fled starvation, a prolonged civil war, and massacres at the hands of the military. When Christmas Eve came, their camp in Honduras burst into joyful celebration. Women baked sweet cinnamon bread in an adobe oven, while men butchered hogs for the making of special pork tamales.

The children made figurines for the Nativity scene out of clay from the river bed, adding local touches to the usual characters: pigs, an armadillo, and baby Jesus sleeping in a hammock rather than a manger. They painted beans and kernels of corn in bright colors and strung them into garlands. They dressed as shepherds and passed from tent to tent, recounting the journey of "Maria" and "Jose" in search of shelter.

"This Christmas we will celebrate as they did," said one mother, "looking for a place where our children can be born."

Practice of **CHARITY**

BIND UP THE BROKENHEARTED. Healing both physical and spiritual wounds is part of the mission that Jesus entrusts to us. There are many groups that work to heal people, but two that are obvious, close and always in need of help are hospitals and nursing homes. Consider becoming part of your local hospital guild, or doing hospital visits through your parish. You can become a communion minister to the hospitalized, or you can simply visit them. Does your parish have an organized ministry to a local nursing home? If so, volunteer. If not, contact an area nursing home and talk with the activities director about helping. You can try this for a limited period of time—once a week for a month, for example—and then decide whether or not to continue.

Weekday Reading
Numbers 24:2–4, 15–17; Zephaniah 3:1–2, 9–13; Isaiah 45:6–8, 18, 21–25; Isaiah 54:1–10; Genesis 49:2, 8–10; Jeremiah 23:5–8

DECEMBER 19, 1993
FOURTH SUNDAY OF ADVENT

READING I   *2 Samuel 7:1–5, 8–11, 16*

Now when King David dwelt in his house, and the LORD had given him rest from all his enemies round about, the king said to Nathan the prophet, "See now, I dwell in a house of cedar, but the ark of God dwells in a tent." And Nathan said to the king, "Go, do all that is in your heart; for the LORD is with you."

But that same night the word of the LORD came to Nathan, "Go and tell my servant David, 'Thus says the LORD: Would you build me a house to dwell in? I took you from the pasture, from following the sheep, that you should be prince over my people Israel; and I have been with you wherever you went, and have cut off all your enemies before you; and I will make for you a great name, like the name of the great ones of the earth. And I will appoint a place for my people Israel, and will plant them, that they may dwell in their own place, and be disturbed no more; and the children of violence shall afflict them no more, as formerly, from the time that I appointed judges over my people Israel; and I will give you rest from all your enemies. Moreover the LORD declares to you that the LORD will make you a house. And your house and your dominion shall be made sure for ever before me; your throne shall be established for ever.'"

READING II   *Romans 16:25–27*

Now to the one who is able to strengthen you according to my gospel and the preaching of Jesus Christ, according to the revelation of the mystery which was kept secret for long ages but is now disclosed and through the prophetic writings is made known to all nations, according to the command of the eternal God, to bring about the obedience of faith—to the only wise God be glory for evermore through Jesus Christ! Amen.

GOSPEL   *Luke 1:26–38*

In the sixth month the angel Gabriel was sent from God to a city of Galilee named Nazareth, to a virgin betrothed to a man whose name was Joseph, of the house of David; and the virgin's name was Mary. And the angel came to her and said, "Hail, O favored one, the Lord is with you!" But she was greatly troubled at the saying, and considered in her mind what sort of greeting this might be. And the angel said to her, "Do not be afraid, Mary, for you have found favor with God. And behold, you will conceive in your womb and bear a son, and you shall call his name Jesus.

"He will be great, and will be called the Son of the Most High; and the Lord God will give to him the throne of his ancestor David, and he will reign over the house of Jacob for ever; and of his dominion there will be no end."

And Mary said to the angel, "How shall this be, since I am a virgin?" And the angel said to her,

"The Holy Spirit will come upon you, and the power of the Most High will overshadow you; therefore the child to be born will be called holy, the Son of God. "And behold, your kinswoman Elizabeth in her old age has also conceived a son; and this is the sixth month with her who was called barren. For with God nothing will be impossible." And Mary said, "Behold, I am the serving maid of the Lord; let it be to me according to your word." And the angel departed from her.

REFLECTION

David's dynasty came to an end when Jerusalem fell (587 BCE) and its people were deported. It lasted barely 400 years. Yet descent from David is claimed for Jesus and the prophecy in the first reading suggests that David and his line have more significance than a mere succession of kings. Before Saul was made first king, Israel was divided over the question of having a king. Some thought that only God could be king of Israel. Others believed that through a human king, God would bless and unite the people into a holy nation. David was seen as the ideal king, servant of the servants of God; the model of righteousness and upholder of justice. The quality of the relationship between David and God formed the bedrock of promises to all the people.

The writer of 2 Samuel plays with the word "house." Explaining why the great king didn't build God a temple (his son Solomon did), the author uses "house" sometimes to mean temple, but also to mean palace, dynasty or family rank. It is the trusting relationship of a father and a son that is the everlasting "house" of David—the house into which Jesus is born. The royal messiah, Jesus inherits the best qualities of his "father," David, and perfects them.

1. In later centuries, Mary was named *theotokos* or "God-bearer." How does life within your parish prepare you to bear God to the world?

2. How would you now describe the "house" that David was promised? Jesus said, "In my Father's house, there are many dwellings" (John 14:2). What kind of "house" was he talking about? The church? Heaven? Your community?

Practice of FAITH

THE ANGELUS. Here is a prayer that summarizes today's gospel:
I: The angel of the Lord declared unto Mary.
II: And she conceived by the Holy Spirit.
I/II: Hail Mary . . .
I: Behold the handmaid of the Lord.
II: Be it done unto me according to your word.
I/II: Hail Mary . . .
I: The Word was made flesh.
II: And dwelt among us.
I/II: Hail Mary . . .
I: Pray for us, O holy mother of God,
II: that we may be made worthy of the promises of Christ.
I: Let us pray.
Pour forth, we beseech you, O Lord,
your grace into our hearts, that as we have known
the incarnation of Christ, your Son,
by the message of an angel,
so by his passion and cross
may we be brought to the glory of his resurrection.
Through the same Christ our Lord.
II: Amen.

Practice of HOPE

WITH GOD NOTHING WILL BE IMPOSSIBLE. It was Christmas Eve in an overnight shelter for homeless women in downtown Washington, D.C. An argument erupted in one corner, with Sheila accusing Mary of stealing her coat. The shouting match went on until Mary yelled, "I'm an aristocrat of the highest order—with the Rothschilds on my mother's side and the Three Wise Men on my father's!" End of discussion—Sheila couldn't top that.

I thought of God's astonishing choice to come to us as a baby, vulnerable and poor; to live among the outcasts and the needy, among the sick and marginal ones of society. Another Mary, whose song of praise we remember this season, understood better than anyone the meaning of God's coming in human form: "You have put down the mighty from their thrones, and exalted those of low degree."

Practice of CHARITY

THAT THEY MAY DWELL IN THEIR OWN PLACE. As we light the fourth candle on our Advent wreath, let us remember those who have no place to dwell. Think about Mary and Joseph and their experience in Bethlehem. If there is a shelter in your neighborhood, volunteer to take a shift. Or go as a family to help serve a meal at a soup kitchen on Christmas day. This will help give you a better understanding of homelessness in our land. Make a commitment to become informed about homelessness by writing the National Coalition Against Homelessness, 1612 K Street NW, Suite 1004, Washington DC 20006.

Weekday Reading
2 Samuel 7:1–5, 8–11; Isaiah 7:10–14; Song of Songs 2:8–14 or Zephaniah 3:14–18; 1 Samuel 1:24–28; Malachi 3:1–4, 23–24; 2 Samuel 7:1–5, 8–11, 16; (Sa—Christmas)

Christmastime

The Lord our God comes,
comes to rule the earth!

Sing to the Lord a new song,
the Lord of wonderful deeds.
Right hand and holy arm
brought victory to God.

God made that victory known,
revealed justice to nations,
remembered a merciful love
loyal to the house of Israel.

The ends of the earth have seen
the victory of our God.
Shout to the Lord, you earth,
break into song, into praise!

Sing praise to God with a harp,
with a harp and sound of music.
With sound of trumpet and horn,
shout to the Lord, our king.

Let roar the sea with its creatures,
the world and all that live there!
Let rivers clap their hands,
the hills ring out their joy!

The Lord our God comes,
comes to rule the earth,
justly to rule the world,
to govern the peoples aright.

—Psalm 98

When people witness deeds like these—
mercy winning victories
and justice welcomed in the public
 places—
then the earth itself will be an orchestra
and all creatures a choir,
and we shall sing together a song
that announces you,
God of poor shepherds and stargazers.
Rehearse us now in that Christmas song:
Like those shepherds may we know where
 to look,
like the magi may we know when to listen
 to the powerful
and when to mere dreams.
Come, Lord, and lift us up in song.

—*Prayer of the Season*

DECEMBER 25, 1993
CHRISTMAS

READING I   *Isaiah 9:2–7*

The people who walked in darkness
   have seen a great light;
those who dwelt in a land of deep darkness,
   on them has light shined.
You have multiplied the nation,
   you have increased its joy;
they rejoice before you
   as with joy at the harvest,
   as they rejoice when dividing spoil.
For the yoke of their burden,
   and the staff of their shoulders,
   the rod of their oppressor,
   you have broken as on the day of Midian.
For every boot of the tramping warrior
   in battle tumult
   and every garment rolled in blood
   will be burned as fuel for the fire.
For to us a child is born,
   to us a son is given;
and the government will be upon his shoulder,
   and his name will be called
"Wonderful Counselor, Mighty God,
   Everlasting Father, Prince of Peace."
Of the greatness of his government and of peace
   there will be no end,
upon the throne and dominion of David,
   to establish it, and to uphold it
with justice and with righteousness
   from this time forth and for evermore.
The zeal of the LORD of hosts will do this.

READING II   *Titus 2:11–14*

The grace of God has appeared for the salvation of all people, training us to renounce irreligion and worldly passions, and to live sober, upright, and godly lives in this world, awaiting our blessed hope, the appearing of the glory of the great God and our Savior Jesus Christ, who gave himself for us to redeem us from all iniquity and to purify for himself a chosen people who are zealous for good deeds.

GOSPEL   *Luke 2:1–14*

In those days a decree went out from Caesar Augustus that all the world should be enrolled. This was the first enrollment, when Quirinius was governor of Syria. And all went to their own city to be enrolled. And Joseph also went up from Galilee, from the city of Nazareth, to Judea, to the city of David, which is called Bethlehem, because he was of the house and lineage of David, to be enrolled with Mary, his betrothed, who was with child. And while they were there, the time came for her to deliver. And she gave birth to her firstborn son and wrapped him in swaddling cloths, and laid him in a manger, because there was no place for them in the inn.

And in that region there were shepherds out in the field, keeping watch over their flock by night. And an angel of the Lord appeared to them, and the glory of the Lord shone around them, and they were filled with fear. And the angel said to them, "Be not afraid; for behold, I bring you good news of a great joy which will come to all the people; for to you is born this day in the city of David a Savior, who is Christ the Lord. And this will be a sign for you: you will find an infant wrapped in swaddling cloths and lying in a manger." And suddenly there was with the angel a multitude of the heavenly host praising God and saying,

"Glory to God in the highest,
   and peace to God's people on earth."

These readings are for Christmas Midnight Mass. Other Christmas readings are:

VIGIL MASS
Isaiah 62:1–5   Our Creator will marry us.
Acts 13:16–17, 22–25   With a mighty arm we are saved.
Matthew 1:1–25   This is how the birth of Jesus came about. . . .

MASS AT DAWN
Isaiah 62:11–12   Your savior comes.
Titus 3:4–7   We are saved through new birth in the Spirit.
Luke 2:15–20   Let us go to Bethlehem.

MASS DURING THE DAY
Isaiah 52:7–10   All the ends of the earth have seen salvation.
Hebrews 1:1–6   You are my son; today I have begotten you.
John 1:1–18   In the beginning was the word.

REFLECTION

King David had been a shepherd, the youngest of Jesse's sons, who was almost overlooked when Samuel came in search of God's chosen one. But David became Israel's ideal king, a prototype of the messiah—the anointed savior of the people. When Jesus is born, the good news of his birth to David's house and in David's city—Bethlehem—comes first to shepherds. This new king also will be a shepherd. He shares the humble origins of his illustrious ancestor and inherits his glory and more.

While the shepherds learn right away of Jesus' birth, it will be a long time before the Roman emperor and the other worldly powers even hear of Jesus, born in Bethlehem. Luke is careful to give a genealogy of Jesus and make historical references to the rulers Augustus and Quirinius. He insists that the messiah is born into human history and will change that history forever. The irony in the story as we read it now is this: Although the powerful of this world—symbolized by the Romans—didn't even hear about Jesus' birth, it was Jesus' birth that would eventually undo their empire.

The story of the angels and the shepherds speaks of reconciliation between the highest, the hosts of heaven, and the lowest, the shepherds (the poor). The gospel that unfolds from this story shows a Jesus whose mission is precisely that. People are reconciled to God and to each other. They are healed by an anointed shepherd king. The reign of God is accessible to all, highest and lowest. But it appears that the lowest are most ready to receive God's coming; the highest of this world continue to wallow in darkness.

1. Read the choice of David as king (1 Samuel 16:1–16). Using the details of Jesus' birth as found in the Gospel of Luke, how is Jesus' humble beginning like David's?

2. Where and who are the "lowest," the shepherds of our time? Will they hear the angelic good news tonight? Who will deliver the good news?

Practice of FAITH

GLORY TO GOD. The acclamation of the angels becomes our prayer for the whole season of Christmas, which began with the Midnight Mass last night and ends at nightfall on January 9. Memorize the two lines: "Glory to God in the highest/and peace to God's people on earth." Let it be your first and last prayer of each day until January 9. Say the first part as you take a deep breath and hold it a second. Imagine that the breath filling your lungs is God's glory. Say the second part as you slowly and quietly breathe out. Imagine that the breath leaving you is God's peace, breathed out on all the world. When you pray with others—before meals, for example—have a leader say the first part and all others respond with the second. Then add your other prayers.

Practice of HOPE

GLORY TO GOD IN THE HIGHEST. Four-year-old Kyle was reciting the Christmas story. He faltered when he got to his favorite part, the angels' message to the shepherds. But suddenly his face brightened and he started in again: "Glory to God in the highest . . . and I'll huff and I'll puff and I'll blow your house down!"

We live in an age when the huffing and puffing seems to have reached gale force. Bulldozers raze shanties from Central America's jungles to South Africa's squatter camps; land speculation and greed force the poor from their homes in America's inner cities and farmers from our rural lands; war and famine around the world have created untold numbers of refugees.

But we have this hope, this promise from God: "Peace to God's people on earth."

Practice of CHARITY

ON THEM HAS LIGHT SHINED. The luminarias and lights of Christmas light up our darkness on this most beautiful night as we gather with family and friends. But there are places in our world where people dwell in the deep darkness of fear or poverty or violence. Take a moment on this night to light a candle and remember those who dwell in the darkness of injustice or oppression, and resolve to write Amnesty International this week. Let them know of your concern and of your desire to work to put an end to the darkness. Amnesty International, 322 Eighth Avenue, New York NY 10001; 212-807-8400.

Weekday Reading
2 Samuel 7:1–5, 8–11; Isaiah 7:10–14; Song of Songs 2:8–14 or Zephaniah 3:14–18; 1 Samuel 1:24–28; Malachi 3:1–4, 23–24; 2 Samuel 7:1–5, 8–11, 16; (Sa—Christmas)

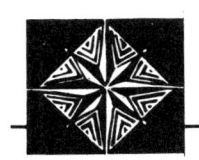

DECEMBER 26, 1993
THE HOLY FAMILY

READING I *Sirach 3:2–6, 12–14*

For the Lord honored the father above the children,
 and confirmed the right of the mother
  over her sons.
Honoring one's father atones for sins,
 and glorifying one's mother is like
  laying up treasure.
Those who honor their father will be gladdened
  by their own children,
 and when they pray they will be heard.
Those who glorify their father will have long life,
 and those who obey the Lord will
  refresh their mother.
O child, help your father in his old age,
 and do not grieve him as long as he lives;
even if he is lacking in understanding,
  show forbearance;
 in all your strength do not despise him.
For kindness to a father will not be forgotten,
 and against your sins it will be credited to you.

READING II *Colossians 3:12–21*

Put on then, as God's chosen ones, holy and beloved, compassion, kindness, lowliness, meekness, and patience, forbearing one another and, if one has a complaint against another, forgiving each another; as the Lord has forgiven you, so you also must forgive. And above all these put on love, which binds everything together in perfect harmony. And let the peace of Christ rule in your hearts, to which indeed you were called in the one body. And be thankful. Let the word of Christ dwell in you richly, teach and admonish one another in all wisdom, and sing psalms and hymns and spiritual songs with thankfulness in your hearts to God. And whatever you do, in word or deed, do everything in the name of the Lord Jesus, giving thanks to God, the Father, through him.

Wives, be subject to your husbands, as is fitting in the Lord. Husbands, love your wives, and do not be harsh with them. Children, obey your parents in everything, for this pleases the Lord. Parents, do not provoke your children, lest they become discouraged.

GOSPEL *Luke 2:22–35*

When the time came for their purification according to the law of Moses, Mary and Joseph brought Jesus up to Jerusalem to present him to the Lord (as it is written in the law of the Lord, "Every male that opens the womb shall be called holy to the Lord") and to offer a sacrifice according to what is said in the law of the Lord, "a pair of turtledoves, or two young pigeons." Now there was in Jerusalem a person named Simeon, who was righteous and devout, looking for the consolation of Israel, and the Holy Spirit was upon him. And it had been revealed to him by the Holy Spirit that he should not see death before he had seen the Lord's Christ. And inspired by the Spirit Simeon came into the temple; and when the parents brought in the child Jesus, to do for him according to the custom of the law, he took Jesus up in his arms, and blessed God and said,

"Lord, now you let your servant go in peace;
 your word has been fulfilled.
My own eyes have seen the salvation
 which you have prepared in the sight
  of every people:
a light to reveal you to the nations
 and the glory of your people Israel."

And his father and his mother marveled at what was said about Jesus; and Simeon blessed them and said to Mary his mother,

"Behold, this child is set for the fall and rising
  of many in Israel,
 and for a sign that is spoken against
 (and a sword will pierce
  through your own soul also),
that thoughts out of many hearts may be revealed."

[Complete reading: Luke 2:22–40]

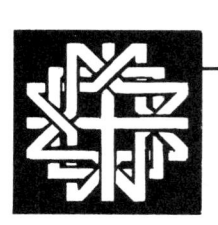

Mary, the Mother of God
Saturday, January 1, 1994

Numbers 6:22–27 The Lord let his face shine on you!
Galatians 4:4–7 You are no longer slaves, but children of God.
Luke 2:16–21 Mary pondered these things in her heart.

Our merry Christmastime unfolds with the blessing of a new year, with the astonishing good news of peace on earth, and with the treasures pondered within the heart of Mary.

REFLECTION

"I am a slave set free!" So says Simeon as his aged eyes behold the salvation present in the child Jesus. Simeon calls himself *doulos*, "slave." But Luke calls him "righteous" and "devout," one "looking for the consolation of Israel." The Holy Spirit was upon him. With the prophet Anna he represents that element in old Israel that was faithful, trusting, and patiently waiting for God to fulfill ancient promises. Theirs had been a long Advent.

When the old man held the child in his arms, blessing God, he knew he was no longer a slave of time and its slow passing. What God had promised was happening: Darkness was shattered by a new light. Freedom illuminates Simeon's old age, transforms his patient waiting into excited, joyful rest. Because of this child, the human family can be holy; Christ renews the relationship between God and all the sons and daughters of earth.

Later in the Gospel of Luke (8:19–21), Jesus appears to abandon his immediate family, and they appear to reject him. His response is to point to the larger dimensions of God's holy family. It transcends the limits of biological bonds. Simeon sees this dimension of the child's life, a meaning that stretches beyond their immediate situation. "This child is set for the fall and rising of many in Israel." Gifted with the Spirit, the old sage sees beyond a baby to a different kind of new birth. It is birth that also brings pain, the pain experienced when hearts are truly opened and their truths revealed when the light shines.

1. Read the whole passage (Luke 2:22–40) from which today's gospel is excerpted. It includes the important prophet, Anna. For Luke to call her a "prophetess" scandalized those who thought that only men could be prophets. Why? What evidence do you see of similar attitudes toward women in the church?

2. When someone is brought for baptism, he or she adds another facet to the holiness of your parish. How do you acknowledge and support a new member? How do you nurture faith and growth and a missionary spirit? How does a newly baptized person fire your communal hopes or satisfy old longings?

Practice of FAITH

NIGHT SONG. When old Simeon finally saw the Savior, he sang a song that the church has sung every night for centuries. Before bedtime, the Canticle of Simeon reminds us that, in many ways throughout the day now done, God offered salvation. You can sing Simeon's song to the tune of "O God Our Help in Ages Past" or "Land of Rest" before you go to sleep, perhaps standing in front of your Nativity set:

Lord, bid your servant go in peace
Your word is now fulfilled.
These eyes have seen salvation's dawn,
This child so long foretold.
This is the Savior of the world,
The gentiles' promised light,
God's glory dwelling in our midst,
The joy of Israel.

Then say "Glory to God in the highest and peace to God's people on earth."

Practice of HOPE

SO YOU ALSO MUST FORGIVE. Gerard Kiely was a university student, just 19 years old, when he was killed as he attended Mass at St. Brigid's Church in Belfast, Northern Ireland. His mother, Maura Kiely, realized then that "nothing could ever be the same again." She committed herself to working with bereaved families, both Catholic and Protestant. She founded the Cross Group, named to reflect the belief that no cross could be heavier to bear than to lose a loved one to the senseless tragedy of war.

The families meet to share their pain and their memories, commemorate anniversaries of the deaths of loved ones, and write personal notes of sympathy to others affected by the violence.

Their common pain has been a force for reconciliation, transcending the differences that have caused other citizens to kill one another. "People say that time heals," reflects Maura Kiely. "Time itself does not heal. It is what we do with time that can heal."

Practice of CHARITY

FORGIVING EACH OTHER. Our families might be where we find nurturing and growth and where we come to be who we are. At the same time, our families are often a source of pain. Perhaps it is time to sit around the table with your family and talk openly and honestly about those hurts. Work at forgiving each other. Instead of covering things up, bring them to the surface. If you're far away, pick up the phone and try to reconcile with a member of your family with whom you have had difficulty. Peace on earth begins here.

Weekday Reading
1 John, chapters 1–3

JANUARY 2, 1994
THE EPIPHANY OF THE LORD

READING I *Isaiah 60:1–6*

Arise, shine; for your light has come,
   and the glory of the LORD has risen upon you.
For behold, darkness shall cover the earth,
   and thick darkness the peoples;
but the LORD will arise upon you,
   and the glory of the LORD will be seen upon you.
And nations shall come to your light,
   and rulers to the brightness of your rising.
Lift up your eyes round about, and see;
   they all gather together, they come to you;
your sons shall come from far,
   and your daughters shall be carried in the arms.
Then you shall see and be radiant,
   your heart shall thrill and rejoice;
because the abundance of the sea shall be
    turned to you,
   the wealth of the nations shall come to you.
A multitude of camels shall cover you,
   the young camels of Midian and Ephah;
   all those from Sheba shall come.
They shall bring gold and frankincense,
   and shall proclaim the praise of the LORD.

READING II *Ephesians 3:2–3, 5–6*

Assuming that you have heard of the stewardship of God's grace that was given to me for you, how the mystery was made known to me by revelation, as I have written briefly, which was not made known to people of other generations as it has now been revealed to his holy apostles and prophets by the Spirit; that is, how the Gentiles are heirs with us, members of the same body, and partakers of the promise in Christ Jesus through the gospel.

GOSPEL *Matthew 2:1–12*

Now when Jesus was born in Bethlehem of Judea in the days of Herod the king, behold, magi from the East came to Jerusalem, saying, "Where is he who has been born king of the Jews? For we have seen his star in the East, and have come to worship him." When Herod the king heard this, he was troubled, and all Jerusalem with him; and assembling all the chief priests and scribes of the people, he inquired of them where the Christ was to be born. They told him, "In Bethlehem of Judea; for so it is written by the prophet:

'And you, O Bethlehem, in the land of Judah,
are by no means least among the rulers of Judah;
for from you shall come a ruler
who will govern my people Israel.'"

Then Herod summoned the magi secretly and ascertained from them what time the star appeared; and he sent them to Bethlehem, saying, "Go and search diligently for the child, and when you have found him bring me word, that I too may come and worship." When they had heard the king they went their way; and lo, the star which they had seen in the East went before them, till it came to rest over the place where the child was. When they saw the star, they rejoiced exceedingly with great joy; and going into the house they saw the child with Mary his mother, and they fell down and worshiped him. Then, opening their treasures, they offered him gifts, gold and frankincense and myrrh. And being warned in a dream not to return to Herod, they departed to their own country by another way.

REFLECTION

Jerusalem is an important locale in the gospels. Jesus is born near this holy city. He is presented in its Temple, visits throughout his life, and goes there as a fitting finale to his ministry, aware of the suffering that will result. Today's first reading celebrates the restored Jerusalem—Zion—in the time after Israel's exile. God has fulfilled a promise and restored the people to their holy city: Darkness is gone. Light blazes and scattered people flock there in wonder. God is among the people again; they are free to worship and to glory in the riches bestowed upon their city.

Matthew tells the story of the magi traveling a great distance by means of their astrological know-how. They represent the world; just as Isaiah had prophesied, at the coming of the messiah the nations gather and present their wealth as divine light shines forth. But the darkness is still thick. Herod, threatened by the sudden appearance of a rival to his throne, instigates a slaughter for security reasons. He has no idea what power he is taking on, and unwittingly begins the process that will end in Jesus' death in Jerusalem. Herod seeks to extinguish the new light. Later, Annas, Caiaphas, Pilate and the rest will believe they have succeeded in doing this. But the darkness over the earth at Calvary is but the prelude to the glorious light of resurrection.

Jerusalem is the focal point. It is the city of David's royal throne, though now occupied by a puppet of Rome. Later it is taken by its true king proclaimed by a crude sign above his crucified body—"the King of the Jews." The magi, who were foreigners and Gentiles, saw it and understood. They were forerunners in faith of the many Gentiles who came to believe.

The Epiphany discloses God's plan of salvation coming to fruition. It is light and joy to all people. But it is also an apocalypse of pain and suffering, as God struggles to be born into a violent world.

1. Even in the stories about Jesus' birth, Matthew plants the seeds of his passion. Can you spot those seeds in Matthew's first two chapters?

2. What do you think is the difference between the world the child Jesus was born into and the world you and your community seek to deliver him into? Use Matthew 2 as a starter.

Practice of **FAITH**

INTO THE HOUSE. Notice how the magi found God: "... going into the house they saw the child with Mary his mother, and they fell down and worshiped him." The door to your house is the door to where God lives! You can bless your house—and all those friends and strangers who will enter it this new year—by inscribing a prayer above the front door. With a piece of chalk or a lump of charcoal, inscribe this above the doors to your home:

19 + C + M + B + 94

Legend has it that the letters stand for the names of the magi—Caspar, Melchior and Balthasar—those strangers who came seeking God. They are also an abbreviation for "Christ bless this dwelling," in Latin *("Christus mansionem benedicat")*. Blessing your doorways in January is appropriate. The Latin word *janua* means portal or doorway, and January is the doorway to the whole year.

Practice of **HOPE**

ARISE, SHINE, YOUR LIGHT HAS COME. In the black township of Mamelodi, outside of Pretoria, South Africa, I asked a 10-year-old if he believes that apartheid will end in his lifetime. Without hesitation he said "yes." When I asked if he thought his children would grow up without apartheid, he answered confidently, "I will see to it."

Such children are part of the backbone of the freedom struggle. They light candles in windows as signs of their hope. The South African security forces push into homes to blow out the candles, and the children laugh and say, "They are afraid of candles." These children know a greater truth than the power of force: "The light shines in the darkness, and the darkness has not overcome it" (John 1:5).

Practice of **CHARITY**

AND NATIONS SHALL COME TO YOUR LIGHT. Our knowledge of other lands and peoples usually comes to us filtered by mass media. It's usually news of politics or economics. But in order for us to build bridges with our brothers and sisters in other countries we need first to begin to be exposed to their culture, their art, and their music. This is especially true for all of us who live in the Americas. In coming to appreciate another heritage we are a lot less likely to condemn it or destroy it. This week look up Nicaragua in the encyclopedia and learn something about this small country. The Nicaraguan Cultural Alliance and Quixote Center/Quest for Peace publish all-occasion greeting cards by Nicaraguan artists. The proceeds help fund human rights work in Nicaragua. Contact the Nicaraguan Cultural Alliance, Quixote Center, P.O. Box 5051, Hyattsville MD 20782; 301-699-0042.

Weekday Reading
1 John, chapters 4–5

JANUARY 9, 1994
THE BAPTISM OF THE LORD

READING I   *Isaiah 42:1–4, 6–7*

Behold my servant, whom I uphold,
  my chosen, in whom my soul delights,
upon whom I have put my Spirit,
  to bring forth justice to the nations:
not crying out, not lifting up his voice,
  not making it heard in the street,
a bruised reed my servant will not break,
  nor quench a dimly burning wick,
  but will faithfully bring forth justice.
My chosen one will not fail or be discouraged
  till he has established justice in the earth;
  and the coastlands wait for his law.
"I am the LORD, I have called you in righteousness,
  I have taken you by the hand and kept you;
I have given you as a covenant to the people,
  a light to the nations,
  to open the eyes that are blind,
to bring out the prisoners from the dungeon,
  from the prison those who sit in darkness."

READING II   *Acts 10:34–38*

Peter opened his mouth and said: "Truly I perceive that God shows no partiality, but in every nation anyone who is God-fearing and does what is right is acceptable to God. You know the word which God sent to Israel, preaching good news of peace by Jesus Christ (who is Lord of all), the word which was proclaimed throughout all Judea, beginning from Galilee after the baptism which John preached: how God anointed Jesus of Nazareth with the Holy Spirit and with power; how Jesus went about doing good and healing all that were oppressed by the devil, for God was with him."

GOSPEL   *Mark 1:7–11*

And John preached, saying, "After me comes one who is mightier than I, the thong of whose sandals I am not worthy to stoop down and untie. I have baptized you with water; but the one who is coming will baptize you with the Holy Spirit."

In those days Jesus came from Nazareth of Galilee and was baptized by John in the Jordan. And coming up out of the water, immediately Jesus saw the heavens opened and the Spirit descending upon him like a dove; and a voice came from heaven, "You are my son, the beloved one; with you I am well pleased."

REFLECTION

In the prophecy of Isaiah, a mysterious person appears in four poems or songs called the "Servant Songs." The song of the one who suffers is familiar to us from the Good Friday liturgy. From early on, the church understood these songs to be about Jesus.

Today's first reading is the first of the Servant Songs, and many scholars would say it refers not so much to an individual but to a group of people—Israel as a whole. The chosen nation is seen as the servant in whom God delights, charged with a mission to all other peoples.

We hear the first Servant Song today in the context of Jesus' baptism, and it gives occasion for reflection on the meaning of every Christian's baptism. Certainly the event Mark describes concerns the individual Jesus. But the purpose of baptism goes beyond the private interests of one particular human being. It initiates the purpose of Christ's coming—to minister. Mark tells the baptism story at the beginning of his active ministry of healing, teaching, reconciling, suffering and dying and rising. So, it marks a missionary commencement for him—as it does for all believers. Baptism defines the purpose and meaning of the individual. Jesus comes to serve others. The baptized servant—the Son of God in the Gospel of Mark or an anonymous Christian in a remote jungle village—takes on a new role within the missionary body. Just as Jesus fulfills Isaiah's prophecy and becomes the servant of whom the Servant Songs sing, so must the body of the baptized—the church—become Jesus.

Three times in Mark a heavenly voice is reported affirming the integrity of the servant/son. Jesus is empowered with the Holy Spirit, and so are believers who accept freely their baptism and enter into the serving community of disciples.

1. The three other Servant Songs from Isaiah are 49:1–6; 50:4–11; 52:13—53:12. Note one very similar song we heard on December 12—Isaiah 61:1–11. How interchangeable are the roles of individual and community in these songs? How do they apply to your church?

2. How do you understand and carry out your personal mission, your part in the communal mission and the mission of your church? How does this mission spring from baptism?

Practice of FAITH

WATER AND SPIRIT. Do you know the date of your baptism? If not, find out this week. Ask a relative, or write to the parish that baptized you. Write your baptismal date on the new calendar, and resolve to celebrate the anniversary this year by participating in the eucharist and spending some time reflecting on your Christian mission—your part in spreading God's love.

When Jesus was baptized, he came out of the water and heard a heavenly voice say, "You are my beloved one; with you I am well pleased." Listen for this voice this week whenever you "come out of the water"—the shower, the snow or rain, the swimming pool, the sudsy kitchen sink.

Practice of HOPE

I HAVE TAKEN YOU BY THE HAND. Several years ago, a fire—the result of landlord negligence—swept through the tenement in inner-city Washington, D.C., where Naomi Scott lived. She was severely burned and had to spend six months in the hospital on two separate occasions, hovering near death part of the time. She lost several fingers on both hands.

But Naomi Scott feels no bitterness. She says of her traumatic experience, "I just thank God that I can still play the piano," which she does with great ease, despite her loss. She is in great demand for her hymn and gospel playing at all her neighborhood's gatherings.

Practice of CHARITY

YOU ARE MY BELOVED ONE. In order for charity to be a dynamic component of our lives, we must believe that the words God spoke to Jesus as he emerged from the waters are also spoken to us. To believe that each one of us is a son or daughter loved by God is the first step in being able to live in charity and work for justice. Throughout this week repeat this passage from scripture to yourself: You are my beloved one. Allow the words to become part of your daily prayer. Repeat them to yourself each time you spare a quarter, change a diaper or do a favor. See that they describe how God sees the person you encounter and how God sees you, too.

Weekday Reading
1 Samuel, chapters 1–10

Winter Ordinary Time

God speaks, the ice melts;
God breathes,
    the streams flow.

Jerusalem, give glory!
Praise God with song, O Zion!
For the Lord strengthens your gates
guarding your children within,
the Lord fills your land with peace,
giving you golden wheat.

God speaks,
the word speeds forth.
The Lord sends heavy snow,
and scatters frost;
the Lord hurls chunks of hail.
Who can stand such cold?

God speaks, the ice melts;
God breathes, the streams flow.
God speaks the word to Israel,
for Israel, laws and decrees.
God has not done this for others;
no others receive this wisdom.

Hallelujah!
—*Psalm 147:12–20*

Shall we praise you, hail-hurling God,
in winter's splendor,
in the grace of snow
that covers with brightness
and reshapes both your creation and ours?
Or shall we curse the fierce cold
that punishes homeless people
and shortens tempers?
Blessed are you
in the earth's tilt and course.
Blessed are you in the sleep of winter
and in the oncoming lenten spring.
Now and then and always,
fill these lands with peace.

—*Prayer of the Season*

JANUARY 16, 1994
SECOND SUNDAY IN ORDINARY TIME

READING I *1 Samuel 3:3–10, 19*

Samuel was lying down within the temple of the LORD, where the ark of God was. Then the LORD called, "Samuel! Samuel!" and he said, "Here I am!" and ran to Eli, and said, "Here I am, for you called me." But Eli said, "I did not call; lie down again." So Samuel went and lay down. And the LORD called again, "Samuel!" And Samuel arose and went to Eli, and said, "Here I am, for you called me." But Eli said, "I did not call, my son; lie down again." Now Samuel did not yet know the LORD, and the word of the LORD had not yet been revealed to him. And the LORD called Samuel again the third time. And he arose and went to Eli, and said, "Here I am, for you called me." Then Eli perceived that the LORD was calling the boy. Therefore Eli said to Samuel, "Go, lie down; and if the LORD calls you, you shall say, 'Speak, LORD, for your servant hears.'" So Samuel went and lay down in his place.

And the LORD came and stood forth, calling as at other times, "Samuel! Samuel!" And Samuel said, "Speak, for your servant hears."

And Samuel grew, and the LORD was with him and let none of his words fall to the ground.

READING II *1 Corinthians 6:13–15, 17–20*

The body is not meant for immorality, but for the Lord, and the Lord for the body. And God raised the Lord and will also raise us up by divine power. Do you not know that your bodies are physical parts of Christ? But the one who is united to the Lord becomes one spirit with the Lord. Shun immoral sexual conduct. Every other sin which is committed is outside the body; but immoral sexual conduct is sin against one's own body. Do you not know that your body is a temple of the Holy Spirit within you, which you have from God? You are not your own; you were bought with a price. So glorify God in your body.

GOSPEL *John 1:35–42*

John was standing with two of his disciples; and he looked at Jesus walking by, and said, "Behold, the Lamb of God!" The two disciples heard him say this, and they followed Jesus. Jesus turned, and saw them following, and said to them, "What do you seek?" And they said to him, "Rabbi" (which means Teacher), "where are you staying?" Jesus said to them, "Come and see." They came and saw where he was staying; and they stayed with him that day, for it was about the tenth hour. One of the two who heard John speak, and followed him, was Andrew, Simon Peter's brother. He first found his brother Simon, and said to him, "We have found the Messiah" (which means Christ). Andrew brought Simon to Jesus. Jesus looked at him, and said, "So you are Simon the son of John? You shall be called 'Cephas'" (which means Peter).

REFLECTION

The Bible is a variety of accounts of how God and human beings grew into a relationship, how that relationship was strained, even broken, and how reconciliation was achieved—repeatedly. Human beings pictured God in different ways at different times in their relationship: as a warrior (Judges), a savior (Exodus), a king enthroned in glory (Isaiah and Ezekiel), a compassionate spouse (Hosea), a detached and indifferent power (Ecclesiastes) and so on. No monolithic picture of God emerges from the Bible. That there was a caring God involved with a chosen people is never questioned, though. And two things remain consistent: Although the people waver in their faithfulness, God never does.

How God was understood to be present also varied. The ark was a visible symbol of the power and presence of the one who rescued a people from slavery and then dwelt among them. It was a tangible presence that evoked Moses, Sinai, Egypt, slavery, redemption —the whole Exodus. In the book of Numbers the ark is housed in a tent—God "pitched his tent among us" and was present in word and deed.

The first reading speaks of the dark silence out of which the voice of God issues. When the ark later rested in the Jerusalem Temple, the "Holy of Holies" had no windows, and a lamp burned as a reminder of the divine presence. Only the high priest made an annual visit into the blackness. But here the voice bypasses the priest Eli to address the 12-year-old Samuel. Luke uses this material in his scene of Jesus in the Temple: the child teaching his elders. In the Gospel of John, Jesus is the light of the world itself and into his presence he invites people to share in the ministry of the word made flesh. He is the voice speaking the message of life. Samuel was his prophetic forbearer, through whom the voice of God was heard anew in Israel.

1. What is your image of God? What image of God is most common in your parish?

2. The presence of God in our midst affects our personal and communal presence in the world. How does God's message of peace and reconciliation for all speak through us? How is it received?

Practice of FAITH

MARTYRS AGNES AND MARTIN. Friday we remember Agnes, a young woman (perhaps thirteen) who was killed during Diocletian's persecution of Christians in the fourth century. In art, Agnes is shown holding a wooly white lamb, a symbol of her innocence—and a visual pun. Agnes sounds like *agnus,* the Latin word for lamb. (In today's gospel, John calls Jesus "*Agnus Dei*"—Lamb of God.) If you have a lamb-shaped cake mold for Easter, dust it off and bake a cake this week in honor of Agnes.

Tomorrow we remember another martyr, the great African American Martin Luther King, Jr. If your public library is open today, borrow a book of Dr. King's writings. Read the speeches aloud tomorrow. Enjoy the poetry as you heed the prophecy.

Practice of HOPE

SPEAK, LORD, FOR YOUR SERVANT HEARS. God spoke to Samuel and continues to call all manner of reluctant and unexpected prophets. As we once again mark the birthday of Martin Luther King, Jr., let us remember all the anonymous heroes of that turbulent time in our history known as the civil rights era. Let us remember the women, men, and children who bore the insults and the clubs, the water cannons and the dogs, in their fight for equality.

During the Montgomery bus boycott in 1956, a concerned friend suggested to an elderly woman that she should ride the bus anyway. But she was steadfast in her determination to observe the boycott. "My feet are tired, but my soul is rested," she said as she continued walking for freedom. May we be such determined prophets when God calls us.

Practice of CHARITY

A SIN AGAINST ONE'S BODY. Sexuality is a tremendous gift of God's love for us. The abuse of this gift diminishes the beauty of what God has created and severely harms both the abused and the abuser. Both in the church and in larger society, the horror of sexual abuse has manifested itself. We can do three things: 1) If you suspect someone is being sexually abused, immediately contact the sexual assault counseling center in your town or the department of children and family services in your state (check the phone book for numbers); 2) ask that a speaker be brought in to your parish to address the issue; 3) be a healthy example of the beauty of sexuality by the way you live and relate to others.

Weekday Reading
1 Samuel, chapters 15–24

JANUARY 23, 1994
THIRD SUNDAY IN ORDINARY TIME

READING I *Jonah 3:1–5, 10*

The word of the LORD came to Jonah the second time, saying, "Arise, go to Nineveh, that great city, and proclaim to it the message that I tell you." So Jonah arose and went to Nineveh, according to the word of the LORD. Now Nineveh was an exceedingly great city, three days' journey in breadth. Jonah began to go into the city, going a day's journey. And he cried, "Yet forty days, and Nineveh shall be overthrown!" And the people of Nineveh believed God; they proclaimed a fast, and put on sackcloth, from the greatest of them to the least of them.

When God saw what they did, how they turned from their evil way, God repented of the evil which had been threatened; and God did not do it.

READING II *1 Corinthians 7:29–31*

My dear people, the appointed time has grown very short; from now on, let those who are married live as though they were not, and those who mourn as though they were not mourning, and those who rejoice as though they were not rejoicing, and those who buy as though they had no goods, and those who deal with the world as though they had no dealings with it. For the form of this world is passing away.

GOSPEL *Mark 1:14–20*

After John was arrested, Jesus came into Galilee, preaching the gospel of God, and saying, "The time is fulfilled, and the dominion of God is at hand; repent, and believe in the gospel."

And passing along by the Sea of Galilee, Jesus saw Simon and Andrew the brother of Simon casting a net in the sea; for they were fishermen. And Jesus said to them, "Follow me and I will make you fish for human beings." And immediately they left their nets and followed him. And going on a little farther, Jesus saw James the son of Zebedee and John his brother, who were in their boat mending the nets. And immediately Jesus called them; and they left their father Zebedee in the boat with the hired servants, and followed him.

REFLECTION

The Book of Jonah is unusual and amusing. It contains none of the usual prophetic oracles of condemnation, no diatribes against foreign nations, nor any of the lilting poems or sonorous psalms that we find in Isaiah or Jeremiah. Instead the character of Jonah himself takes center stage in this brief book. His message is about the broadness of God's love and mercy which, to Jonah's dismay, even includes the Gentile Ninevites. Jonah is reminded that however reluctant he might be—and he is very reluctant—he has a mission to preach and so preach he must. He is not at all pleased with the resounding success of his ministry, and he is reminded that he is only the instrument of a ministering God.

Similarly, Jesus' initial call to "repent and believe," is met with success. Simon, Andrew, James and John simply stop what they are doing and heed the call. They jump at the time-fulfilling opportunity that Jesus presents—passage into the dominion of heaven.

We have a message of salvation from two very different prophets. Jonah leaves the people to whom he successfully preached, finds a hiding place, and pouts. The main obstacle to God's word had been Jonah, but God's word is not dependent on Jonah. What Jesus delivers is more than God's word. Mark leaves us in no doubt that the relationship between God and Jesus is unique. Their wills are consonant. What God wants, Jesus wants—and makes effective.

We don't know what eventually happened to Jonah. He may have met another large fish! What happened to Jesus as a consequence of his missionary activity is the focal point of the Gospel of Mark. And even in that apparent contradiction—the murder of God's prophet, when all seems like failure—it is the message of love and mercy, the word of God made flesh that springs to new life from a tomb.

1. Read the whole book of Jonah. It's very short. Why is Jonah so reluctant? Tell about a time when you felt the same way.

2. Many people are often reluctant to be teachers, evangelists or sponsors because they believe "success" depends on them. Jonah and Jesus both show that success is entirely the work of God and that apparent "failure" is also part of the drama. What happens when you let God do what God wants?

Practice of FAITH

FISHING FOR HUMAN BEINGS. Has your parish been fishing for human beings lately? More and more parishes now invite and encourage adults who were never baptized to consider becoming Christian. The *catechumenate* is the group of unbaptized people in a parish preparing for baptism; individuals are called *catechumens,* an old Greek name that means "people who learn by word of mouth." The catechumens are cared for by catechists (those who teach "by word of mouth") and sponsors.

It seems too simple, but an unbaptized adult often becomes a Christian because someone *asks* him or her. Do you know someone who has never been baptized? Do you know someone who is searching for meaning in life? Find out if your parish has an inquiry session. Invite the unbaptized person you know to attend the session, and go with him or her.

Practice of HOPE

REPENT AND BELIEVE. Beyers Naude of South Africa was the youngest person ever to join the Broederbond, the secret Afrikaner society that conceived apartheid. Naude became a pastor of the Dutch Reformed Church, and many thought that he would some day be prime minister of South Africa. But when he was in his forties, a dawning of truth came—by "reading the Bible, that's all," according to Naude. He went to areas of black suffering. "Unless you are willing to go to the victims," he said, "you can never discover the full truth of the gospel." For his commitment to the black freedom struggle, the church severed its ties to Naude and the government banned him for seven years. But, he said, "I've gained an inner freedom and an inner peace of mind . . . and the ability to continue to love when others hate."

Practice of CHARITY

LIVE AS THOUGH YOU HAD NO GOODS. If you have a car, park it. If you have a TV, turn it off. If you own a house . . . ? These may be radical considerations for those of us who live in a consumer society where creature comfort is number one. But what if our comfort is slowly destroying the environment? Stewardship is more than just planting a tree on Earth Day. It involves how we live on the earth. Does it mean living without modern technology? Maybe some people will feel called to do so, but for most of us it means making choices to live simply. A great resource is the book *50 Simple Things You Can Do to Save the Earth.* For information write: Earth Works Press, Box 25, 1400 Shattuck Avenue, Berkeley CA 94709 or call 415-841-5866.

Weekday Reading
2 Samuel, chapters 1–12

JANUARY 30, 1994
FOURTH SUNDAY IN ORDINARY TIME

READING I *Deuteronomy 18:15–20*

[Moses said to the people,]

"The LORD your God will raise up for you a prophet like me from among you, from your kinfolk—whom you shall heed—just as you desired of the LORD your God at Horeb on the day of the assembly, when you said, 'Let me not hear again the voice of the LORD my God, or see this great fire any more, lest I die.' And the LORD said to me, 'They have rightly said all that they have spoken. I will raise up for them a prophet like you from among their kin; and I will put my words in his mouth, to speak all that I command. And those who do not give heed to my words which the prophet shall speak in my name, I myself will require it of them. But the prophet who presumes to speak a word in my name which I have not commanded him to speak, or who speaks in the name of other gods, that same prophet shall die.'"

READING II *1 Corinthians 7:32–35*

I want you to be free from anxieties. The unmarried man is anxious about the affairs of the Lord, how to please the Lord; but the married man is anxious about worldly affairs, how to please his wife, and his interests are divided. And the unmarried woman or virgin is anxious about the affairs of the Lord, how to be holy in body and spirit; but the married woman is anxious about worldly affairs, how to please her husband. I say this for your own benefit, not to lay any restraint upon you, but to promote good order and to secure your undivided devotion to the Lord.

GOSPEL *Mark 1:21–28*

Jesus and his followers went into Capernaum; and immediately on the sabbath he entered the synagogue and taught. And they were astonished at his teaching, for Jesus taught them as one who had authority, and not as the scribes. And immediately there was in their synagogue a man with an unclean spirit, who cried out, "What have you to do with us, Jesus of Nazareth? Have you come to destroy us? I know who you are, the Holy One of God." But Jesus rebuked the spirit, saying, "Be silent, and come out of him!" And the unclean spirit, convulsing him and crying with a loud voice, came out of the man. And they were all amazed, so that they questioned among themselves, saying, "What is this? A new teaching! With authority he commands even the unclean spirits, and they obey him." And at once Jesus' fame spread everywhere throughout all the surrounding region of Galilee.

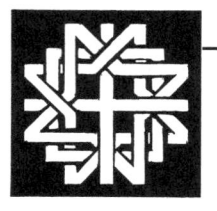

The Presentation of the Lord
Wednesday, February 2, 1994

Malachi 3:1–4 But who can endure the day of his coming?
Hebrews 2:14–18 He became like us in every way.
Luke 2:22–40 Simeon took the child in his arms.

The light of Christmas shone feebly at first, rising to shine brightly from a star at Epiphany. Today this light is placed in our arms. The desire of our hearts and the hope of the world now shine in our flesh and blood. Like Simeon, we are hand in hand with God.

REFLECTION

How do you recognize a real prophet when there are so many fakes around? Behind the four different gospel portraits of Jesus is the powerful figure of Moses, the prophet par excellence, hero of the Exodus, the lawgiver. In the important scene of the transfiguration (Mark 9:2–13), he appears alongside Jesus to give the authority of law and the ancient scriptures to the message and ministry of Jesus.

Authority is a key idea in today's readings. It's how the ordinary folk distinguished Jesus from their more familiar religious leaders. He had genuine authority, an authority that the leaders had forfeited a long time ago. In word and deed this new prophet astonished the crowds. Even unclean spirits obeyed him.

In the first reading is a promise to the people by God through Moses that another prophet like Moses—with the same authority and from among the same people—would follow the great lawgiver. God's word would be in the new prophet's mouth, who will be obedient. There is also a warning to would-be prophets who tell people, "This is what the Lord says," but have no authority to prophesy.

By virtue of how each lived his life, Moses and Jesus had authority from God and they handed it on to others: Moses to Joshua, Jesus to the church. Both lead captives from slavery to freedom. Each one's relationship to God was unique. Deuteronomy 18 is about truth and falsehood. The true prophet is recognizable: His or her words will be brought to fulfillment in line with God's intentions. Jesus and Moses lived in communion with God and were obedient. Their lives revealed the authority of their words and their deeds were thus true.

1. Read some of what scripture has to say about real prophets (Isaiah 48:3–5; Ezekiel 12:21–28; 33:1–9) and about false ones (Deuteronomy 13:1–5; Ezekiel 13:1–16; Jeremiah 23:9–40; Micah 3:5–8). How does Jesus fulfill these expectations of what a real prophet is? How does Moses?

2. Who would you classify as a modern prophet? Remember that what a prophet has to say about the future is based mostly on a truthful, often unwelcome, analysis of the present.

Practice of FAITH

CANDLES AND THROATS. Wednesday is the Solemnity of the Presentation of the Lord. We remember that Mary and Joseph, faithful Jews, took their firstborn son to the Temple to consecrate him to the Lord. When they arrived, the aged prophets Simeon and Anna recognized the little baby as the light of the world. So today the church gives thanks and praise to God for candles that remind us of Christ's light. Even if you can't attend Mass and get blessed candles, light candles at dinner Wednesday night. Did you learn Simeon's song last month (see page 37)? Sing it before you go to bed on Wednesday, if not every night.

Thursday, we remember the bishop and martyr Blase, who saved someone from choking. With the blessed candles of the Presentation arranged in the shape of the cross, we touch each other's throats and pray that God keeps us well this winter.

Practice of HOPE

I WILL RAISE UP FOR THEM A PROPHET. "I have been sick and tired so long that I am sick and tired of being sick and tired." These were the most well-known words of Fannie Lou Hamer, who was born into a family of sharecroppers in the Mississippi delta and later became a prophet of the civil rights movement. She moved her audiences wherever she appeared, because she spoke not only about their frustrations, but also about their determination for justice.

Hamer led a grassroots uprising against racism in the Democratic party and was a leader in the fight to desegregate buses and lunch counters. For her persistence she suffered beatings and other kinds of persecution. Some other words she left with us are those from the song "This Little Light of Mine": "I've got the light of freedom, I'm gonna let it shine."

Practice of CHARITY

A PROPHET AMONG YOU, FROM YOUR KINSFOLK. There are many opportunities for parishes in our country to have sister parishes in third world nations or in other parts of North America. One group that facilitates this is the Adopt a Parish Program founded by Harry Hosey in Old Hickory, Tennessee, over 15 years ago. His program matches parishes in the U.S. and Canada with parishes in Haiti, Guatemala, Panama, Jamaica, Mexico and El Salvador. He has arranged over 330 adoptions. Talk to your parish council or parish peace and justice committee, and ask them to contact Harry & Alice Hosey, Adopt A Parish Program, P.O. Box 111, Old Hickory TN 37138; 615-847-5022.

Weekday Reading
2 Samuel, chapters 13–18, 1 Kings, chapters 1–3, Sirach 47:2–11

FEBRUARY 6, 1994
FIFTH SUNDAY IN ORDINARY TIME

READING I   *Job 7:1–4, 6–7*

[Job answered,]
"Has not a man a hard service upon earth,
 and are not his days like the days of a hireling?
Like a slave who longs for the shadow,
 and like a hireling who looks for wages,
so I am allotted months of emptiness,
 and nights of misery are apportioned to me.
When I lie down I say, 'When shall I arise?'
 But the night is long,
 and I am full of tossing till the dawn.
My days are swifter than a weaver's shuttle,
 and come to their end without hope.
Remember that my life is a breath;
 my eye will never again see good."

READING II   *1 Corinthians 9:16–19, 22–23*

If I preach the gospel, that gives me no ground for boasting. For necessity is laid upon me. Woe to me if I do not preach the gospel! For if I do this of my own will, I have a reward; but if not of my own will, I am entrusted with a commission. What then is my reward? Just this: that in my preaching I may make the gospel free of charge, not making full use of my right in the gospel.

For though I am free from all people, I have made myself a slave to all, that I might win the more. To the weak I became weak, that I might win the weak. I have become all things to all people, that I might by all means save some. I do it all for the sake of the gospel, that I may share in its blessings.

GOSPEL   *Mark 1:29–39*

Immediately Jesus left the synagogue, and entered the house of Simon and Andrew, with James and John. Now Simon's mother-in-law lay sick with a fever, and immediately they told Jesus of her. And Jesus came and took her by the hand and lifted her up, and the fever left her; and she served them.

That evening, at sundown, they brought to Jesus all who were sick or possessed with demons. And the whole city was gathered together about the door. And Jesus healed many who were sick with various diseases, and cast out many demons; and he would not permit the demons to speak, because they knew him.

And in the morning, a great while before day, Jesus rose and went out to a lonely place, and there he prayed. And Simon and those who were with him pursued him, and they found Jesus and said to him, "Every one is searching for you." And Jesus said to them, "Let us go on to the next towns, that I may preach there also; for that is why I came out." And Jesus went throughout all Galilee, preaching in their synagogues and casting out demons.

REFLECTION

Job is innocent—the quintessential good man to whom bad things happen. Eliphaz tries to persuade Job that his suffering is a good discipline that will lead to his healing. But Job will have none of this: His punishment is too harsh. Job confronts God directly with the eternal human question: "Why?"

The Book of Job searches for an answer to this riddle. No neat and tidy answer is given. The Book of Job is not that kind of self-help book.

In Mark, Jesus is the solution—but in a surprising way. In today's excerpt, he is found among the suffering, people who themselves have said, "Why me, God?" Jesus heals people, but that doesn't end all human pain. Up to this point in the gospel, only the demons have truly recognized Jesus for who he is. For others, his suffering and death need to be witnessed—experienced—before they can understand. The issue of suffering surfaces as Jesus predicts his own passion. The disciples are uncomfortable with the idea, even reject it. What kind of Son of God is this that he needs to suffer? Why could not Jesus avoid the pain and suffering that mortals are subject to? Peter wanted him to.

But Jesus lives a complete human life. Into familiar human miseries, Jesus brings a closeness to God that does not deflect the suffering but shows a way through it to a different kind of life. The human situation is not transcended by avoidance or denial of its reality but by embracing it and allowing the power of God to transform it. Jesus died in order to rise. His followers are bound on the same journey. Job's trust, tested ultimately like Jesus', was not acceptable to his "friends." Jesus' trust appeared crazy, too, given the forces he was up against. But God gives the final word in both cases.

1. The mystery of suffering is seen by Mark as a cosmic force, hence his report that demons—supernatural powers—know who Jesus is and are threatened and obedient. How do we or people we know handle suffering? What communal suffering have we witnessed or experienced?

2. A young man with AIDS said: "I realize that this diagnosis of AIDS presents me with a choice: the choice to be a hopeless victim and die of AIDS, or to make my life right now what it always ought to have been." How do transformations like this happen?

Practice of FAITH

OUT TO A LONELY PLACE. Sometimes to grow in spirit we need to do as Jesus did: Go away to pray. In church language, this is called "going on retreat." Most dioceses have a place or two, sometimes out in the country but often right in the middle of the city, where Christians can go for a few hours, a few days or even a few weeks to pray, read, sleep and eat. Some parishes organize group retreats for a weekend, and even help babysit or elder sit to allow someone to go. See if these opportunities are available to you, and plan to avail yourself during the year.

If that is not practical, try setting aside some "retreat time" during your week. Spending a half hour in prayer by yourself in your room can be your way of going out to that lonely place.

Practice of HOPE

CAST OUT MANY DEMONS. Washington, D.C., averages more than one drug-related murder a day. Such violence has a profound effect on children, particularly in a gun- and drug-infested neighborhood like Columbia Heights, where many of these murders occur. The Sojourners Neighborhood Center has committed itself to building their self-esteem and hope. During a program called "We Can Make a Change," the children of Columbia Heights painted a mural of their neighborhood. They decided that they didn't want the "demons" of guns and drugs and broken glass in their mural. They painted rainbows and children playing and notes of music drifting across the tenements. The huge mural hangs on the side of the neighborhood center as a testimony of their dream for a different world.

Practice of CHARITY

THE NIGHT IS LONG. Imagine that you are lost and afraid. You left home because you thought no one cared, and maybe you are right. You think if you can just make it to the city, your life will turn around. Instead what you find is drugs, prostitution, homelessness and more terror. And no one seems to care. Then the light appears. It is the light of people who care and who believe in the gospel to seek and find the forgotten. Those people give you shelter, food and comfort. Most importantly they give you a safe haven in which to get your life on track.

This is the work of the Covenant House, which began in New York City 26 years ago, and now has spread to over 8 cities. Consider making a donation to their work. Consider helping one more son or daughter to realize their life is significant. For information or to send a donation, write to Covenant House, P.O. Box 731, Times Square Station, New York NY 10108; 212-727-4143.

Weekday Reading
1 Kings, chapters 8–12

FEBRUARY 13, 1994
SIXTH SUNDAY IN ORDINARY TIME

READING I   *Leviticus 13:1–2, 44–46*

The Lord said to Moses and Aaron, "When the skin of someone's body has a swelling or an eruption or a spot, and it turns into a leprous disease on the body's skin, then that person shall be brought to Aaron the priest or to one of his descendants the priests.

"If he is a leprous man, he is unclean; the priest must pronounce him unclean; his disease is on his head. The male leper who has the disease shall wear torn clothes and let the hair of his head hang loose, and he shall cover his upper lip and cry, 'Unclean, unclean.' He shall remain unclean as long as he has the disease; he is unclean; he shall dwell alone in a habitation outside the camp."

READING II   *1 Corinthians 10:31—11:1*

Whether you eat or drink, or whatever you do, do all to the glory of God. Give no offense to Jews or to Greeks or to the church of God, just as I try to please every one in everything I do, not seeking my own advantage, but that of many, that they may be saved. Be imitators of me, as I am of Christ.

GOSPEL   *Mark 1:40–45*

A leprous man came, beseeching Jesus, and kneeling said to him, "If you will, you can make me clean." Moved with pity, Jesus stretched out his hand and touched him, and said to him, "I will; be clean." And immediately the leprosy left the man, and he was made clean. And Jesus sternly charged the man, and sent him away at once, saying, "See that you say nothing to any one; but go, show yourself to the priest, and offer for your cleansing what Moses commanded, for a proof to the people." But the one who was cleansed went out and began to talk freely about it, and to spread the news, so that Jesus could no longer openly enter a town, but it was out in the country; and people came to him from every quarter.

Ash Wednesday
Wednesday, February 16, 1994

Joel 2:12–18   Proclaim a fast. Rend your hearts.
2 Corinthians 5:20—6:2   Now is the time to be reconciled.
Matthew 6:1–6, 16–18   Pray, fast and give alms.

The Spirit urges us into the desert discipline of the lenten spring. For 40 days we will strip away everything that separates us from God, beginning today, as we are marked with a cross of ashes: death and life in a single sign!

REFLECTION

Biblical law (Leviticus 13–14) says that lepers, because they were thought to be dangerous to the community, must be isolated. The disease itself is less important than its contagious ritual impurity—to have leprosy means being separated from the worshiping community. The Hebrew word for leprosy used in the Bible includes the disease as we now diagnose it, as well as other skin diseases.

Jesus is in the presence of a leprous man. The man should not have been within range of ritually clean people. However, out of compassion, Jesus actually touches him. The law is broken and Jesus is made ritually impure. That means no more worship, no more association with the community for Jesus until a priest declares him cleansed. By touching the leper, Jesus puts himself in the same situation as the leper. Jesus becomes an outcast by choice.

Why would Jesus command the leper to silence? This healing is a miracle. Why hide it? Mark supplies a solution. Because the man broadcasts the good news of his healing, everybody knows that Jesus had contracted impurity: "Jesus could no longer openly enter a town." He was perhaps looked upon suspiciously by the pious and avoided by those he wished to meet.

Jesus told the man to observe the law by showing himself to the priest. Technically, even though clearly healed, the man was not "cleansed" until the priest said so, after inquiring into the circumstances. The details could have served as ammunition for those who would later seek to destroy Jesus as a law-breaker and blasphemer. No doubt Jesus' ignoring of the law by actually touching the leper came out of his compassion for a suffering man. Such an action also endeared him to the many common folk who already felt alienated from the religious establishment: "People came to him from every quarter."

1. Who are the social and moral "lepers" in the world and in our community? Does their "condition" bar them from God's love at our hands?

2. What religious, political or moral views might, or do, make us outcasts? What does it mean that Jesus, the center of our faith, was regarded by the powers of his day as a religious, moral and political outcast? Jesus is still in that role around the world today. Where? Why?

Practice of FAITH

EXILED IN ASHES. Lent begins this Wednesday: The church gathers to smear ashes on each forehead and admonish each one to believe and repent. The ashes are made by burning the palms we took home last year to tuck behind a crucifix or picture as a sign of faith. As do our best intentions, the palms have become dry and dusty. Again we've wandered off course. So in Lent we find our way back to the basics: prayer, fasting and almsgiving.

An old way of showing that we were lost was to veil the statues in church with purple cloth. Images of Christ and the saints are promises of heaven; the veil reminds us that we've lost sight of our goal. At Easter the veils come off and we see more clearly our destiny. You may want to do this: Cover your cross or holy picture with a simple purple cloth until Easter.

Practice of HOPE

DO ALL TO THE GLORY OF GOD. All of creation speaks to the glory of God. Destruction of our environment indicates our distance from the Creator. But Native Indian Christians are inviting us back to a partnership with the Earth. Theologian George Tinker says that "respect for creation must be our starting point for theological reflection in our endangered world." He speaks of the hope that is carried forward in churches such as his own, with a challenge to those of us who are not native to America:

"Not only do Indians continue to tell the stories, sing the songs, speak the prayers, and perform the ceremonies that root themselves deeply in Mother Earth, they are actually audacious enough to think that their stories and their ways of reverencing creation will someday win over 'the immigrants' and transform them."

Practice of CHARITY

UNCLEAN, UNCLEAN. The Center for Disease Control predicts that, by the mid-1990s, 10,000 residents in Washington, D.C., alone will have AIDS. Our nation's capital is a mirror to the deadly disease now present in over 163 countries and projected to infect over 40 million people worldwide by the year 2000. We cannot shun those who are ill, treating them as lepers. We must respond as Jesus did, touching and being touched by those persons living with AIDS, or those who are HIV-positive. The church has a moral responsibility to teach compassion and to preach about AIDS, and parents and teachers must teach prevention. If you are interested in making a donation, being a friend for a person living with AIDS or helping to educate your parish about this disease, contact The National Catholic AIDS Network, P.O. Box 10092, Washington DC 20018.

Weekday Reading
James 1:1–11; 1:12–18; (We—Ash Wednesday); Deuteronomy 30:15–20; Isaiah 58:1–9; 58:9–14

Lent

Wash away my sin.
Cleanse me from my guilt.

You see me for what I am,
a sinner before my birth.

You love those centered in truth;
in wisdom center me.
Wash me with fresh water;
wash me bright as snow.

Fill me with happy songs;
let my bruised bones dance.
Shut your eyes to my sin;
make my guilt vanish.

Bring back my joy; save me.
Support me, free my spirit.
Then I will teach your way
and sinners will turn to you.

Help me, stop my tears,
and I will sing your goodness.
Lord, give me words
and I will shout your praise.

When I offer a holocaust,
you do not take the gift.
So I offer my shattered spirit;
a changed heart you welcome.

—*Psalm 51:7–11, 14–19*

Like a gift we only want to want,
these forty days surround us once more
and you set about washing us, God.
Scrub and scour these stubborn ashes.
Separate what we are
from what we are not
and so bring on the lenten ordeal:
the prayer by day and night,
the fast that clears our sight,
the alms that set things right.
At the end, when we have lost again,
you alone make dry bones come together
and bruised bones dance
round the cross where sinners live
now and for ever.

—*Prayer of the Season*

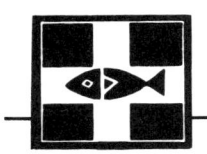

FEBRUARY 20, 1994
FIRST SUNDAY OF LENT

READING I *Genesis 9:8–15*

God said to Noah and to Noah's sons with him, "Behold, I establish my covenant with you and your descendants after you, and with every living creature that is with you, the birds, the cattle, and every beast of the earth with you, as many as came out of the ark. I establish my covenant with you, that never again shall all flesh be cut off by the waters of a flood, and never again shall there be a flood to destroy the earth." And God said, "This is the sign of the covenant which I make between me and you and every living creature that is with you, for all future generations: I set my bow in the cloud, and it shall be a sign of the covenant between me and the earth. When I bring clouds over the earth and the bow is seen in the clouds, I will remember my covenant which is between me and you and every living creature of all flesh; and the waters shall never again become a flood to destroy all flesh."

READING II *1 Peter 3:18–22*

Christ also died for sins once for all, the righteous for the unrighteous, that he might bring us to God, being put to death in the flesh but made alive in the spirit; in which he went and preached to the spirits in prison, who formerly did not obey, when God's patience waited in the days of Noah, during the building of the ark, in which a few, that is, eight persons, were saved through water. Baptism, which corresponds to this, now saves you, not as a removal of dirt from the body but as an appeal to God for a clear conscience, through the resurrection of Jesus Christ, who has gone into heaven and is at the right hand of God, with angels, authorities, and powers subject to him.

GOSPEL *Mark 1:12–15*

The Spirit immediately drove Jesus out into the wilderness. And Jesus was in the wilderness forty days, tempted by Satan, and was with the wild beasts; and the angels ministered to him.

Now after John was arrested, Jesus came into Galilee, preaching the gospel of God, and saying, "The time is fulfilled, and the dominion of God is at hand; repent, and believe in the gospel."

REFLECTION

Our universe has death and resurrection at its very core. From the randomness at the sub-atomic level to the macrocosmic inevitability of the Earth's end, change is constant: One thing passes away so that something new can be born. We humans have been telling stories about it forever. We still do.

A very ancient death and resurrection story is that of the Deluge, the story of Noah. Our first reading today is part of the whole saga (Genesis 5:32—9:29). God brings to an end the known creation. It dies in a flood. Out of its dying comes new life and a rainbow as reassurance that destruction will never happen this way again.

Flood waters connect Noah, Jesus and ourselves. Baptism washed away what used to be—our old self dies—and up out of the waters comes a new life. In Jesus' baptism, as Mark reports it, the first event in the emergent new life was the opening of heaven. Mark's language is powerful. *"Schizomenous,"* he writes: The heavens were torn apart. The Spirit of God hovers over the waters of chaos. In the first Genesis creation story, the Spirit descends like the dove that Noah released, a sign of new life on the earth, a sign of peace between God and people.

The voice declares that this new life is freshly grafted to God. One issues from the other. That which is made of clay—humanity—is charged with divine life—the breath of God.

Temptation follows, that familiar internal battle that has to be settled in each human being if peace is ever to reign—the choice for life or death. Jesus' action, after the issue is settled in the desert, is to go out and announce, "New life with God is available. Make your choice (repent). Do it now (time is fulfilled). Believe what I say (I've been through it. I know the way to God)."

Baptized we may be. Yet the choice is a daily one: life or death!

1. Lent's 40 days prepare us for Easter's 50. What has to be washed away from you so that new life can begin?

2. What examples of death and resurrection going on around you can you identify? How are you part of it? What does Christ's resurrection affirm in your experience?

Practice of FAITH

BAPTISM SAVES YOU. Are some people in your parish preparing to be baptized at Easter? Have their names been published in the bulletin or on a prayer card? If so, stick the names in your Bible or on your refrigerator so that you will remember to pray for them. Today they will see the bishop, who will "elect" (choose) them for the Easter sacraments of baptism, confirmation and eucharist. Thus they will be called "the elect" (those chosen). Say this prayer from the Rite of Christian Initiation of Adults for them:

Lord God,
you desire that all be saved
and come to the knowledge of truth.
Enliven with faith those who are preparing for baptism;
bring them into the fold of your Church,
there to receive the gift of eternal life.
We ask this through Christ our Lord. Amen.

Practice of HOPE

I SET MY BOW IN THE CLOUD. The Monday night women's Bible study at Sojourners Neighborhood Center was just dispersing. The participants, many of them mothers, had shared the difficulties of raising their children in their violent, Washington, D.C., neighborhood. One had asked, "How can we be faithful to Jesus in the most murderous neighborhood in the most murderous city in the most murderous nation in the world?"

The mood was somber as we walked out the front door. One of the women lamented that the city had ignored their complaints for months about a street light in front of the center that was burned out, making it more dangerous for the children. But then she looked into the sky. There was an amazing rainbow encircling a full moon. It disappeared as we moved onto more well lit streets. The woman smiled and said, "I guess God is watching after this neighborhood after all."

Practice of CHARITY

REPENT AND BELIEVE IN THE GOSPEL. The Israelites had their golden calf and each one of us has his or hers. Lent gives us the opportunity to renounce our idols. Whatever stands in the way of our entering into a covenant with God must be purified. Smash your golden calf, whether it is materialism, sexism, racism, addictions or lack of self-love. Genuine charity begins here. It flows from a selflessness that comes from conversion.

An old spiritual practice some use to overcome an imperfection is to do its opposite: If you eat too much, then fast a lot. Eventually you find the happy medium. Another help in removing your personal idols is to have a spiritual companion, someone with whom you meet on a regular basis to talk about your spiritual life. Practice these acts of charity toward yourself this Lent.

Weekday Reading
Leviticus 19:1–2, 11–18; 1 Peter 5:1–4; Jonah 3:1–10; Esther 14:12, 14–16, 23–25; Ezra 18:21–28; Deuteronomy 26:16–19

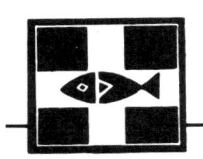

FEBRUARY 27, 1994

SECOND SUNDAY OF LENT

READING I   *Genesis 22:1–2, 9, 10–13, 15–18*

After these things God tested Abraham, and said to him, "Abraham!" And he said, "Here am I." God said, "Take your son, your only son Isaac, whom you love, and go to the land of Moriah, and offer him there as a burnt offering upon one of the mountains of which I shall tell you."

When they came to the place of which God had told him, Abraham built an altar there, and laid the wood in order. Then Abraham put forth his hand, and took the knife to slay his son. But the angel of the LORD called to him from heaven, and said, "Abraham, Abraham!" And he said, "Here am I." The angel said, "Do not lay your hand on the lad or do anything to him; for now I know that you fear God, seeing you have not withheld your son, your only son, from me." And Abraham lifted up his eyes and looked, and behold, behind him was a ram, caught in a thicket by its horns; and Abraham went and took the ram, and offered it up as a burnt offering instead of his son.

And the angel of the LORD called to Abraham a second time from heaven, and said, "By myself I have sworn, says the LORD, because you have done this, and have not withheld your son, your only son, I will indeed bless you, and I will multiply your descendants as the stars of heaven and as the sand which is on the seashore. And your descendants shall possess the gate of their enemies, and by your descendants shall all the nations of the earth bless themselves, because you have obeyed my voice."

READING II   *Romans 8:31–34*

If God is for us, who is against us? God did not spare God's own Son, but gave him up for us all; how shall God then not give us all things, along with the Son? Who shall bring any charge against God's elect? It is God who justifies; who is to condemn? It is Christ Jesus who died, yes, who was raised from the dead, who is at the right hand of God, who indeed intercedes for us.

GOSPEL   *Mark 9:2–10*

After six days Jesus took with him Peter and James and John, and led them up a high mountain apart by themselves; and he was transfigured before them, and his garments became glistening, intensely white, as no fuller on earth could bleach them. And there appeared to them Elijah with Moses; and they were talking to Jesus. And Peter said to Jesus, "Rabbi, it is well that we are here; let us make three booths, one for you and one for Moses and one for Elijah." For he did not know what to say, for they were exceedingly afraid. And a cloud overshadowed them, and a voice came out of the cloud, "This is my Son, the beloved one; listen to him." And suddenly looking around they no longer saw anyone with them but Jesus only.

And as they were coming down the mountain, Jesus charged them to tell no one what they had seen, until the Man of Heaven should have risen from the dead. So they kept the matter to themselves, questioning what the rising from the dead meant.

REFLECTION

Like Isaac before him, Jesus is being prepared to be sacrificed. Abraham's child almost died because of his father's obedience to God. Jesus will die in obedience to his Father: a free choice on his part. At this point in Mark's plan, the "lamb of sacrifice" is being prepared. The disciples puzzle about what rising from the dead might mean. Oddly, they don't seem fazed by Jesus' reference to dying. Peter had reacted strongly to the idea earlier in the gospel (see Mark 8:31–33), but here the notion of Jesus having to die seems to be ignored if not rejected. The disciples are interested in the resurrection but not the death. They are mystified by Jesus.

Just as when Jesus was baptized (see Mark 1:11), here again we are told who Jesus is by a voice from heaven. Attending this revelation are the lawgiver Moses and the great prophet Elijah. This is the Son of God, verified by two giants of scripture. Although the disciples witness this, they have little idea of its implication. God's son will be sacrificed. The disciples will have to witness and accept that before they arrive at the kind of trust in Jesus that Abraham had in God.

Both Jesus and Isaac are beloved sons. They differ in that Abraham and his child are snatched from the horror of sacrifice, but Jesus is not. Jesus' trust in God goes beyond his dying to a belief that suffering and death are not the final human experience. New life—resurrection of every kind—lies beyond all varieties of death.

1. God challenges Abraham's trust at the very core of Abraham's being, in his love for Isaac. Where and when has God challenged your trust most painfully and productively?

2. The transfiguration is a kind of foretaste of Jesus' resurrection for the disciples. What are your foretastes of new life and resurrection?

Practice of FAITH

HERE AM I. Faith requires ultimate sacrifice. Abraham and Sarah's life and love was their child. In their old age, they would literally depend on Isaac to survive. Yet when he thought that God was requiring that they sacrifice Isaac, Abraham did not hesitate. He was willing to give up anything in order to love and serve God.

What is your life and love? Are you able to let go of it or give it up if living faithfully some day requires it? At the end of our lives, we will have to let go of life as we know it. The smaller sacrifices beforehand are a rehearsal for that ultimate offering we will make of ourselves. This Lent, practice letting go of or giving up smaller things.

Practice of HOPE

LET US MAKE THREE BOOTHS. The apostle Peter wanted to build three booths in order "to hang around for a long time and capture the moment," according to Gordon Cosby, pastor of the ecumenical Church of the Saviour in Washington, D.C. Cosby said the same is often true in our Christian lives; it's hard to let go of a particularly graced moment and move on. But, he said, "You have to trust that the same power that produced it will be there for the next moment, and the next moment, and the next. The indwelling of the Spirit is not fragile; human beings are fragile."

Practice of CHARITY

COMING DOWN THE MOUNTAIN. We've all had those mountain-top experiences when time stands still during an experience we want never to end. But, alas, we must come down the mountain and get on with the ordinariness of life. Yet, life has now changed. In that mountain-top experience is a powerful glimpse of our relationship with God. And we carry that glimpse with us when we descend the mountain.

Those who do mission work here in our country and abroad carry that glimpse of God with them and share it in the ordinariness of life. This weekend in many parishes a collection will be taken up for the Propagation of the Faith. Do two things: 1) Reflect on your own mountain-top experience and keep that memory with you this week, and 2) support the work of missionaries by making a donation to the Propagation of the Faith collection.

Weekday Reading
Daniel 9:4–10; Isaiah 1:10, 16–20; Jeremiah 18:18–20; Jeremiah 17:5–10; Genesis 37:3–4, 12–13, 17–28; Micah 7:14–20

MARCH 6, 1994
THIRD SUNDAY OF LENT

READING I   *Exodus 20:1–17*

God spoke all these words, saying,

"I am the LORD your God, who brought you out of the land of Egypt, out of the house of bondage.

"You shall have no other gods before me.

"You shall not make for yourself a graven image, or any likeness of anything that is in heaven above, or that is in the earth beneath, or that is in the water under the earth; you shall not bow down to them or serve them; for I the LORD your God am a jealous God, visiting the iniquity of the parents upon the children to the third and the fourth generation of those who hate me, but showing steadfast love to thousands of those who love me and keep my commandments.

"You shall not take the name of the LORD your God in vain; for the LORD will not hold guiltless one who takes in vain the divine name.

"Remember the sabbath day, to keep it holy. Six days you shall labor, and do all your work; but the seventh day is a sabbath to the LORD your God; in it you shall not do any work, you, or your son, or your daughter, your manservant, or your maidservant, or your cattle, or the sojourner who is within your gates; for in six days the LORD made heaven and earth, the sea, and all that is in them, and rested the seventh day; therefore the LORD blessed the sabbath day and hallowed it.

"Honor your father and your mother, that your days may be long in the land which the LORD your God gives you.

"You shall not kill.

"You shall not commit adultery.

"You shall not steal.

"You shall not bear false witness against
 your neighbor.

"You shall not covet your neighbor's possessions: you shall not covet your neighbor's wife, or manservant, or maidservant, or ox, or ass, or anything that is your neighbor's."

READING II   *1 Corinthians 1:22–25*

The Jews demand signs and Greeks seek wisdom, but we preach Christ crucified, a stumbling block to Jews and folly to Gentiles, but to those who are called, both Jews and Greeks, Christ [is] the power of God and the wisdom of God. For the foolishness of God is wiser than human wisdom, and the weakness of God is stronger than human strength.

GOSPEL   *John 2:13–25*

The Passover of the Jewish people was at hand, and Jesus went up to Jerusalem. In the temple he found those who were selling oxen and sheep and pigeons, and the money-changers at their business. And making a whip of cords, he drove them all, with the sheep and oxen, out of the temple; and he poured out the coins of the money-changers and overturned their tables. And Jesus told those who sold the pigeons, "Take these things away; you shall not make my Father's house a house of trade." His disciples remembered that it was written, "Zeal for your house will consume me." The Judeans then said to him, "What sign have you to show us for doing this?" Jesus answered them, "Destroy this temple, and in three days I will raise it up." The Judeans then said, "It has taken forty-six years to build this temple, and will you raise it up in three days?" But Jesus spoke of the temple of his body. When therefore he was raised from the dead, his disciples remembered that he had said this; and they believed the scripture and the word which Jesus had spoken.

Now when Jesus was in Jerusalem at the Passover feast, many believed in his name when they saw the signs which he did; but Jesus did not trust himself to them, because he knew them all and needed no one to bear witness concerning humankind; for he himself knew what was in the human heart.

REFLECTION

God covets our hearts. The word of God strikes at the heart—at the heart of everything. From both Exodus and the Fourth Gospel, we have readings about hearts.

The Ten Commandments are the heart of biblical law, of the Exodus encounter with God, of a covenant between a loving God and a wayward people. Heart speaks to heart. In the gospel, Jesus is found at the heart of his nation's life—the Temple in Jerusalem. There he "scrutinizes" his people's religious life and finds it wanting and ready for radical change.

Interestingly, John is the only canonical gospel writer who places the "cleansing of the temple" at the beginning rather than the end of Jesus' ministry. Why? One reason is that it stands as a sign or symbol of his whole ministry about to begin. Look at what he does and says. It was Passover—the feast of liberation, of deliverance from bondage. He says the Temple is a house of trade. The heart of religion had a dangerous blockage: its prayer chamber was not operating smoothly or purposefully. The writer quotes Psalm 93:10: "Zeal for your house will consume me," a prayer of gratitude for deliverance expressing enthusiasm for the rebuilding of the Temple after Israel's exile in Babylon. The sign and authority for Jesus doing what he does is his own death (exile) and resurrection (restoration—and more). When this is accomplished, there will be no more need for the physical Temple. All people, all of creation will be drawn to him when he is lifted up. People then will worship in spirit and in truth, for Christ is the way, the truth and the life.

Those who love Jesus keep his commandments. He doesn't change the original commandments, but he does give a new one: "Love one another."

1. The second reading places Christ's crucifixion at the center of attention for believers—the heart of Christian mystery. How is a humiliated, crucified Christ the power and wisdom of God for you?

2. An old children's hymn sings, "Gentle Jesus, meek and mild. . . ." This is not the Jesus of today's gospel. Does your image of Jesus allow for his anger, indignation, impatience and sharpness? What would the cleansing of the Temple look like today, if Jesus were to come to your home town on such a mission?

Practice of FAITH

OVERTURNING TABLES. Each Lent, the Bible movies play on television and evil Pharisees plot with hardhearted Romans to crucify Jesus. If the cleansing of the Temple is shown, a self-righteous Jesus thrashes some sleazy merchants and no one seems to mind. But some people suggest that Jesus' actions struck at the heart of big religion's cooperation with the big military: The money-changing was a service to the military government, which in turn allowed the Temple to function. Some suggest that it was Jesus' action in the Temple that led the Romans to execute him.

To follow Jesus better, we need to study this gospel episode more. A good start is a book by Bill Wylie Kellerman, *Seasons of Faith and Conscience*, published in 1991 by Orbis Books (800-258-5838; 914-941-7686).

Practice of HOPE

WE PREACH CHRIST CRUCIFIED. Karl Gaspar, a redemptorist brother, spent almost two years in a Philippine prison during the reign of Ferdinand Marcos. Gaspar spoke of "a desolate darkness" as a result of the persecution he suffered and witnessed. But, he said:

"We still find embers of hope across the haunting horizon. . . . Anchored in the faith that we are always in his care, and that he saves us from our enemies, our hope in the Lord takes on characteristics of fire. It tears apart the bleak darkness of hopelessness, warms the battered heart, and raises to the heavens the prayer for strength and courage."

Practice of CHARITY

YOU SHALL NOT KILL. The command has been given to us, handed on as a treasure from generation to generation. When will we learn the power of these words? All life, from womb to tomb, is sacred. God, and not the human person, is the one who decides when life shall end. "By what right do men touch that unknown thing?" asks Bishop Bienvenu speaking of the gallows in Victor Hugo's *Les Miserables*. We have our own gallows. Our bishops have condemned the use of the death penalty, yet ask the Sunday congregation who is for the death penalty and almost every hand will raise. The death penalty solves nothing; it is vengeance. No restitution is made to the victim's family, no victim is brought back, no change happens in society. To find out more or get involved, write the National Coalition to Abolish the Death Penalty, 1325 G Street NW, Washington DC 20005; 202-347-2411.

Weekday Reading
2 Kings 5:1–15; Daniel 3:25, 34–43; Deuteronomy 4:1, 5–9; Jeremiah 7:23–28; Hosea 14:2–10; 6:1–6

MARCH 13, 1994
FOURTH SUNDAY OF LENT

READING I   *2 Chronicles 36:14–17, 19–23*

All the leading priests and the people likewise were exceedingly unfaithful, following all the abominations of the nations; and they polluted the house of the LORD which had been hallowed in Jerusalem.

The LORD, the God of their forebears, persistently sent messengers to them, because the LORD had compassion on the chosen people and on the sacred house; but they kept mocking God's messengers, despising God's words, and scoffing at the prophets, till the wrath of the LORD rose against the chosen people, till there was no remedy.

Therefore the LORD brought up against them the king of the Chaldeans, who slew their enlisted men with the sword in the house of their sanctuary, and had no compassion on young men or virgin women, old people or aged folk; God gave them all into the king's hand. And they burned the house of God, and broke down the wall of Jerusalem, and burned all its palaces with fire, and destroyed all its precious vessels. The king took into exile in Babylon those who had escaped from the sword, and they became servants to him and to his descendants until the establishment of the realm of Persia, to fulfill the word of the LORD by the mouth of Jeremiah, until the land had enjoyed its sabbaths. All the days that it lay desolate it kept sabbath, to fulfill seventy years.

Now in the first year of Cyrus king of Persia, that the word of the LORD by the mouth of Jeremiah might be accomplished, the LORD stirred up the spirit of Cyrus king of Persia so that he made a proclamation throughout all his realm and also put it in writing: "Thus says Cyrus king of Persia, 'The LORD, the God of heaven, has given me all the realms of the earth, and has charged me to build a house for God at Jerusalem, which is in Judah. Those among you who are of God's people, may the LORD their God be with them. Let them go up.'"

READING II   *Ephesians 2:4–10*

Even when we were dead through our trespasses, God, who is rich in mercy, made us alive together with Christ (by grace you have been saved) out of the great love with which God loved us. With Christ God raised us up and enthroned us in the heavenly places in Christ Jesus, that in the coming ages might be shown the immeasurable riches of God's grace in kindness toward us in Christ Jesus. For by grace you have been saved through faith; and this is not your own doing, it is the gift of God—not because of works, lest anyone should boast. For we are God's handiwork, created in Christ Jesus for good works, which God prepared beforehand, that we should walk in them.

GOSPEL   *John 3:14–21*

As Moses lifted up the serpent in the wilderness, so must the Man of Heaven be lifted up, that whoever believes in him may have eternal life.

For God loved the world in this way, that God gave the Son, the only begotten one, that whoever believes in him should not perish but have eternal life. For God sent the Son into the world, not to condemn the world, but that through the Son the world might be saved. Those who believe in him are not condemned; those who do not believe are condemned already, because they have not believed in the name of the only Son of God. And this is the judgment, that the light has come into the world, and people loved darkness rather than light, because their deeds were evil. For all those who do evil hate the light, and do not come to the light, lest their deeds should be exposed. But they who do what is true come to the light, that it may be clearly seen that their deeds have been wrought in God.

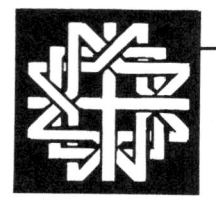

Joseph, the Husband of Mary
Saturday, March 19, 1994

2 Samuel 7:4–5, 12–14, 16   I will make David's throne endure.
Romans 4:13, 16–18, 22   He is father of us all.
Matthew 1:16, 18–21, 24   Joseph, Son of David, fear not!

On the final day of winter, as the earth is about to waken from its sleep, we tell the story of Joseph. In the Book of Genesis, Joseph is "the dreamer of dreams." In the Book of Matthew, Joseph dreamed of the coming kingdom. Then he awoke to find himself the father of the king.

REFLECTION

God abandoned the people! That's how 2 Chronicles sees the tragic collapse of religious, political and moral life when the chosen people suffered at the hands of Nebuchadnezzar, the Chaldean king from Babylon. Jerusalem and the Temple were razed and King Zedekiah was tortured and deported to Babylon along with nobles and clergy, scholars and lawyers, merchants and artists. The reason? The opening verses of the first reading explain: Israel's unfaithfulness, the pollution of the Temple and its adopting the inappropriate customs of foreign peoples. Out of compassion, God sent messengers like Jeremiah with warnings, but the people mocked both the prophets and the compassion of God. There was "no other remedy" but Nebuchadnezzar.

The reading from the Gospel of John points out that there is no condemnation, unless a person chooses to bring it on himself or herself. This summary of what God was doing in Jesus calmly states that it is love for people that motivates God. The Son is a gift and a focus for faith, a living, breathing example of God's intended relationship to each human being in community. John's message is that in the presence of Jesus there is truth—the truth of who people really are. The light of that truth scrutinizes people, illuminating good and casting evil into the shadows. So people see themselves truly and have to choose light or darkness, life or death. Opting for the light is belief; choosing darkness is unbelief and therein lies the judgment. If there is condemnation of "the world," the realm of darkness, it is not God's but the "world's" own free choice to remain in comfortable and familiar darkness.

At the Easter Vigil we will gather around the paschal candle, the symbol of Christ our saving light. God abides with us and we can bask in the light of the risen Christ. Eternal life is available now. The choice is both personal and communal. God does not abandon people, but people are still free to abandon God.

1. Read 2 Kings 23:30b—25:21, an earlier version of the Chronicles story heard today. What differences do you detect between these two versions?

2. Many have made the journey from darkness to light. What have been the significant times when, as some still say, you "saw the light"? What changed? Did it happen instantly or gradually? Consider some "darknesses" like grief, anger, addiction or illness. How do light and liberation apply to those?

Practice of FAITH

ST. JOSEPH. The Solemnity of St. Joseph next Saturday gives us a break from fasting. The tradition of having a St. Joseph's table is an act of Lenten charity, too. The idea is to celebrate Joseph's memory by having a feast and inviting the hungry to share it with you. In thanksgiving for being saved from famine, Sicilians cooked up a feast and invited the poor and the homeless. Can you think of someone in need to invite to your house next Saturday? Do you know someone who perhaps eats alone and would relish a meal with company? Could you spare a few hours to work at a soup kitchen? If your parish holds a St. Joseph table as a fundraiser, you might suggest that a certain percentage of the tickets be quietly given to hungry people in your neighborhood.

Practice of HOPE

BY GRACE YOU HAVE BEEN SAVED. Mary Glover's prayer as she serves on the Saturday morning food line at the Sojourners Neighborhood Center begins with thankfulness, and it ends with this petition: "Lord, we know you are coming through this line today, so help us to treat you right." She possesses that wonderful grace that allows her to see Jesus in everyone, especially the "least of these." She takes to heart the mandate of love found in Matthew 25: "Whatever you do to them, you do to me," said Jesus. Mary Glover lives her life in testimony to the joyful requirement of faith: to feed, clothe, shelter, and visit those in need.

Practice of CHARITY

GOD'S HANDIWORK. Today a collection is taken up for Catholic Relief Services, an agency dedicated to promulgating the gospel throughout the world by distributing emergency aid and promoting development projects. Your gift truly can make a difference. Added to those of many other generous people, it can enable CRS to provide hope when the power of evil seems to have won. CRS helps victims of everything from disease and illiteracy to famine, war and natural disasters. For more information about the work of Catholic Relief Services, write 209 W. Fayette St., Baltimore MD 21201-3403.

Weekday Reading
Isaiah 65:17–21; Ezra 47:1–9, 12; Isaiah 49:8–15; Exodus 32:7–14; Wisdom 2:1, 12–22; 2 Samuel 7:4–5, 12–14, 16

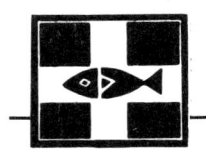

MARCH 20, 1994
FIFTH SUNDAY OF LENT

READING I *Jeremiah 31:31–34*

"Behold, the days are coming, says the LORD, when I will make a new covenant with the house of Israel and the house of Judah, not like the covenant which I made with their forebears when I took them by the hand to bring them out of the land of Egypt, my covenant which they broke, though I was married to them, says the LORD. But this is the covenant which I will make with the house of Israel after those days, says the LORD: I will put my law within them, and I will write it upon their hearts; and I will be their God, and they shall be my people. And no longer shall they, each of them, teach their neighbor and their kin, saying, 'Know the LORD,' for they shall all know me, from the least of them to the greatest, says the LORD; for I will forgive their iniquity, and I will remember their sin no more."

READING II *Hebrews 5:7–9*

In the days of his flesh, Jesus offered up prayers and supplications, with loud cries and tears, to the one who was able to save him from death, and for being God-fearing Jesus was heard. Although being a Son, Jesus learned obedience through what he suffered; and being made perfect Jesus became the source of eternal salvation to all who obey him.

GOSPEL *John 12:20–33*

Among those who went up to worship at the feast were some Greeks. So these came to Philip, who was from Bethsaida in Galilee, and said to him, "Sir, we wish to see Jesus." Philip went and told Andrew; Andrew went with Philip and they told Jesus. And Jesus answered them, "The hour has come for the Man of Heaven to be glorified. Truly, truly, I say to you, unless a grain of wheat falls into the earth and dies, it remains alone; but if it dies, it bears much fruit. They who love their life lose it, and they who hate their life in this world will keep it for eternal life. Those who serve me must follow me; and where I am, there shall my servants be also; those who serve me, the Father will honor.

"Now is my soul troubled. And what shall I say? 'Father, save me from this hour'? No, for this purpose I have come to this hour. Father, glorify your name." Then a voice came from heaven, "I have glorified it, and I will glorify it again." The crowd standing by heard it and said that it had thundered. Others said, "An angel has spoken to him." Jesus answered, "This voice has come for your sake, not for mine. Now is the judgment of this world, now shall the ruler of this world be cast out; and I, when I am lifted up from the earth, will draw the whole world to myself." Jesus said this to show by what death he was to die.

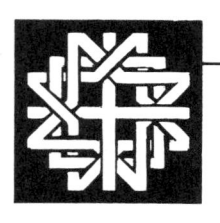

The Annunciation of the Lord
Friday, March 25, 1994

Isaiah 7:10–14   A virgin will bear a child.
Hebrews 10:4–10   I come to do God's will.
Luke 1:26–38   Rejoice, O highly favored daughter!

Because pregnancy without marriage was punishable by death, Mary's yes to the angel is acceptance of death. But in this death, the risen Spirit conquers death. Mary's mortal body conceives the Immortal One. The paschal victory is won.

REFLECTION

At the wedding at Cana, Jesus told his mother that his "hour had not yet come" (John 2:4). In today's excerpt from John, the hour has come. The hour refers to the point in time when Jesus is fully disclosed as the Son of God. This time is fulfilled when he is "lifted up" for the world to see and be drawn to him: at the point of death when he can say, "It is accomplished." The new covenant or relationship, dreamed of centuries before by Jeremiah (see the first reading) is finally established, not just *by* Jesus but *in* him.

Why should his "hour" be at this stage of the gospel? It is the arrival of the two Greeks, Gentiles, who approach the two disciples with Greek names—Phillipos ("lover of horses") and Andreas ("manly one")—that proclaims the beginning of the "hour." The time had come for Jesus' own people to reject him and for him to be received by others.

The Gospel of John doesn't have a Gethsemane prayer scene (see, for example, Mark 14:32–42). According to John, all that happens in the garden is Jesus' arrest. In the second part of today's gospel reading we seem to have John's oblique reference to Jesus' prayer-suffering in Gethsemane. He cannot pray for "this cup to pass" (Mark 14:35) even though his soul is troubled because that would contradict his purpose in coming into the world—to glorify the Father. He would do this by his obedient death. His trust is affirmed by a divine voice that sounds like thunder to others. His death is a judgment on the world, not a Roman judgment on Jesus. John loves irony!

Jeremiah's prophecy of a new covenant is accomplished. There is a new bond forged between heaven and earth when the word becomes flesh and the only Son is suspended on a cross between earth and sky. In Jesus all can know God, sins are forgiven and life is available in a new relationship to God.

1. Read the whole gospel section for the full story of the Gentiles' approach to Jesus and his response to them—John 12:20–36. What do you think are some major differences, without being judgmental of others, between "children of the light" and those "who walk in the darkness"?

2. Is the good news getting beyond the confines of your faith community? What form does this evangelization take? Do you offer this new and loving covenant relationship to a caring and forgiving God? How do you help those who are afraid of God?

Practice of FAITH

THE ANNUNCIATION. This Friday, we remember that the angel Gabriel visited Mary, who said yes to God and conceived Jesus. This week, be an angel to an expectant or new mother. If you know someone expecting a child or someone who has recently given birth, offer to help in some way: with the wash, the grocery shopping or house cleaning. Find out what services are available for unwed mothers in your area and make a donation of time or money. Pray the Angelus on Friday; it's on page 31.

Friday is also the fourteenth anniversary of the death of Archbishop Oscar Romero of San Salvador. An advocate for the poor, he was gunned down during Mass. A good movie about his life, *Romero,* is available at many video stores. Rent it and watch it. Or purchase a copy from Palisades Home Video, 153 Waverly Place, New York NY 10014; 212-243-0600.

Practice of HOPE

IF A GRAIN OF WHEAT DIES, IT BEARS MUCH FRUIT. "It seems as if during Lent, the suffering of Jesus becomes very acute. It is not unlike the suffering my own son went through." These words were spoken by Alice Biko, mother of Steve Biko, the proponent of "black consciousness" who was brutally murdered in 1977 while in the custody of the South African police.

In one of her last conversations with her son, Alice Biko told him how difficult it was to live with her fears for him. He responded by reminding her that Jesus had come to set his people free. "Are you Jesus?' she had asked impatiently. "No, I'm not," her son answered, "but I'm going to do the same job." The martyrdom of Steve Biko deepened the freedom struggle that still goes on today.

Practice of CHARITY

I WILL PUT MY LAW WITHIN THEM. How do we know when we are doing what God wants? How are we certain we are walking the way of Jesus? We have church teaching and the Bible, the sacraments and preaching from the pulpit. How else might we gain insight to the practice of charity? How can we stay informed? *Salt* magazine, published by the Claretians, is an excellent resource "for Christians who seek social justice." The monthly magazine features articles on people who make a difference, ideas for working with justice issues, and success stories of individuals and groups who are living the gospel. Subscriptions are $15 a year for ten issues. To subscribe, write: *Salt,* Subscription Manager, 205 West Monroe St, Chicago IL 60606.

Weekday Reading
Daniel 13:1–9, 15–17, 19–30, 33–62 or 13:41–62; Numbers 21:4–9; Daniel 3:14–20, 91–92, 95; Genesis 17:3–9; Isaiah 7:10–14; Ezra 37:21–28

MARCH 27, 1994
THE PASSION OF THE LORD

READING I   *Isaiah 50:4–7*

The Lord God has given me
  the tongue of those who are taught,
that I may know how to sustain with a word
  those who are weary.
Morning by morning the Lord God wakens,
  wakens my ear,
to hear as those who are taught.
The Lord God has opened my ear,
  and I was not rebellious,
  I turned not backward.
I gave my back to the smiters,
  and my cheeks to those who pulled out the beard;
I hid not my face
  from shame and spitting.
For the Lord God helps me;
  therefore I have not been confounded;
therefore I have set my face like a flint,
  and I know that I shall not be put to shame.

READING II   *Philippians 2:6–11*

Have this mind among yourselves, which is yours in Christ Jesus, who, being in the form of God, did not count equality with God a thing to be grasped, but gave it up, taking the form of a servant, being born in human likeness. And being found in human form he humbled himself and became obedient unto death, even death on a cross. Therefore God has highly exalted him and bestowed on him the name which is above every name, that at the name of Jesus every knee should bow, in heaven and on earth and under the earth, and every tongue confess that Jesus Christ is Lord, to the glory of God, the Father.

GOSPEL   *Mark 14:1—15:47*

It was now two days before the Passover and the feast of Unleavened Bread. And the chief priests and the scribes were seeking how to arrest Jesus by stealth, and kill him; for they said, "Not during the feast, lest there be a tumult of the people."

And while Jesus was at Bethany in the house of Simon the leper as he sat at table, a woman came with an alabaster flask of ointment of pure nard, very costly, and she broke the flask and poured it over Jesus' head. But there were some who said to themselves indignantly, "Why was the ointment thus wasted? For this ointment might have been sold for more than three hundred denarii, and given to the poor."

And they reproached her. But Jesus said, "Let her alone, why do you trouble her? She has done a beautiful thing to me. For you always have the poor with you, and whenever you will, you can do good to them; but you will not always have me. She has done what she could; she has anointed my body beforehand for burying. And truly, I say to you, wherever the gospel is preached in the whole world, what she has done will be told in memory of her."

Then Judas Iscariot, who was one of the twelve, went to the chief priests in order to betray Jesus to them. And when they heard it they were glad, and promised to give Judas money. And he sought an opportunity to betray Jesus. And on the first day of Unleavened Bread, when they sacrificed the passover lamb, Jesus' disciples said to him, "Where will you have us go and prepare for you to eat the passover?" And Jesus sent two of his disciples, and said to them, "Go into the city, and someone carrying a jar of water will meet you; follow him, and wherever he enters, say to the householder, 'The Teacher says, Where is my guest room, where I am to eat the passover with my disciples?' The householder will show you a large upper room furnished and ready; there prepare for us."

And the disciples set out and went to the city, and found it as Jesus had told them; and they prepared the passover. And when it was evening he came with the twelve. And as they were at table eating, Jesus said, "Truly, I say to you, one of you will betray me, one who is eating with me." They began to be sorrowful, and to say to him one after another, "Is it I?"

He said to them, "It is one of the twelve, one who is dipping bread into the dish with me. For the Man of Heaven as it is written of him, but woe to that person by whom the Man of Heaven is betrayed! It would have been better for that person if he had not been born."

And as they were eating, Jesus took bread, and blessed, and broke it, and gave it to them, and said, "Take; this is my body." And he took a cup, and having given thanks he gave it to them, and they drank all of it. And he said to them, "This is my blood of the covenant, which is poured out for many. Truly, I say to you, I shall not drink again of the fruit of the vine until that day when I drink it new in the dominion of God."

And when they had sung a hymn, they went out to the Mount of Olives.

Jesus said to them, "You will all fall away; for it is written, I will strike the shepherd, and the sheep will be scattered. But after I am raised up, I will go before you to Galilee." Peter said to him, "Even though they all fall away, I will not." And Jesus said to him, "Truly, I say to you, this very night before the cock crows twice, you will deny me three times." But Peter said vehemently, "If I must die with you, I will not deny you." And they all said the same.

And they went to a place which was called Gethsemane; and Jesus said to his disciples, "Sit here, while I pray." And Jesus took with him Peter and James and John, and began to be greatly distressed and troubled. And he said to them, "My soul is very sorrowful, even to death; remain here, and watch." And going a little farther, he fell on the ground and prayed that, if it were possible, the hour might pass from him. And he said, "Abba, Father, all things are possible to you; remove this cup from me; yet not what I will, but what you will."

And Jesus came and found them sleeping, and said to Peter, "Simon, are you asleep? Could you not watch one hour? Watch and pray that you may not enter into temptation; the spirit indeed is willing, but the flesh is weak." And again Jesus went away and prayed, saying the same words. And again he came and found them sleeping, for their eyes were very heavy; and they did not know what to answer him. And he came the third time, and said to them, "Are you still sleeping and taking your rest? It is enough; the hour has come; the Man of Heaven is betrayed into the hands of sinners. Rise, let us be going; see, my betrayer is at hand." And immediately, while Jesus was still speaking, Judas came, one of the twelve, and with him a crowd with swords and clubs, from the chief priests and the scribes and the elders. Now the betrayer had given them a sign, saying, "Whomever I shall kiss is the one; seize him and lead him away under guard." And when Judas came, he went up to Jesus at once, and said, "Master!" And he kissed him. And they laid hands on Jesus and seized him. But one of those who stood by drew his sword, and struck the slave of the high priest and cut off his ear. And Jesus said to them, "Have you come out as against a robber, with swords and clubs to capture me? Day after day I was with you in the temple teaching, and you did not seize me. But let the scriptures be fulfilled." And they all forsook him and fled.

And a young man followed Jesus with nothing but a linen cloth about his body; and they seized him, but he left the linen cloth and ran away naked.

And they led Jesus to the high priest; and all the chief priests and the elders and the scribes were assembled. And Peter had followed him at a distance, right into the courtyard of the high priest, and was sitting with the guards, warming himself at the fire. Now the chief priests and the whole council sought his testimony against Jesus to put him to death; but they found none. For many bore false witness against Jesus and their witness did not agree. And some stood up and bore false witness against him saying, "We heard him say, I will destroy this temple that is made with hands, and in three days I will build another, not made with hands." Yet even so did their testimony agree. And the high priest stood up in the midst, and asked Jesus, "Have you no answer to make? What is it that these people testify against you?" But Jesus was silent and made no answer. Again the high priest asked him, "Are you the Christ, the Son of the Blessed?" And Jesus said, "I am; and you will see the Man of Heaven seated at the right hand of Power, and coming with the clouds of heaven." And the high priest tore his garments, and said, "Why do we still need witnesses? You have heard his blasphemy. What is your decision?" And they all condemned him as deserving death. And some began to spit on him, and to cover his face, and to strike him, saying to him, "Prophesy!" And the guards received him with blows.

And as Peter was below in the courtyard, one of the maids of the high priest came, and seeing Peter warming himself, she looked at him and said, "You were also with the Nazarene, Jesus." But he denied it, saying, "I neither know nor understand what you mean." And Peter went out into the gateway. And the maid saw him, and began again to say to the bystanders, "This man is one of them." But again he denied it. And after a little while again the bystanders said to Peter, "Certainly you are one of them; for you are a Galilean." But he began to invoke a curse on himself and to swear, "I do not know this one of whom you speak." And immediately the cock crowed a second time. And Peter remembered how Jesus had said to them, "Before the cock crows twice, you will deny me three times." And he broke down and wept.

And as soon as it was morning the chief priests, with the elders and scribes, and the whole council held a consultation; and they bound Jesus and led him away and delivered him to Pilate. And Pilate asked him, "Are you King of the Jews?" And Jesus answered him, "You have said so." And the chief priests accused him of many things. And Pilate again asked him, "Have you no answer to make? See how many charges they bring against you." But Jesus made no further answer, so Pilate wondered.

Now at the feast Pilate used to release for them one prisoner for whom they asked. And among the rebels in prison, who had committed murder in the insurrection, there was someone called Barabbas. And the crowd came up and began to ask Pilate to do as he was wont to do for them. And he answered them, "Do you want me to release you for the King of the Jews?" For he perceived that it was out of envy that the chief priests had delivered him up. But the chief priests stirred up the crowd to have Pilate release for them Barabbas instead. And Pilate again said to them, "Then what shall I do with the one whom you call the King of the Jews?" And they cried out again "Crucify him." And Pilate said to them, "Why, what evil has he done?" But they shouted all the more, "Crucify him." So Pilate, wishing to satisfy the crowd, released for them Barabbas, and having scourged Jesus, delivered him to be crucified.

And the soldiers led Jesus away inside the palace (that is, the praetorium); and they called together the whole battalion. And they clothed him in a purple cloak, and plaiting a crown of thorns they put it on him. And they began to salute him, "Hail, King of the Jews!" And they struck his head with a reed, and spat upon him, and they knelt down in homage to him. And when they had mocked him, they stripped him of the purple cloak, and put his own clothes on him. And they led him out to crucify him.

And they compelled a passer-by, Simon of Cyrene, who was coming in from the country, the father of Alexander and Rufus, to carry his cross. And they brought him to the place called Golgotha (which means the place of a skull). And they offered Jesus wine mingled with myrrh; but he did not take it. And they crucified him, and divided his garments among them, casting lots for them, to decide what each side should take. And it was the third hour, when they crucified him. And the inscription of the charge against him read, "The King of the Jews." And with him they crucified two robbers, one on his right and one on his left. And those who passed by derided him, wagging their heads, and saying, "Aha! You who would destroy the temple and build it in three days, save yourself, and come down from the cross!" So also the chief priests mocked him to one another with the scribes, saying, "He saved others; he cannot save himself. Let the Christ, the King of Israel, come down now from the cross, that we may see and believe." Those who were crucified with him also reviled him.

And when the sixth hour had come there was darkness over the whole land until the ninth hour. And at the ninth hour Jesus cried with a loud voice, "Eloi, Eloi, lama sabachthani?" which means, "My God, my God, why have you forsaken me?" And some of the bystanders hearing it said, "Behold, he is calling Elijah." And one ran and, filling a sponge full of vinegar, put it on a reed and gave it to him to drink, saying, "Wait, let us see whether Elijah will come to take him down." And Jesus uttered a loud cry, and breathed his last, And the curtain of the temple was torn in two, from top to bottom.

And when the centurion, who stood facing him, saw that Jesus thus breathed his last, he said, "Truly this man was the Son of God!"

There were also two women looking on from afar, among whom were Mary Magdalene, and Mary the mother of James the younger and of Joses, and Salome, who, when Jesus was in Galilee, followed him, and ministered to him; and also many other women who came up with Jesus to Jerusalem.

And when evening had come, since it was the day of Preparation, that is, the day before the sabbath, Joseph of Arimathea, a respected member of the council, who was also himself looking for the dominion of God, took courage and went to Pilate, and asked for the body of Jesus. And Pilate wondered if Jesus were already dead; and summoning the centurion, Pilate asked him whether he was already dead. And when Pilate learned from the centurion that Jesus was dead, he granted the dead body to Joseph. And Joseph bought a linen shroud, and taking him down, wrapped him in the linen shroud, and laid him in a tomb which had been hewn out of the rock; and Joseph rolled a stone against the door of the tomb. Mary Magdalene and Mary the mother of Joses saw where he was laid.

REFLECTION

Mark's telling of the passion of Jesus occupies about a third of the gospel. Why did Mark give so much space to the events of just a few days? Perhaps, even in Mark's day, Christians forgot that suffering and sacrifice go hand in hand with mission.

In Mark's passion narrative, all the disciples abandon Jesus. The only people near the cross are those who mock him. Mark mentions the faithful women, but they look on "from afar." Perhaps not everyone wants salvation if it means too much disruption of familiar patterns of living—a disruption that we get some taste of this week if we participate fully in worship with our parish.

Despite the fact that most of the disciples abandoned him the mission of Jesus is nonetheless given to them—to us. Like Jesus, his disciples must teach, heal and combat evil. Like Jesus, his disciples must suffer and die.

Here is Mark's message: This story of Jesus' passion is a disciple's story, too—each disciple's story. To be a disciple is not to be a pious observer, but a participant in the drama begun by Jesus—the routing of evil by the healing, freeing, teaching, compassionate power of God made flesh.

In the Three Days of our Pasch, we celebrate the passover of each disciple and all disciples as they are found in the passover of Jesus. The passion—the suffering—of all those who are baptized is the passion of Christ, and to die with Christ means that we will live forever with Christ in an unending Easter.

1. In the Gospel of Mark, John the Baptist, Jesus and the disciples suffer because of their mission. You have your own passion story that flows from your own discipleship—your living out your baptismal vows. Reflect on your personal passion story.

2. Although the Father (the voice from heaven) identifies Jesus as the Son of God at his baptism and again at his transfiguration, only once in Mark's gospel does a human being call Jesus the Son of God. (See Mark 15:39.) Who is this person? Why is he the only one to acknowledge Jesus' identity? What does this remarkable profession of faith mean?

Practice of FAITH

PILGRIM'S PALMS. Medieval Christians who went on pilgrimages to shrines were called "palmers," because they carried leafy branches from trees as signs of their religious purpose. The procession with palms in today's liturgy foreshadows important processions we'll make later this week: the procession with gifts for the poor and the procession with the eucharist on Thursday; the procession with and to the cross on Friday; the procession behind the Easter candle, the procession to the font and the procession to share eucharist at the Vigil. Processions are important signs of our willingness to live as pilgrims. Like Israelites in the desert, we only wander through this earthly life for a time. Like the itinerant Christ, we go from place to place with good news. So join in the Triduum processions with devotion. If your parish doesn't do them, ask why not.

Practice of HOPE

THERE WERE ALSO WOMEN. In the scriptures, women are often portrayed as peripheral; many are unnamed; and under Hebrew law they were considered the property of either their fathers or husbands. But the passion narrative reminds us that they stayed by Jesus to the end, even when the other disciples had abandoned him. And they were the first witnesses to the resurrection.

Today, around the world, women are joining together out of tragedy to demand justice. In Argentina, the Mothers of the Disappeared march in the Plaza de Mayo, demanding information about their loved ones. In South Africa, the Detainees' Parents Support Committee ministers to detained children and their families. In our own country, mothers whose children have been killed in Detroit's street violence have founded Save Our Sons and Daughters, pushing for an end to the terror of guns and drugs. Suffering women are still witnesses to hope.

Practice of CHARITY

TO SUSTAIN WITH A WORD THOSE WHO ARE WEARY. A comforting word from someone can be so uplifting. As our lenten observance draws to a close this week, take time to look around your neighborhood and find someone who is weary. Perhaps it is someone caring for the elderly or sick, perhaps it is a mother with children, perhaps it is a single person who seems lonely, perhaps it is a family that is struggling. Reach out to the weary and offer words of comfort; or better yet, put those words into action and offer to help out in some way. You'll feel good about ending Lent in this way. It will help prepare you to enter into the Holy Triduum.

Weekday Reading
Isaiah 42:1–7; 49:1–6; 50:4–9; 61:1–9

Paschal Triduum

Holy is God!
Holy and strong!
Holy, immortal One,
have mercy on us!

All you sheltered by God Most High,
who live in the Almighty's shadow,
say to the Lord, "My refuge, my fortress,
my God in whom I trust!"

God will free you from hunters' snares,
will save you from deadly plague,
will cover you like a nesting bird.
God's wings will shelter you.

No nighttime terror shall you fear,
no arrows shot by day,
no plague that prowls the dark,
no wasting scourge at noon.

A thousand may fall at your side,
ten thousand at your right hand.
But you shall live unharmed:
God is sturdy armor.

You have only to open your eyes
to see how the wicked are repaid.
You have the Lord as refuge,
have made the Most High your stronghold.

No evil shall ever touch you,
no harm come near your home.
God instructs angels
to guard you wherever you go.

With their hands they support you
so your foot will not strike a stone.
On lion and viper you shall tread,
trample tawny lion and dragon.

"I will deliver all who cling to me,
raise the ones who know me,
answer those who call me,
be with those in trouble.
These I will rescue and honor,
satisfy with long life,
and show my power to save."

—*Psalm 91*

Holy God,
praise be yours for this tree of Paradise,
this tree that made Noah's saving Ark,
this tree whose branches embraced Jesus
and so shade and shelter us all.
Here may all the weary rest
these holy days,
hungry and thirsty for your word,
eating and drinking only your word
until, in the darkness between
Saturday and Sunday,
heaven and earth shall here be wed.
Then drowning waters shall be
waters of life
and the Savior's blood a banquet.
Holy God, praise be yours.

—*Prayer of the Triduum*

MARCH 31, 1994
HOLY THURSDAY

READING I *Exodus 12:1–8, 11–14*

The Lord said to Moses and Aaron in the land of Egypt, "This month shall be for you the beginning of months; it shall be the first month of the year for you. Tell all the congregation of Israel that on the tenth day of this month they shall each take a lamb according to their ancestors' houses, a lamb for a household; and if the household is too small for a lamb, then neighbors shall take according to the number of persons; according to what each can eat you shall make your count for the lamb. Your lamb shall be without blemish, a male a year old; you shall take it from the sheep or from the goats; and you shall keep it until the fourteenth day of this month, when the whole assembly of the congregation of Israel shall kill their lambs in the evening. Then they shall take some of the blood, and put it on the two doorposts and the lintel of the houses in which they eat them. They shall eat the flesh that night, roasted; with unleavened bread and bitter herbs they shall eat it. In this manner you shall eat it: your loins girded, your sandals on your feet, and your staff in your hand; and you shall eat it in haste. It is the LORD's passover. For I will pass through the land of Egypt that night, and I will smite all the firstborn in the land of Egypt, both human and animal; and on all the gods of Egypt I will execute judgments: I am the LORD. The blood shall be a sign for you, upon the houses where you are; and when I see the blood, I will pass over you, and no plague shall fall upon you to destroy you, when I smite the land of Egypt.

"This day shall be for you a memorial day, and you shall keep it as a feast to the LORD; throughout your generations you shall observe it as an ordinance forever."

READING II *1 Corinthians 11:23–26*

For I received from the Lord what I also delivered to you, that the Lord Jesus on the night when he was betrayed took bread, and having given thanks, broke it, and said, "This is my body which is for you. Do this in remembrance of me." In the same way also the cup, after supper, saying, "This cup is the new covenant of my blood. Do this, as often as you drink it, in remembrance of me." For as often as you eat this bread and drink the cup, you proclaim the Lord's death until he comes.

GOSPEL *John 13:1–15*

Now before the feast of the Passover, when Jesus knew that his hour had come to depart out of this world to the Father, having loved his own who were in the world, he loved them to the end. And during supper, when the devil had already put it into the heart of Judas Iscariot, Simon's son, to betray him, Jesus, knowing that the Father had given all things into his hands, and that he had come from God and was going to God, rose from supper, laid aside his garments, and girded himself with a towel. Then he poured water into a basin, and began to wash the disciples' feet, and to wipe them with the towel with which he was girded. Jesus came to Simon Peter; and Peter said to him, "Lord, do you wash my feet?" Jesus answered him, "What I am doing you do not know now, but afterward you will understand." Peter said to him, "You shall never wash my feet." Jesus answered him, "If I do not wash you, you have no part in me." Simon Peter said to him, "Lord, not my feet only but also my hands and my head!" Jesus said to him, "Those who have bathed do not need to wash, except for their feet, but they are clean all over; and you are clean, but not every one of you." For Jesus knew who was to betray him; that was why he said, "You are not all clean."

When Jesus had washed their feet, and taken his garments, and resumed his place, he said to them, "Do you know what I have done to you? You call me Teacher and Lord; and you are right, for so I am. If I then, your Lord and Teacher, have washed your feet, you also ought to wash one another's feet. For I have given you an example, that you should do as I have done to you."

APRIL 1, 1994
GOOD FRIDAY

READING I *Isaiah 52:13 — 53:12*

Behold, my servant shall prosper,
   shall be exalted and lifted up,
   and shall be very high.
As many were astonished at the one
   whose appearance was so marred, beyond
     human semblance,
   and whose form was beyond that of humanity,
so shall my servant startle many nations;
   rulers shall shut their mouths because of him;
for that which has not been told them they shall see,
   and that which they have not heard
     they shall understand.
Who has believed what we have heard?
   And to whom has the arm of the LORD
     been revealed?
For the servant grew up before the LORD
   like a young plant,
   and like a root out of dry ground,
having no form or comeliness for us to behold,
   and no beauty for us to desire.
He was despised and rejected by men and women,
   a man of sorrows, and acquainted with grief;
and as one from whom people hid their faces
   He was despised, and we esteemed him not.
Surely he has borne our griefs
   and carried our sorrows;
yet we esteemed him stricken,
   smitten by God, and afflicted.
But he was wounded for our transgressions,
   and was bruised for our iniquities;

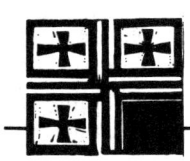

the chastisement that made us whole was upon him,
   by whose stripes we are healed.
All we like sheep have gone astray;
   we have turned each one to our own way,
and the LORD has laid on this servant
   the iniquity of us all.
This servant was oppressed and was afflicted,
   yet opened not his mouth;
like a lamb that is led to slaughter,
   and like a ewe that before her shearers is dumb,
   so he opened not his mouth.
By oppression and judgment
   the servant was taken away;
   and as for his generation, who considered
that he was cut off out of the land of the living,
   stricken for the transgression of my people?
He was given a grave with the wicked,
   and was with the rich in death,
although having done no violence,
   having never spoken deceit.
Yet it was the will of the LORD to bruise this servant;
   the LORD has put him to grief;
making himself an offering for sin,
   the servant shall see offspring
      and shall prolong his days;
the will of the LORD shall prosper
   in the hand of the servant,
   who shall see the fruit of the travail of his soul
      and be satisfied;
by his knowledge shall the righteous one, my servant,
   make many to be accounted righteous;
   my servant shall bear their iniquities.
Therefore I will divide a portion with the great
   for my servant
   who shall divide the spoil with the strong;
because my servant poured out his soul to death,
   and was numbered with the transgressors;
yet he bore the sin of many,
   and made intercession for the transgressors.

READING II   *Hebrews 4:14–16; 5:7–9*

Since then we have a great high priest who has passed through the heavens, Jesus, the Son of God, let us hold fast our confession. For we have not a high priest who is unable to sympathize with our weaknesses, but one who in every respect has been tempted as we are, yet without sin. Let us then with confidence draw near to the throne of grace, that we may receive mercy and find grace to help in time of need.

In the days of his flesh, Jesus offered up prayers and supplications, with loud cries and tears, to the one who was able to save him from death, and for being God-fearing Jesus was heard. Although being a Son, Jesus learned obedience through what he suffered; and being made perfect Jesus became the source of eternal salvation to all who obey him.

GOSPEL   *John 18:1 — 19:42*

When Jesus had spoken these words, he went forth with his disciples across the Kidron Valley, where there was a garden, which he and his disciples entered. Now Judas, who betrayed him, also knew the place; for Jesus often met there with his disciples. So Judas, procuring a band of soldiers and some officers from the chief priests and the Pharisees, went there with lanterns and torches and weapons. Then Jesus, knowing all that was to befall him, came forward and said to them, "Whom do you seek?"

They answered him, "Jesus of Nazareth."

Jesus said to them, "Here I am."

Judas, who betrayed Jesus, was standing with them. When Jesus said to them, "Here I am," they drew back and fell to the ground. Again Jesus asked them, "Whom do you seek?"

And they said, "Jesus of Nazareth."

Jesus answered, "I told you here I am, so, if you seek me, let these others go."

This was to fulfill the word which Jesus had spoken, "Of those whom you gave me I lost not one." Then Simon Peter, having a sword, drew it and struck the high priest's slave and cut off his right ear. The slave's name was Malchus. Jesus said to Peter, "Put your sword into its sheath; shall I not drink the cup which the Father has given me?"

So the band of soldiers and their captain and the officers of the Judeans seized Jesus and bound him. First they led him to Annas, the father-in-law of Caiaphas, who was high priest that year. It was Caiaphas who had given counsel to the Judeans that it was expedient that one person should die for the people.

Simon Peter followed Jesus, and so did another disciple. Being known to the high priest, that disciple entered the court of the high priest along with Jesus, while Peter stood outside at the door. So the other disciple, who was known to the high priest, went out and spoke to the maid who kept the door, and brought Peter in. The maid who kept the door said to Peter, "Are you not also one of this man's disciples?"

He said, "I am not."

Now the servants and officers had made a charcoal fire, because it was cold, and they were standing and warming themselves; Peter also was with them, standing and warming himself.

The high priest then questioned Jesus about his disciples and his teaching. Jesus answered the high priest, "I have spoken openly to the world; I have always taught in synagogues and in the temple, where all the Judeans come together; I have said nothing secretly. Why do you ask me? Ask those who have heard me, what I said to them; they know what I said."

When he had said this, one of the officers standing by struck Jesus with his hand, saying, "Is that how you answer the high priest?"

Jesus answered the officer, "If I have spoken wrongly, bear witness to the wrong; but if I have spoken rightly, why do you strike me?"

Annas then sent Jesus bound to Caiaphas the high priest. Now Simon Peter was standing and warming himself. They said to Peter, "Are you not also one of his disciples?"

He denied it and said, "I am not."

One of the servants of the high priest, a relative of the man whose ear Peter had cut off, asked, "Did I not see you in the garden with him?"

Peter again denied it, and at once the cock crowed.

Then they led Jesus from the house of Caiaphas to the praetorium. It was early. They themselves did not enter the praetorium, so that they might not be defiled, but might eat the passover. So Pilate went out to them and said, "What accusation do you bring against this man?"

They answered Pilate, "If this man were not an evildoer, we would not have handed him over."

Pilate said to them, "Take him yourselves and judge him by your own law."

The Judeans said to him, "It is not lawful for us to put any one to death."

This was to fulfill the word which Jesus had spoken to show by what death he was to die.

Pilate entered the praetorium again and called Jesus, saying, "Are you King of the Jews?"

Jesus answered, "Do you say this of your own accord, or did others say it to you about me?"

Pilate answered, "Am I Jewish? Your own nation and the chief priests have handed you over to me; what have you done?"

Jesus answered, "My kingship is not of this world; if my kingship were of this world, my servants would fight, that I might not be handed over to the Judeans; but my kingship is not from this world."

Pilate said to him, "So you are a king?"

Jesus answered, "You say that I am a king. For this I was born, and for this I have come into the world, to bear witness to the truth. Everyone who is of the truth hears my voice."

Pilate said to Jesus, "What is the truth?"

Having said this, Pilate went out to the Judeans again, and told them, "I find no crime in him. But you have a custom that I should release one person for you at the Passover; will you have me release for you the King of the Jews?"

They cried out again, "Not this man, but Barabbas!"

Now Barabbas was a robber.

Then Pilate took Jesus and scourged him. And the soldiers plaited a crown of thorns, and put it on his head, and arrayed him in a purple robe; they came up to Jesus, saying, "Hail, King of the Jews!" and struck him with their hands. Pilate went out again, and said to them, "See, I am bringing him out to you, that you may know that I find no crime in him."

So Jesus came out, wearing the crown of thorns and the purple robe. Pilate said to them, "Behold the man."

When the chief priest and the officers saw him, they cried out, "Crucify him, crucify him!"

Pilate said to them, "Take him yourselves and crucify him, for I find no crime in him."

The Judeans answered him, "We have a law, and by that law he ought to die, because he has made himself the Son of God."

When Pilate heard these words, he was the more afraid, he entered the praetorium again and said to Jesus, "Where are you from?"

But Jesus gave no answer. Pilate therefore said to him, "You will not speak to me? Do you know that I have the power to release you, and the power to crucify you?"

Jesus answered him, "You would have no power over me unless it had been given you from above; therefore the one who delivered me to you has the greater sin."

Upon this Pilate sought to release him, but the Judeans cried out, "If you release this man, you are not Caesar's friend; everyone who makes himself a king sets himself against Caesar."

When Pilate heard these words, he brought Jesus out and sat down on the judgment seat at a place called The Pavement, and in Hebrew, Gabbatha. Now it was the day of Preparation of the Passover; it was about the sixth hour. He said to the Judeans, "Behold your king!"

They cried out, "Away with him, away with him, crucify him."

Pilate said to them, "Shall I crucify your king?"

The chief priest answered, "We have no king but Caesar."

Then Pilate handed Jesus over to them to be crucified. So they took Jesus, and he went out, bearing his own cross, to the place called the place of a skull, which is called in Hebrew Golgotha. There they crucified him, and with him two others, one on either side, and Jesus between them. Pilate also wrote a title and put it on the cross; it read, "Jesus of Nazareth, the King of the Jews." Many of the Judeans read this title, for the place where Jesus was crucified was near the city; and it was written in Hebrew, in Latin and in Greek. The chief priests then said to Pilate, "Do not write, 'The King of the Jews,' but 'This man said, I am King of the Jews.'"

Pilate answered, "What I have written I have written."

When the soldiers had crucified Jesus they took his garments and made four parts, one for each soldier;

also the tunic. But his tunic was without seam, woven from top to bottom; so they said to one another, "Let us not tear it, but cast lots for it to see whose it shall be."

This was to fulfill the scripture, "They parted my garments among them, and for my clothing they cast lots."

So the soldiers did this. But standing by the cross of Jesus were his mother, and his mother's sister, Mary the wife of Clopas, and Mary Magdalene. When Jesus saw his mother, and the disciple whom he loved stand near, he said to his mother, "Woman, behold your son!" Then he said to the disciple, "Behold, your mother!"

And from that hour the disciple took her to his own home. After this Jesus, knowing that all was not finished, said (to fulfill the scripture), "I thirst."

A bowl of vinegar stood there; so they put a sponge full of vinegar on hyssop and held it to his mouth. Having received the vinegar, Jesus said, "It is finished"; and he bowed his head and gave over the spirit.

Since it was the day of Preparation, in order to prevent the bodies from remaining on the cross on the sabbath (for that sabbath was a high day), the Judeans asked Pilate that their legs might be broken, and that they might be taken away. So the soldiers came and broke the legs of the first, and of the other who had been crucified with him; but when they came to Jesus and saw that he was already dead, they did not break his legs. But one of the soldiers pierced his side with a spear, and at once there came out blood and water. He who saw it, whose testimony is true, and who knows that he tells the truth, has borne witness that you also may believe. For these things took place that the scripture might be fulfilled, "Not a bone of him shall be broken." And again another scripture says, "They shall look upon the one whom they have pierced."

After this Joseph of Arimathea, who was a disciple of Jesus, but secretly, for fear of the Judeans, asked Pilate that he might take away the body of Jesus, and Pilate gave him leave. So Joseph came and took away Jesus' body. Nicodemus also, who had at first come to Jesus by night, came bringing a mixture of myrrh and aloes, about a hundred pounds' weight. They took the body of Jesus, and bound it in linen cloths with the spices, as is the Jewish burial custom. Now in the place where Jesus was crucified there was a garden, and in the garden a new tomb where no one had ever been laid. So because of the Jewish day of Preparation, as the tomb was close at hand, they laid Jesus there.

APRIL 2, 1993
THE EASTER VIGIL

READING I   *Genesis 1:1 — 2:3*

In the beginning God created the heavens and the earth. The earth was without form and void, and darkness was upon the face of the deep; and the Spirit of God was moving over the face of the waters.

And God said, "Let there be light"; and there was light. And God saw that the light was good; and God separated the light from the darkness. God called the light Day, and the darkness God called Night. And there was evening and there was morning, one day.

And God said, "Let there be a firmament in the midst of the waters, and let it separate the waters from the waters." And God made the firmament and separated the waters which were under the firmament from the waters which were above the firmament. And it was so. And God called the firmament Heaven. And there was evening and there was morning, a second day.

And God said, "Let the waters under the heavens be gathered together in one place, and let the dry land appear." And it was so. God called the dry land Earth, and the waters that were gathered together God called Seas. And God saw that it was good. And God said, "Let the earth put forth vegetation, plants yielding seed, and fruit trees bearing fruit in which is their seed, each according to its kind, upon the earth." And it was so. The earth brought forth vegetation, plants yielding seed according to their own kinds, and trees bearing fruit in which is their seed, each according to its kind. And God saw that it was good. And there was evening and there was morning, a third day.

And God said, "Let there be lights in the firmament of the heavens to separate the day from the night; and let them be for signs and for seasons and for days and years, and let them be lights in the firmament of the heavens to give light upon the earth." And it was so. And God made the two great lights, the greater light to rule the day, and the lesser light to rule the night; God made the stars also. And God set them in the firmament of the heavens to give light upon the earth, to rule over the day and over the night, and to separate the light from the darkness. And God saw that it was good. And there was evening and there was morning, a fourth day.

And God said, "Let the waters bring forth swarms of living creatures, and let birds fly above the earth across the firmament of the heavens." So God created the great sea monsters and every living creature that moves, with which the waters swarm, according to their kinds, and every winged bird according to its kind. And God saw that it was good. And God blessed them, saying, "Be fruitful and multiply and fill the waters in the seas, and let birds multiply on the earth." And there was evening and there was morning, a fifth day.

And God said, "Let the earth bring forth living creatures according to their kinds: cattle and creeping things and beasts of the earth according to their kinds." And it was so. And God made the beasts of the earth according to their kinds and the cattle according to their kinds, and everything that creeps upon the ground according to its kind. And God saw that it was good.

Then God said, "Let us make humankind in our image, after our likeness; and let them have dominion over the fish of the sea, and over the birds of the air, and over the cattle, and over all the earth, and over every creeping thing that creeps upon the earth." So

God created humankind in the divine image; in the image of God humankind was created; male and female God created them. And God blessed them, and God said to them "Be fruitful and multiply, and fill the earth and subdue it; and have dominion over the fish of the sea and over the birds of the air and over every living thing that moves upon the earth." And God said, "Behold, I have given you every plant yielding seed which is upon the face of all the earth, and every tree with seed in its fruit; you shall have them for food.

"And to every beast of the earth, and to every bird of the air, and to everything that creeps on the earth, everything that has the breath of life, I have given every green plant for food." And it was so. And God saw everything that had been made, and behold, it was very good. And there was evening and there was morning, a sixth day.

Thus the heavens and the earth were finished, and all the host of them. And on the seventh day God finished the work which had been done, and God rested on the seventh day from all the work which God had done. So God blessed the seventh day and hallowed it, because on it God rested from all the work which God had done in creation.

READING II *Genesis 22:1–18*

After these things God tested Abraham, and said to him, "Abraham!" And he said, "Here am I." God said, "Take your son, your only son Isaac, whom you love, and go to the land of Moriah, and offer him there as a burnt offering upon one of the mountains of which I shall tell you." So Abraham rose early in the morning, saddled his donkey, and took two of his servants with him, and his son Isaac; and he cut the wood for the burnt offering, and arose and went to the place of which God had told him. On the third day Abraham lifted up his eyes and saw the place afar off. Then Abraham said to his servants, "Stay here with the donkey; I and the lad will go yonder and worship, and come again to you." And Abraham took the wood of the burnt offering, and laid it on Isaac his son; and he took in his hand the fire and the knife. So they went both of them together. And Isaac said to his father Abraham, "My father!" And he said, "Here am I, my son." Isaac said, "Behold, the fire and the wood, but where is the lamb for a burnt offering?" Abraham said, "God will provide the lamb for a burnt offering to God, my son." So they went both of them together.

When they came to the place of which God had told him, Abraham built an altar there, and laid the wood in order, and bound Isaac his son and laid him on the altar, upon the wood. Then Abraham put forth his hand, and took the knife to slay his son. But the angel of the LORD called to him from heaven, and said, "Abraham, Abraham!" And he said, "Here am I." The angel said, "Do not lay your hand on the lad or do anything to him; for now I know that you fear God, seeing you have not withheld your son, your only son, from me." And Abraham lifted up his eyes and looked, and behold, behind him was a ram, caught in a thicket by its horns; and Abraham went and took the ram, and offered it up as a burnt offering instead of his son. So Abraham called the name of that place The LORD will provide, as it is said to this day, "On the mount of the LORD it shall be provided."

READING III *Exodus 14:15 — 15:2*

The LORD said to Moses, "Why do you cry to me? Tell the people of Israel to go forward. Lift up your rod, and stretch out your hand over the sea and divide it, that the people of Israel may go on dry ground through the sea. And I will harden the hearts of the Egyptians so that they shall go in after them, and I will get glory over Pharaoh and all his host, his chariots and his charioteers. And the Egyptians shall know that I am the LORD, when I have gotten glory over Pharaoh, his chariots and his charioteers."

Then the angel of God who went before the host of Israel moved and went behind them; and the pillar of cloud moved from before them and stood behind them, coming between the host of Egypt and the host of Israel. And there was the cloud and the darkness; and the night passed without one coming near the other all night.

Then Moses stretched out his hand over the sea; and the LORD drove the sea back by a strong east wind all night, and made the sea dry land, and the waters were divided. And the people of Israel went into the midst of the sea on dry ground, the waters being a wall to them on their right hand and on their left. The Egyptians pursued, and went in after them into the midst of the sea, all Pharaoh's horses, his chariots and his charioteers. And in the morning watch the LORD in the pillar of fire and of cloud looked down upon the host of the Egyptians, and discomfited the host of the Egyptians, clogging their chariot wheels so that they drove heavily; and the Egyptians said, "Let us flee from before Israel, for the LORD fights for them against the Egyptians."

The LORD said to Moses, "Stretch out your hand over the sea, that the water may come back upon the Egyptians, upon their chariots, and upon their charioteers." So Moses stretched forth his hand over the sea, and the sea returned to its wonted flow when the morning appeared; and the Egyptians fled into it, and the LORD routed the Egyptians in the midst of the sea. The waters returned and covered the chariots and the charioteers and all the host of Pharaoh that had followed them into the sea; not so much as one of them remained. But the people of Israel walked on dry ground through the sea, the waters being a wall to them on the right hand and on their left.

Thus the LORD saved Israel that day from the hand of the Egyptians; and Israel saw the Egyptians dead upon the seashore. And Israel saw the great work which the LORD did against the Egyptians, and the people feared the LORD; and they believed in the LORD and in Moses, the servant of the LORD.

Then Moses, Miriam and the people of Israel sang this song to the LORD, saying,

"I will sing to the LORD who has triumphed gloriously; the horse and its rider have been thrown into the sea."

READING IV *Isaiah 54:5–14*

For your Maker is your husband,
   whose name is the LORD of hosts;
and the Holy One of Israel is your redeemer,
   who is called the God of the whole earth.
For the LORD has called you
   like a wife forsaken and grieved in spirit,
like a wife of youth when she is cast off,
   says your God.
For a brief moment I forsook you,
   But with great compassion I will gather you.
In overflowing wrath for a moment
   I hid my face from you,
but with everlasting love
   I will have compassion on you,
   says the LORD, your Redeemer.
For this is like the days of Noah to me:
   as I swore that the waters of Noah
   should no more go over the earth,
so I have sworn that I will not be angry with you
   and will not rebuke you.
For the mountains may depart
   and the hills be removed,
but my steadfast love shall not depart from you,
   and my covenant of peace shall not be removed,
   says the LORD, who has compassion on you.
"O afflicted one, storm-tossed and not comforted,
   behold, I will set your stones in antimony,
   and lay your foundations with sapphires.
I will make your pinnacles of agate,
   your gates of carbuncles,
   and all your walls of precious stones.
All your children shall be taught by the LORD,
   and great shall be the prosperity
     of your offspring.
In righteousness you shall be established;
   you shall be far from oppression,
     for you shall not fear;
and from terror, for it shall not come near you."

READING V *Isaiah 55:1–11*

"Ho, everyone who thirsts,
   come to the waters;
and whoever has no money,
   come, buy and eat!
Come, buy wine and milk
   without money and without price.
Why do you spend your money for that
     which is not bread,
   and your labor for that which does not satisfy?
Hearken diligently to me, and eat what is good,
   and delight yourselves in fatness.
Incline your ear, and come to me:
   hear, that your soul may live;
and I will make with you an everlasting covenant,
   my steadfast, sure love for David.
Behold, I made him a witness to the peoples,
   a leader and commander for the peoples.
Behold, you shall call nations that you know not,
   and nations that knew you not shall run to you,
because of the LORD your God,
   and of the Holy One of Israel,
   for the LORD had glorified you.
Seek the LORD while the LORD may be found,
   call upon God, while God is near;
let the wicked forsake their ways,
   and the unrighteous their thoughts;
let them return to the LORD, who will have mercy
     on them,
   and to our God, who will abundantly pardon.
For my thoughts are not your thoughts,
   neither are your ways my ways, says the LORD.
For as the heavens are higher than the earth,

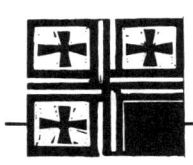

so are my ways higher than your ways
  and my thoughts than your thoughts.
For as the rain and the snow come down from heaven,
  and return not thither but water the earth,
making it bring forth and sprout,
  giving seed to the sower and bread to the eater,
so shall my word be that goes forth from my mouth;
  it shall not return to me empty,
but it shall accomplish that which I purpose,
  and prosper in the thing for which I sent it."

READING VI   *Baruch 3:9—4:4*

Hear the commandments of life, O Israel;
  give ear, and learn wisdom!
Why is it, O Israel, why is it that you are in the land
    of your enemies,
  that you are growing old in a foreign country,
that you are defiled with the dead,
  that you are counted among those in Hades?
You have forsaken the fountain of wisdom.
If you had walked in the way of God,
  you would be dwelling in peace for ever.
Learn where there is wisdom,
  where there is strength,
  where there is understanding,
that you may at the same time discern
  where there is length of days, and life,
  where there is light for the eyes, and peace.
Who has found the place of Wisdom?
  And who has entered her storehouses?
The one who knows all things knows her,
  and found her through understanding.
The one who prepared the earth for all time
  filled it with four-footed creatures;
the one who sends forth the light, and it goes,
  called it, and it harkened in fear;
the stars shone in their watches, and were glad;
  God called them, and they said, "Here we are!"
  They shone with gladness for the one
    who made them.
This is our God,
  with whom none other can be compared.
God found the whole way to knowledge,
  and gave her to Jacob, God's servant,
  and to Israel, the one whom God loved.
Afterward she appeared upon earth
  and lived among humankind.
She is the book of the commandments of God,
  and the law that endures for ever.
All who hold her fast will live,
  and those who forsake her will die.
Turn, O Jacob, and take her;
  walk toward the shining of her light.
Do not give your glory to another,
  or your advantages to an alien people.
Happy are we, O Israel,
  for we know that is pleasing to God.

READING VII   *Ezekiel 36:16–28*

The word of the LORD came to me: "Son of man, when the house of Israel dwelt in their own land, they defiled it by their ways and their doings; their conduct before me was unclean. So I poured out my wrath upon them for the blood which they had shed in the land, for the idols with which they defiled it. I scattered them among the nations, and they were dispersed through the countries; in accordance with their conduct and their deeds I judged them. But when they came to the nations, wherever they came, they profaned my holy name, in that strangers said of them, 'These are the people of the LORD, and yet they had to go out of God's land.' But I had concern for my holy name, which the house of Israel caused to be profaned among the nations to which they came.

"Therefore say to the house of Israel, Thus says the Lord GOD: It is not for your sake, O house of Israel, that I am about to act, but for the sake of my holy name, which you have profaned among the nations to which you came. And I will vindicate the holiness of my great name, which has been profaned among the nations, and which you have profaned among them; and the nations will know that I am the LORD, says the Lord GOD, when through you I vindicate my holiness before their eyes. For I will take you from the nations, and gather you from all the countries, and bring you into your own land. I will sprinkle clean water upon you, and you shall be clean from all your uncleannesses, and from all your idols I will cleanse you. A new heart I will give you, and a new spirit I will put within you; and I will take out of your flesh the heart of stone and give you a heart of flesh. And I will put my spirit within you, and cause you to walk in my statutes and be careful to observe my ordinances. You shall dwell in the land which I gave to your ancestors; and you shall be my people, and I will be your God."

READING VIII   Romans 6:3–11

Do you not know that all of us who have been baptized into Christ Jesus were baptized into his death? We were buried therefore with Christ by baptism into death, so that as Christ was raised from the dead by the glory of the Father, we too might walk in newness of life.

For if we have been united with Christ in death, we shall certainly be united with Christ in resurrection. We know that our old self was crucified with Christ so that the sinful body might be destroyed, and we might no longer be enslaved to sin. For whoever has died is freed from sin. But if we have died with Christ, we believe that we shall also live with Christ. For we know that Christ being raised from the dead will never die again; death no longer has dominion over him. The death he died he died to sin, once for all, but the life he lives he lives to God. So you also must consider yourselves dead to sin and alive to God in Christ Jesus.

GOSPEL   Mark 16:1–7

When the sabbath was past, Mary Magdelene, and Mary the mother of James, and Salome, bought spices, so that they might go and anoint Jesus. And very early on the first day of the week they went to the tomb when the sun had risen. And they were saying to one another, "Who will roll away the stone for us from the door of the tomb?" And looking up, they saw that the stone was rolled back — it was very large. And entering the tomb, they saw a youth sitting on the right side, dressed in a white robe; and they were amazed. And the youth said to them, "Do not be amazed; you seek Jesus of Nazareth, who was crucified. He has risen, he is not here; see the place where they laid him. But go, tell his disciples and Peter that he is going before you to Galilee; there you will see him, as he told you." And they went out and fled from the tomb; for trembling and astonishment had come upon them; and they said nothing to any one, for they were afraid.

APRIL 3, 1994

EASTER SUNDAY

READING I *Acts 10:34, 37–43*

Peter opened his mouth and said: "The word which was proclaimed throughout all Judea, beginning from Galilee after the baptism which John preached: how God anointed Jesus of Nazareth with the Holy Spirit and with power; how Jesus went about doing good and healing all that were oppressed by the devil, for God was with him. And we are witnesses to all that Jesus did both in the country of the Judeans and in Jerusalem. They put him to death by hanging him on a tree; but God raised Jesus on the third day and made him manifest; not to all the people but to us who were chosen by God as witnesses, who ate and drank with Jesus after he rose from the dead. And Jesus commanded us to preach to the people; and to testify that he is the one ordained by God to be judge of the living and the dead. To this Jesus all the prophets bear witness that everyone who believes in him receives forgiveness of sins through his name."

READING II *Colossians 3:1–4*

If then you have been raised with Christ, seek the things that are above, where Christ is, seated at the right hand of God. Set your minds on things that are above, not on things that are on earth. For you have died, and your life is hid with Christ in God. When Christ who is our life appears, then you also will appear with him in glory.

GOSPEL *John 20:1–9*

Now on the first day of the week Mary Magdalene came to the tomb early, while it was still dark, and saw that the stone had been taken away from the tomb. So she ran, and went to Simon Peter and the other disciple, the one whom Jesus loved, and said to them, "They have taken the Lord out of the tomb, and we do not know where they have laid him." Peter then came out with the other disciple, and they went toward the tomb. They both ran, but the other disciple outran Peter and reached the tomb first; and stooping to look in, he saw the linen cloths lying there, but did not go in. Then Simon Peter came, following him, and went into the tomb; he saw the linen cloths lying, and the napkin, which had been on Jesus' head, not lying with the linen cloths but rolled up in a place by itself. Then the other disciple, who reached the tomb first, also went in, and he saw and believed; for as yet they did not know the scripture, that Jesus must rise from the dead.

REFLECTION

When Jesus cried to Lazarus to "come out" of the tomb, Lazarus struggled with the grave bindings and had to be helped out. When Peter entered Jesus' tomb, the grave bindings were neatly folded: Jesus needed no help in leaving his grave. This is why John alone mentions this curious little detail about the folded linens—to draw the contrast between Jesus' new life and the restoration of Lazarus's old life. The raising of Lazarus was a "sign"—a foreshadowing—of Jesus' resurrection, but Lazarus would die again! In fact, John tells us, the officials used the raising of Lazarus as an excuse in the death plot against Jesus. But Jesus' rising from the grave was unique. He is the resurrection and the life. He was not brought back to a life in which another death still awaited him. The risen life of Jesus is of a different, unprecedented order. He had described it as a journey back to the Father.

What Peter and the other disciple witnessed, the empty tomb, was, like all the signs of Jesus in the Gospel of John, a sign that life and light are victorious. Still, none of them fully understood. And neither do we. But what they knew and what we know is that at the heart of Christian faith is an uncompromising and unambiguous affirmation of life.

1. Read the raising of Lazarus in John 11. Besides the symbolism of the grave linens and bindings, what other contrasts could you point to?

2. The Colossians reading says, "you have died, and your life is hid with Christ in God." What does that mean? How have you died? How is your life "hidden" in Christ?

Practice of FAITH

EASTER VESPERS. Although in the Gospel of John Mary Magdalene sees Jesus on Easter morning, the risen Lord does not appear to the other disciples until evening. In the Gospel of Luke the disciples on the road to Emmaus say to Christ, "Stay, Lord, for it is evening. . . ." A natural time for prayer is when day gives way to evening. A great way to keep Easter as our foremost holy day is to celebrate vespers, or evening prayer. If your parish is having Easter vespers, join in. If not, use the evening prayer found on page 12 at Easter dinner, sharing it with all those present. You can use the Easter psalm on page 13, too. Light a candle before you begin. To make your prayer even more beautiful, sing an alleluia or an Easter carol that everyone knows.

Next week, take a jar to church in order to bring home some Easter holy water.

Practice of HOPE

IF YOU HAVE BEEN RAISED WITH CHRIST. "If I am killed, I will rise again in the people of El Salvador." Archbishop Oscar Romero proclaimed these words just days before a gunman cut him down while he was celebrating Mass. Romero had been outspoken in his denunciation of the violence of the Salvadoran military and the unjust distribution of wealth and land that consigned masses of Salvadorans to abject poverty.

Twelve years after Romero's death, in January 1992, the Salvadoran government and the opposition guerrillas signed a peace agreement. It ended a civil war that had claimed tens of thousands of lives, many of them church people who had worked for justice. In San Salvador's packed square during the victory celebration, these words graced a large banner bearing Romero's image: "I *have* risen again in the Salvadoran people."

Practice of CHARITY

MAGDALENE CAME TO THE TOMB EARLY. Mary Magdalene's love for Jesus called her to go to the tomb early that first Easter morning. She did not know what she would find, but she went out of love, out of hope, out of a deep sorrow over the agony and death of Jesus. It was her love that brought her to the Easter joy. We need to have that same love whenever we perform an act of kindness or justice. It is this love that overcomes our fear of failure, cynicism, anger, or despair. It is love that brings us to the Easter faith when we know that all to whom we reach out are our brothers and sisters in Christ. Ponder the depth of this love that calls us all to go to the tomb early.

Weekday Reading
Acts, chapters 2–3

Eastertime

Christ is risen!
Christ is truly risen!

Alleluia!
Give thanks, the Lord is good,
"God is lasting love!"
Now let Israel say,
"God is lasting love!"

I was pushed to falling,
but the Lord gave me help.
My strength, my song is the Lord
who has become my Savior.

I shall not die but live
to tell the Lord's great deeds.
The Lord punished me severely,
but did not let me die.

The stone the builders rejected
has become the cornerstone.
This is the work of the Lord,
how wonderful in our eyes.

This is the day the Lord has made,
let us rejoice and be glad.
Lord, grant us salvation,
Lord, grant us success.

Blest be the one who comes,
who comes in the name of the Lord.
We bless you from the Lord's house.
The Lord God is our light:
adorn the altar with branches.

I will thank you, my God,
will praise you highly, Lord.
Give thanks, the Lord is good,
"God is lasting love!"

—*Psalm 118:1-2, 13–14, 17–18, 22–29*

The heavens rumble alleluias,
earth dances to the tune
and the wail of the graves
itself becomes song.
All are singing with you, savior God,
at this wedding feast
for you have turned the world around,
inside out and upside down.
Now the homeless are at home
and the martyred embrace their assassins
and the rulers and bosses wonder
whose world this is after all.
After all, let us stand and sing
with the heavens and earth and the graves
and so proclaim that we live now only
in Christ who is Lord for ever and ever.

—*Prayer of the Season*

APRIL 10, 1994
SECOND SUNDAY OF EASTER

READING I *Acts 4:32–35*

Now the company of those who believed were of one heart and soul, and they all said that the things which they possessed were not their own, but they had everything in common. And with great power the apostles gave their testimony to the resurrection of the Lord Jesus, and great grace was upon them all. There was not a needy person among them, for as many as were possessors of lands or houses sold them, and brought the proceeds of what was sold and laid it at the apostles' feet; and distribution was made to each as any had need.

READING II *1 John 5:1–6*

Everyone who believes that Jesus is the Christ is a child of God, and everyone who loves the parent loves the child. By this we know that we love the children of God, when we love God and obey God's commandments. For this is the love of God, that we keep God's commandments, which are not burdensome. For whatever is born of God overcomes the world; and this is the victory that overcomes the world, our faith. Who is it that overcomes the world but anyone who believes that Jesus is the Son of God?

This is the one who came by water and blood, Jesus Christ, not with the water only but with the water and the blood.

GOSPEL *John 20:19–31*

On the evening of that day, the first day of the week, the doors being shut where the disciples were, for fear of the Judeans, Jesus came and stood among them and said to them, "Peace be with you." Having said this, Jesus showed them his hands and his side. Then the disciples were glad when they saw the Lord. Jesus said to them again, "Peace be with you. As the Father has sent me, even so I send you." Having said this, Jesus breathed on them, and said to them, "Receive the Holy Spirit. If you forgive the sins of any, they are forgiven; if you retain the sins of any, they are retained."

Now Thomas, one of the twelve, called the Twin, was not with them when Jesus came. So the other disciples told Thomas, "We have seen the Lord." But he said to them, "Unless I see in his hands the print of the nails, and place my finger in the mark of the nails, and place my hand in his side, I will not believe."

Eight days later, Jesus' disciples were again in the house, and Thomas was with them. The doors were shut, but Jesus came and stood among them, and said, "Peace be with you." Then Jesus said to Thomas, "Put your finger here, and see my hands; and put out your hand, and place it in my side; do not be faithless, but believing." Thomas answered Jesus, "My Lord and my God!" Jesus said to him, "Have you believed because you have seen me? Blessed are those who have not seen and yet believe."

Now Jesus did many other signs in the presence of the disciples, which are not written in this book; but these are written that you may believe that Jesus is the Christ, the Son of God, and that believing you may have life in his name.

REFLECTION

Thomas was clearly a man of action. In the Lazarus story he was among the disciples who were bemused by Jesus wanting to return to Judea and the threat of death. Even though Jesus makes clear that there is profound business afoot, Thomas seems to go for the apparent bravado of the plan when he calls to the others, "Let us also go, that we may die with him."

In the famous post-resurrection story we hear today, Thomas demands hard evidence for the others' claim that they had "seen the Lord." He was absent when the rest saw Jesus. They had received his gift of peace when he breathed the Holy Spirit on them on the evening of that first Easter. Jesus gently reprimands the Twin, whose words of faith, "My Lord and my God," round off the fourth gospel's identification of Jesus. Jesus' words to Thomas the Twin validate the faith of Christians who could never physically experience their Lord as the original disciples did. The faith of all believers is equally valid, affirmed in the gift of the same Spirit shared by all. One's situation in space, time and physical proximity to Jesus is irrelevant.

In the original closing words of the gospel, John has told the story, and not all of it, so that "you may believe that Jesus is the Christ, the son of God and that in believing you may have life in his name." That's why John wrote his book and why those who receive Jesus' blessing at the end are those like yourself, "who have not seen and yet believe."

1. That first reading is a very idealistic picture of the earliest community of believers. Read Acts 15:1–35 and Galatians 2. What do these additional passages suggest about early Christian communities? How are they like/unlike your own?

2. In what ways do individuals and groups demand proof before they're prepared to believe? Is it possible to "prove" matters of faith as if they were matters of cold logic?

Practice of FAITH

PEACE BE WITH YOU. The gospel read today is echoed in every Mass at the sign of peace with the prayer that begins: "Lord, Jesus Christ, you said to your apostles 'Peace I leave with you; my peace I give to you.' Look not on our sins, but on the faith of your church . . ." Because it is a ritual, the hug or handshake becomes automatic. That's not bad, but sometimes we do it without being aware of what it means. Try to be aware of what you are doing the next time you share the sign of peace. Look the other person in the eyes. Don't rush. Feel in the warmth of hand or hug the warmth of the risen Lord.

Practice of HOPE

ONE HEART AND SOUL AND EVERYTHING IN COMMON. Habitat for Humanity sponsored a project to build a dozen homes in a very economically depressed area of Mexico. All of the families that would eventually move in joined in the construction of all of the houses. Special care went into the building of each home, and for a very specific reason. When the work was completed, all the keys to the homes were placed in a large basket. Each family picked a key and found their new home.

These were metaphorically "keys to the kingdom." Surely God didn't intend for some of us to live in mansions and others in shanties. In a little corner of Mexico, that truth became a way of life, as all learned to share and look out for the well-being of the others.

Practice of CHARITY

DISTRIBUTION TO EACH AS ANY HAD NEED. What does your parish do for those in need? Does it have a St. Vincent de Paul Society? Find out how you can assist in its important work. It might mean cleaning out closets and donating good used clothing; it might mean buying some extra groceries this month to give to the food pantry, or giving some of your time and talent. St. Vincent de Paul Society members go out two by two to visit those in need. Besides delivering groceries and money, they find out what the causes of poverty are, and they try to help people in planning for the future. For more information about the St. Vincent de Paul Society or to make a donation, write the national office: St. Vincent de Paul, 4140 Lindell Boulevard, St. Louis MO 63108; 314-533-2223.

Weekday Reading
Acts, chapters 4–5

APRIL 17, 1994

THIRD SUNDAY OF EASTER

READING I   *Acts 3:13–15, 17–19*

[Peter said to the people,]

"The God of Abraham and of Isaac and of Jacob, the God of our forebears, glorified Jesus, the servant of God, whom you delivered up and denied in the presence of Pilate, when Pilate had decided to release him. But you denied the Holy and Righteous One, and asked for a murderer to be granted to you, and killed the Author of life, whom God raised from the dead. To this we are witnesses.

"And now, my dear people, I know that you acted in ignorance, as did also your rulers. But what God foretold by the mouth of all the prophets, that the Christ of God should suffer, was thus fulfilled. Repent, therefore, and turn again, that your sins may be blotted out, that times of refreshing may come from the presence of the Lord."

READING II   *1 John 2:1–5*

My little children, I am writing this to you so that you may not sin; but if anyone does sin, we have an advocate with the Father, Jesus Christ the righteous, who is the expiation for our sins, and not for ours only but also for the sins of the whole world. And by this we may be sure that we know God, if we keep God's commandments. They who say "I know God" but disobey God's commandments are liars, and the truth is not in them; but those who keep God's word, in them truly love for God is perfected.

GOSPEL   *Luke 24:35–48*

The two disciples told what had happened on the road, and how Jesus was known to them in the breaking of the bread.

As they were saying this, Jesus himself stood among them. But they were startled and frightened, and supposed that they saw a spirit. And Jesus said to them, "Why are you troubled, and why do questionings rise in your hearts? See my hands and my feet, that it is I myself; handle me, and see; for a spirit has not flesh and bones as you see that I have." And while they still disbelieved for joy, and wondered, Jesus said to them, "Have you anything here to eat?" They gave him a piece of broiled fish, and he took it and ate before them.

Then Jesus said to them, "These are my words which I spoke to you, while I was still with you, that everything written about me in the law of Moses and the prophets and the psalms must be fulfilled." Then Jesus opened their minds to understand the scriptures, and said to them, "Thus it is written, that the Christ should suffer and on the third day rise from the dead, and that repentance and forgiveness of sins should be preached in the name of Christ to all nations, beginning from Jerusalem. You are witnesses of these things."

REFLECTION

Last week we heard of Thomas and his need for proof. Luke's story this week has a similar theme. The first preachers of the risen Lord had to explain that he was real flesh and not a "ghost" whom they claimed had risen.

Today's appearance story comes immediately after the Emmaus tale in which Jesus was recognized by two unnamed disciples in "the breaking of the bread." That physical sign is followed by other physical signs—reassurances of Jesus' abiding presence within the believing community. Luke, having indicated Jesus' presence in the eucharist, retells to the disciples a traditional story of a physical appearance of Jesus that wasn't in the eucharist. Luke edits this story to suit the point he needs to make and provides details not found in Matthew or John. Jesus has hands and feet with holes (but no pierced side) and he eats (ghosts don't get hungry). Jesus' resurrection, in other words, was the resurrection of a real physical body—more than just a "spiritual" experience. These details are important enough for Luke to include, probably because he and his community (circa 80 CE) were dealing with doubts about the physical resurrection of Jesus.

Like the Gospel of John, the Gospel of Luke is concerned with how Jesus is still recognizably present among believers after his death and resurrection. The story of Emmaus gives the eucharist as one experience of his presence. But this is underscored by the other disciples' encounter with an undoubtedly physical risen one. In Acts, the physical signs of the resurrection of Jesus, including the empty tomb, are complemented by the greatest sign, the giving of the Holy Spirit. Jesus left believers behind as witnesses and shared with them the same Spirit given him at baptism, the Spirit that impelled his mission, passion and resurrection.

1. What are the most important tangible signs of Jesus' presence in your life and in your community's life?

2. How are Jesus' resurrection and yours connected? How do you already experience the benefits of Christ's resurrection? What does his physical resurrection suggest about the holiness of the human body?

Practice of FAITH

THE PSALMS MUST BE FULFILLED. A faithful Jew, Jesus prayed the psalms throughout his life; his dying words were from Psalm 22. Early Christians were especially fond of the psalms; they saw in these holy songs hints about who Jesus really is: the one who delights in the law of the Lord (Psalm 1), the good shepherd (Psalm 23), the king of glory (Psalm 24), the one who comes in the name of the Lord and the rejected one who becomes the cornerstone (Psalm 118).

Get to know the psalms. A few years ago, a group of faithful scholars, the International Committee on English in the Liturgy (ICEL) prepared a fresh English translation of the psalms. Some of them are printed throughout this book. Find them. Pray them over and over until you know them by heart. Know that as you pray the psalms, Jesus prays through you.

Practice of HOPE

THEY DISBELIEVED FOR JOY. A small group of peasants in Brazil was being pushed off their land once more, a seizure made legal by a vote in parliament. They knew that their children would starve if they could not stay with their crops, but every time they resisted, the police came in and killed some of them.

The women had a courageous idea. Each went, with her children, to the luxurious home of a parliament member, where they sat on the lawn. The parliament members' wives tried to offer the ragged women money or food. But the mothers said, "We want no money or bread. We are going to die. And since this is such a nice place, we thought we would like to die here." When the wives asked why, the mothers explained. Before long, the parliament phones were buzzing. Every wife pleaded with her husband. The peasants kept their land and their future.

Practice of CHARITY

WHY ARE YOU TROUBLED? Daily living, with its tensions and pressures, can be too much for some people. Depression, anxiety, eating disorders, and the abuse of alcohol and drugs are common responses of those who feel trapped.

The Humanistic Foundation, a national group based in Long Beach, California, provides wholistic programs at licensed hospitals for the treatment of alcohol and drug abuse, depression, anxiety, and similar disorders. It is also a charitable foundation that can help people with their financial problems. For help or more information call toll-free 1-800-333-4444 or 1-800-333-1116. All calls are private and confidential.

Weekday Reading
Acts, chapters 6–10

APRIL 24, 1994
FOURTH SUNDAY OF EASTER

READING I   *Acts 4:8–12*

Peter, filled with the Holy Spirit, said to them, "Rulers of the people and elders, if we are being examined today concerning a good deed done to a crippled man, by what means this man has been healed, be it known to you all, and to all the people of Israel, that by the name of Jesus Christ of Nazareth, whom you crucified, whom God raised from the dead, by Jesus Christ this man is standing before you well. This is the stone which was rejected by you builders, but which has become the head of the corner. And there is salvation in no one else, for there is no other name under heaven given among humankind by which we must be saved."

READING II   *1 John 3:1–2*

See what love the Father has given us, that we should be called children of God; and so we are. The reason why the world does not know us is that it did not know God. Beloved, we are God's children now; it does not yet appear what we shall be, but we know that when it appears we shall be like God, for we shall see God as God is.

GOSPEL   *John 10:11–18*

[At that time Jesus said,]

"I am the good shepherd, the good shepherd who lays down his life for the sheep. The one who is a hireling and not a shepherd, whose own the sheep are not, sees the wolf coming and leaves the sheep and flees; and the wolf snatches them and scatters them. The hireling flees, caring nothing for the sheep. I am the good shepherd; I know my own and my own know me, as the Father knows me and I know the Father; and I lay down my life for the sheep. And I have other sheep, that are not of this fold; I must bring them also, and they will heed my voice. So there shall be one flock, one shepherd. For this reason the Father loves me, because I lay down my life, that I may take it again. No one takes it from me, but I lay it down of my own accord. I have power to lay it down, and I have power to take it again; this charge I have received from my Father."

REFLECTION

Shepherds in the Gospel of Luke signify the low level of society with which Jesus was associated all during his life on earth. The child is identified with common folk—"earthy" people. The Gospel of John opens by saying the same thing—"the word was made flesh"—and later uses the shepherd image powerfully. In the Fourth Gospel, especially in today's assigned portion of it, God comes among ordinary people as a shepherd, the one who cares for and protects his flock. Without him, the flock would be easily scattered and would be in constant danger from predators.

The divine-shepherd image comes from the Hebrew scriptures: See the Book of Ezekiel, for example. But if this is the source for the Gospel of John, the gospel gives the borrowed image a unique twist. The beginning of the fourth gospel has John the Baptist identify Jesus as the lamb of God. Later the lamb calls himself the good shepherd. Jesus is both sheep and shepherd.

Significantly, in the Fourth Gospel Jesus' condemnation to death comes precisely at the hour when the Passover lambs are being prepared for slaughter. That's why St. John is so careful to mention the actual time. Jesus, the good shepherd, becomes the sacrificial lamb who sheds his blood for the life of the flock. In the words of the Baptist, the lamb "takes away the sins of the world." No one preaches repentance in the fourth gospel. The sacrifice of Jesus the lamb, the death of Jesus the shepherd takes away sin. His is an act of grace on behalf of the sheep. And all of this meaning is packed into the seemingly simple phrase that Jesus utters in today's passage: "I am the good shepherd."

1. Read some of the references to God being a shepherd in the Hebrew scriptures—Ezekiel 34 and Jeremiah 23. Is the image of the shepherd still useful for people who may never have known sheep or shepherds? What are some equally good images?

2. A Scottish shepherd once said that his sheep's greatest safety lay in their ability to recognize and follow his voice alone, no one else's. How do you recognize the voice of the true good shepherd?

Practice of **FAITH**

GOOD SHEPHERD SUNDAY. The fourth Sunday of Easter is called Good Shepherd Sunday because the gospel refers to Christ with this title, a favorite of the early Christians. (When Christians first drew pictures of Christ, they drew him as the good shepherd.) If you can, whether at a farm or at a zoo, look at some sheep today or bake a cake using your lamb mold as an Easter season treat. Go back to the first reading for Holy Thursday, found on page 72. Then read today's gospel again. Discuss what light these two scriptures shed on each other. Memorize Psalm 23. And before you go to bed, say or sing this prayer from the Mass: "Lamb of God, you take away the sins of the world have mercy on/grant us peace."

Practice of **HOPE**

I LAY DOWN MY LIFE. Penny Lernoux was a Christian journalist of rare integrity and courage. She traveled throughout Latin America articulating "the cry of the people," which was the title of her most well-known book. In the closing words of her last book, Lernoux left us this challenge: "The Third World will continue to beckon to the First, reminding it of the Galilean vision of Christian solidarity. As a young Guatemalan said, a few months before she was killed by the military, 'What good is life unless you give it away—unless you can give it for a better world, even if you never see that world but have only carried your grain of sand to the building site? Then you're fulfilled as a person.'"

Practice of **CHARITY**

WE ARE GOD'S CHILDREN NOW. Being a child of God means caring for other children of God: Sisters and brothers take care of each other. ince 1985, Christ House, a ministry of The Church of the Saviour and affiliated with Columbia Road Health Services, has been caring for the medical needs of the homeless and destitute in Washington, D.C. It is a convalescent home where patients can stay as long as they need to in order to get well. Care for a typical patient comes to about $68 a day. Money and volunteers are always needed. Write or call Dr. Janelle Goetcheus, Christ House Medical Director, 1717 Columbia Road NW, Washington DC 20009-2803.

Weekday Reading
Acts, chapters 11–14

MAY 1, 1994
FIFTH SUNDAY OF EASTER

READING I *Acts 9:26–31*

When Saul had come to Jerusalem, he attempted to join the disciples; and they were all afraid of him, for they did not believe that he was a disciple. But Barnabas took him, and brought him to the apostles, and declared to them how on the road Saul had seen the Lord, who spoke to him, and how at Damascus he had preached boldly in the name of Jesus. So Saul went in and out among them at Jerusalem, preaching boldly in the name of the Lord. And he spoke and disputed against the Hellenists; but they were seeking to kill him. And when the community knew it, they brought him down to Caesarea, and sent him off to Tarsus.

So the church throughout all Judea and Galilee and Samaria had peace and was built up; and walking in the fear of the Lord and in the comfort of the Holy Spirit it was multiplied.

READING II *1 John 3:18–24*

Little children, let us not love in word or speech but in deed and in truth.

By this we shall know that we are of the truth, and reassure our hearts before God whenever our hearts condemn us; for God is greater than our hearts and knows everything. Beloved, if our hearts do not condemn us, we have confidence before God; and we receive from God whatever we ask, because we keep the commandments and do what is God-pleasing. And this is God's commandment, that we should believe in the name of Jesus Christ, the Son of God, and love one another, just as Jesus has commanded us. All who keep God's commandments abide in God, and God in them. And by this we know that God abides in us, by the Spirit which God has given us.

GOSPEL *John 15:1–8*

[At that time Jesus said,]

"I am the true vine, and my Father is the vinedresser. Every branch of mine that bears no fruit, my Father takes away, and every branch that does bear fruit my Father prunes, that it may bear more fruit. You are already made clean by the word which I have spoken to you. Abide in me, and I in you. As the branch cannot bear fruit by itself, unless it abides in the vine, neither can you, unless you abide in me. I am the vine, you are the branches. They who abide in me, and I in them, it is they that bear much fruit, for apart from me you can do nothing. Those who do not abide in me are cast forth as branches and wither; and the branches are gathered, thrown into the fire and burned. If you abide in me, and my words abide in you, ask whatever you will, and it shall be done for you. By this my Father is glorified, that you bear much fruit and so prove to be my disciples."

REFLECTION

Most Christians have never actually seen Jesus, so how do they relate to him? This is a problem that surfaced in the community that gave birth to the Gospel of John. That gospel was composed about 100CE—a long time after the events it's based upon. Probably there was no one still alive who had actually seen Jesus or any of the original disciples. So how was Jesus still present among believers? It's a very important question.

Each of the four gospels seeks to answer some version of this question. The fourth gospel has its solution—a collection of images, that of the vine is one, that embody the nature of the believers's connection to Jesus. "I am the vine, you are the branches." The connection is one of total dependence. A branch separated from the rooted vine dies. A believer separated from Jesus also dies.

Jesus further develops the image when he reminds the believing community that a vine puts out many branches and all these different branches exist only in their connection to the vine. They share the same source of life. That makes them close relatives! A believer cannot live in isolation—spiritual, intellectual or physical. Connection is necessary—connection to Jesus and the community. Thus to bear fruit is a collective experience. A vine is, by definition, a gathering of fruit producing individual branches. Apart from the vine there is no fruit, no life.

In a natural vine, it is sap, the juice, that conducts life, nutrition and growth to the whole. In John's image of Jesus as the vine, it is the Holy Spirit who conveys life to the whole. This shared Spirit is Jesus' parting gift to the church, guaranteeing the believers a connection to Jesus even though they cannot see him any more.

1. Look up some other vine images in the Bible: Ezekiel 15:1–8; Isaiah 5:1–7; Jeremiah 2:21. What does the image of the vine suggest about Jesus compared to other images in John's gospel: Jesus as bread of life (John 6), light of the world (John 8) or good shepherd (John 10)?

2. As a branch of the vine, when do you feel the need for pruning? What forms does pruning take? Why is it needed? How do you resist it?

Practice of FAITH

O QUEEN BE JOYFUL! In the Easter season, the month of May in the Catholic imagination is dedicated to Mary, who pondered at Christ's birth, understood his teachings, suffered his agony and rejoiced in his victory. Set up a May shrine: Place an image of Mary in a prominent place, and put candles and flowers by it. Use this Easter-season prayer, the *Regina Caeli*, this month:

O Queen of heaven, be joyful, alleluia!
For he whom you have humbly borne for us, alleluia!
Has risen, as he promised, alleluia!
Offer now our prayer to God, alleluia!

If you can find someone (or a recording) to teach you the Latin chant, *you'll* be joyful—it's beautiful.

Practice of HOPE

IN DEED AND IN TRUTH. Sanctuary worker Jack Elder was charged with transporting "illegal aliens" because he had helped some Salvadoran refugees to safety in Texas. During his trial, Rev. Donovan Cook testified on Elder's behalf, quoting the mandate in Matthew 25 to care for the "least of these." The judge responded something like this: "You are talking about feeding and clothing and visiting needy people, but the Bible says nothing about transporting them."

Cook looked squarely at the judge and responded, "The Good Samaritan found a wounded man in the road. He bound up his wounds, put him on his beast, and *transported* him to the nearest place of shelter."

Practice of CHARITY

THAT YOU MAY BEAR MUCH FRUIT. How is the work that you do fruitful? How do you utilize the gifts the God has given you in your job? Work is an important component in our lives. It gives us dignity. Those who are unemployed or underemployed need job training or employment opportunities so that their gifts may be fully actualized. It is our task as Christians in the work place and as owners of businesses to do what we can to create and preserve jobs. What might you do locally to help alleviate unemployment in your area? You can always write your state representative about the need to create jobs in your area. Or suggest that your parish establish an employment bulletin board with a space for job postings and a space for those seeking jobs to post their availability. If some would prefer anonymity, assign numbers to them and post the numbers instead of their names.

Weekday Reading
Acts, chapters 15–18

MAY 8, 1994
SIXTH SUNDAY OF EASTER

READING I *Acts 10:25–26, 34–35, 44–48*

When Peter entered, Cornelius met him and fell down at his feet and worshiped him. But Peter lifted him up, saying, "Stand up; I too am a human being."

And Peter opened his mouth and said: "Truly I perceive that God shows no partiality, but in every nation anyone who is God-fearing and does what is right is acceptable to God."

While Peter was still saying this, the Holy Spirit fell on all who heard the word. And the believers from among the Jewish people who came with Peter were amazed, because the gift of the Holy Spirit had been poured out even on the Gentiles. For they heard them speaking in tongues and extolling God. Then Peter declared, "Can anyone forbid water for baptizing these people who have received the Holy Spirit just as we have?" And Peter commanded them to be baptized in the name of Jesus Christ. And they asked him to remain for some days.

READING II *1 John 4:7–10*

Beloved, let us love one another; for love is of God, and everyone who loves is born of God and knows God. One who does not love does not know God; for God is love. In this the love of God was made manifest among us, that God sent into the world God's only Son, so that we might live through him. In this is love, not that we loved God but that God loved us and sent the Son to be the expiation for our sins.

GOSPEL *John 15:9–17*

[At that time Jesus said,]

"As the Father has loved me, so have I loved you; abide in my love. If you keep my commandments, you will abide in my love, just as I have kept my Father's commandments and abide in my Father's love. These things I have spoken to you, that my joy may be in you, and that your joy may be full.

"This is my commandment, that you love one another as I have loved you. Greater love has no one than this, that a man lay down his life for his friends. You are my friends if you do what I command you. No longer do I call you slaves, for slaves do not know what their master is doing; but I have called you friends, for all that I have heard from my Father I have made known to you. You did not choose me, but I chose you and appointed you that you should go and bear fruit and that your fruit should abide; so that whatever you ask the Father in my name, the Father may give it to you. This I command you, to love one another."

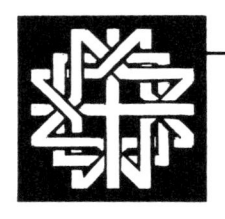

The Ascension of the Lord
Thursday, May 12, 1994 (U.S.A.)
Sunday, May 15, 1994 (CANADA)

Acts 1:1–11 Why stand staring at the skies?
Ephesians 1:17–23 The fullness of Christ has filled the universe.
Mark 16:15–20 Go into the whole world.

On this fortieth day of Easter we are told to stop cloud-gazing and start spreading the good news. The resurrection of Christ didn't end with Jesus' resurrection. All creation is ascending into glory. All the universe is becoming divine.

REFLECTION

Moses's name crops up quite often in the Gospel of John. In the prologue we are told, "The law was given by Moses; grace and truth come through Jesus Christ." At the outset, John establishes a contrast between law and grace/truth. The appearance of Moses at the transfiguration serves also to establish the authority of Jesus and his relationship to Moses.

Jesus replaces Moses, giving new "law," a new commandment. The giving of commandments is a divine prerogative. In the Exodus story Moses first "received," and only then "gave" the law. But Jesus initiates, of his own authority, a new commandment: "Love one another, as I have loved you." The newness lies less in the words used—they may be found in the Hebrew scriptures—than in Jesus' assuming God's role as the origin of commandments.

The Gospel of John seeks to reveal the identity of Jesus. The first images are those of the vine, the living water and the bread of life. In today's passage, Jesus is presented as one with the authority to initiate new commandments.

The love referred to is *agape*, one of several Greek words for love. It refers specifically to the kind of love characteristic of the believing community—not erotic love (*eros*) or the love of siblings (*adelphos*). This love is the Spirit. It charges with life and action the community grafted to Christ and to one another. It is the air Christians breathe. It is the human experience of God's life manifested in community and, again, one of the features marking the continuing real presence of the Risen one.

1. How can love be legislated or commanded? Laws often restrict our behaviors. How does the commandment to love set us free?

2. In Matthew's gospel, Jesus said he came not to abolish the law but to fulfill it. Read the ten commandments (the law of Moses) in Exodus 20. How does Jesus *fulfill* that law?

Practice of
FAITH

THE FIRST NOVENA. The Acts of the Apostles tells us that after Jesus ascended into heaven, the disciples prayed nine days for the coming of the Holy Spirit, the Advocate and Comforter that Jesus promised he would send them. These nine days of prayer made up the very first novena, and throughout the ages Christians developed other nine-day periods of prayer called novenas. Begin your own novena this Ascension Thursday. Pray for the coming of the Holy Spirit every day from Thursday until the great solemn feast of Pentecost on May 22. Use these words from eucharistic prayer III and pray for your parish: "Grant that we, who are nourished by his body and blood, may be filled with his Holy Spirit, and become one body, one spirit in Christ."

Practice of
HOPE

THAT YOUR JOY MAY BE FULL. A Salvadoran refugee in Honduras asked U.S. church worker Yvonne Dilling why she always looked so sad and burdened. Dilling talked about all the grief and terror the refugees were experiencing. "Only people who expect to go back to North America in a year work the way you do," the Salvadoran woman said. "You cannot be serious about our struggle unless you play and celebrate and do those things that make it possible to give a lifetime to it."

She reminded Dilling that each time the refugees were displaced, they immediately formed three committees: a construction committee, an education committee, and the *comité de alegría*—"the committee of joy."

Practice of
CHARITY

GOD SHOWS NO PARTIALITY. Charity knows no skin color, gender or religion. It is not stopped by national boundaries. Its desire is to feed the hungry, clothe the naked, teach the illiterate, empower the destitute. This is what the Maryknoll fathers, brothers, sisters, and lay missioners have been doing since 1911. They were established by the U.S. Bishops to recruit and train, American missionaries for service overseas. If you would like to support their work, send a contribution to: Maryknoll Fathers and Brothers, PO Box 301, Maryknoll NY 10545-9989, or to Maryknoll Sisters, PO Box 317, Maryknoll NY 10545-0317.

Weekday Reading
Acts, chapters 19–24

MAY 15, 1994
SEVENTH SUNDAY OF EASTER

READING I   *Acts 1:15–17, 20–26*

In those days Peter stood up within the community (the company of people was in all about a hundred and twenty), and said, "My dear people, the scripture had to be fulfilled, which the Holy Spirit spoke beforehand by the mouth of David, concerning Judas who was guide to those who arrested Jesus. For Judas was numbered among us, and was allotted his share in this ministry. For it is written in the book of Psalms,

'His office let another take.'

So one of the men who have accompanied us during all the time that the Lord Jesus went in and out among us, beginning from the baptism of John until the day when Jesus was taken up from us—one of these companions must become with us a witness to his resurrection." And they put forward two, Joseph called Barsabbas, who was surnamed Justus, and Matthias. And they prayed and said, "Lord, who knows the hearts of all, show which one of these two you have chosen to take the place in this ministry and apostleship from which Judas turned aside, to go to his own place." And they cast lots for them, and the lot fell on Matthias; and he was enrolled with the eleven apostles.

READING II   *1 John 4:11–16*

Beloved, if God so loved us, we also ought to love one another. No one has ever seen God; if we love one another, God abides in us and God's love is perfected in us.

By this we know that we abide in God and God in us, because we have been given of God's own Spirit. And we have seen and testify that the Father has sent the Son as the Savior of the world. Those who confess that Jesus is the Son of God, God abides in them, and they in God. So we know and believe the love God has for us. God is love, and they who abide in love abide in God, and God abides in them.

GOSPEL   *John 17:11–19*

[At that time Jesus said,]

"Holy Father, keep in your name the ones whom you have given me, that they may be one, even as we are one. While I was with them, I kept them in your name, which you have given me; I have guarded them, and none of them is lost but the son of perdition, that the scripture might be fulfilled. But now I am coming to you; and these things I speak in the world, that they may have my joy fulfilled in themselves. I have given them your word; and the world has hated them because they are not of the world, even as I am not of the world. I do not pray that you should take them out of the world, but that you should keep them from the evil one. They are not of the world, even as I am not of the world. Sanctify them in the truth; your word is truth. As you sent me into the world, so I have sent them into the world. And for their sake I consecrate myself, that they also may be consecrated in truth."

Pentecost Vigil
Saturday night through Sunday dawn, May 21–22, 1994

Genesis 11:1–9   At Babel the Lord confused their speech.
Exodus 19:3–8, 16–20   Fire and wind descended on Sinai.
Ezekiel 37:1–14   O spirit, breathe on the dead!
Joel 3:1–5   On the Day of the Lord I will impart my own spirit.
Romans 8:22–27   We have the Spirit as firstfruits.
John 7:37–39   Let the thirsty come to drink of living waters.

We end Eastertime the way we began it, with a nighttime vigil, poring over the scriptures. We keep watch on Mount Sinai, where we meet God face to face, where we receive the life-giving Spirit. Our paschal journey, begun so long ago in ashes, is finished in fire.

REFLECTION

Jesus is praying for you! This passage is the second (of three) parts of what is often called the "priestly prayer" of Jesus for his disciples. He prayed it before he freely gave himself over to death. To the world, his death looks like the miserable end of a pretentious "messiah." To people of faith, his death is the hour of his glory and his return to the Father.

Jesus is leaving those whom the Father "has given" him. Disciples are a prized gift to Jesus from God. What does he ask the Father for on your behalf?

Unity is first. As he is one with his Father, Jesus prays that his disciples will be one with each other and with him. Second is sanctity. Being "anointed" in truth sanctifies the disciples. One who is anointed takes on a new life. Part of that new life is living out a mission—a desire to share the truth with others. This final prayer of Jesus has dynamic missionary activity in view for all believers.

Jesus consecrates himself in truth. This requires obedience to the will of the Father—facing Good Friday in trust. The life of the Son obedient to his Father is truth in action. In baptism and in death, with the receiving and the breathing out of the spirit, Jesus is consecrated—for disciples, for the church, for you and your community.

1. Does unity mean everybody has to think, believe and behave in exactly the same way? How can unique human beings live in the unity Jesus prays for?

2. Truth is another thing Jesus asks his Father for on our behalf. In John's gospel Pontius Pilate asks, "What is truth?" Having read chapter 17 of John, how would you respond to Pilate? Jesus didn't answer him; what might you, a disciple, say?

Practice of FAITH

THEY CAST LOTS FOR THEM. The leadership of the early church was *collegial* or *conciliar;* in other words, a college or council of leaders—like the twelve apostles themselves—collaborated in making decisions about church life. If your parish has a parish council, it is an attempt to be faithful to this tradition of collegiality. If you are asked to vote for members of your parish council, remember today's reading from Acts. When the apostles needed to replace one of their number (Judas), they prayed to God and then "voted" by casting lots. Participate in your parish council, at least by voting for members when they are needed. Pray for your parish council, too, that it will be inspired by the Holy Spirit.

And keep praying your novena prayer (see page 97) this week until Pentecost.

Practice of HOPE

THAT THEY MAY BE ONE. In 1964 in France, Jean Vanier founded the L'Arche movement, which now includes dozens of communities around the world serving mentally and physically handicapped people. Vanier said this of those with whom he has shared his life, many of whom suffered great brokenness and isolation before coming into community: "They are a real gift. . . . They call us to humanity." He added, "Maybe the less success we have, the more we have to be attentive to the present and the celebration of bonding. Just as we are, in our brokenness, our pain, we celebrate that we're united together. And that is our comfort, our joy, and our gift."

Practice of CHARITY

GOD IS THERE. Every Sunday, all over the world, millions of Christians gather together in assemblies small and large to call to mind and to make present what Jesus has done for us. This is an awesome responsibility. Going to Mass is not just a matter of "me and Jesus," but an action of a community that transcends time and space. It includes the saints of long ago as well as living Christians. All are part of every eucharist. This Sunday take a good look at those who celebrate eucharist with you. When you enter the church, greet not only the Lord (by genuflecting or bowing to the altar), but also greet those with whom you sit. This is one of the ways we know that the Lord is truly present. In the words of an ancient Christian hymn: "Where charity and love are found, God is there."

Weekday Reading
Acts, chapters 24–28

MAY 22, 1994
PENTECOST

READING I *Acts 2:1–11*

When the day of Pentecost had come, the company was all together in one place. And suddenly a sound came from heaven like the rush of a mighty wind, and it filled all the house where they were sitting. And there appeared to them tongues as of fire, distributed and resting on each one of them. And they were all filled with the Holy Spirit and began to speak in other tongues, as the spirit gave them utterance.

Now there were dwelling in Jerusalem Jewish people, devout people from every nation under heaven. And at this sound the multitude came together, and they were bewildered, because all heard them speaking in their own language. And they were amazed and wondered, saying, "Are not all these who are speaking Galileans? And how is it that we hear, all of us in our own native language? Parthians and Medes and Elamites and residents of Mesopotamia, Judea and Cappadocia, Pontus and Asia, Phrygia and Pamphylia, Egypt and the parts of Libya belonging to Cyrene, and visitors from Rome, both Jewish born and proselytes, Cretans and Arabians, we hear them telling in our own tongues the mighty works of God."

READING II *1 Corinthians 12:3–7, 12–13*

No one can say "Jesus is Lord" except by the Holy Spirit.

Now there are varieties of gifts, but the same Spirit; and there are varieties of service, but the same Lord; and there are varieties of working, but it is the same God who inspires them all in everyone. To each is given the manifestation of the Spirit for the common good.

For just as the body is one and has many parts, and all the parts of the body, though many, are one body, so it is with Christ. For by one Spirit we were all baptized into one body—Jews or Greeks, slaves or free—and all were made to drink of one Spirit.

GOSPEL *John 20:19–23*

On the evening of that day, the first day of the week, the doors being shut where the disciples were, for fear of the Judeans, Jesus came and stood among them and said to them, "Peace be with you." Having said this, Jesus showed them his hands and his side. Then the disciples were glad when they saw the Lord. Jesus said to them again, "Peace be with you. As the Father has sent me, even so I send you." Having said this, Jesus breathed on them, and said to them, "Receive the Holy Spirit. If you forgive the sins of any, they are forgiven; if you retain the sins of any, they are retained."

REFLECTION

Luke and John provide us with two views, two traditions, relating to when and how the Spirit was shared with the young company of believers.

Luke places the event on the Jewish festival of Pentecost, the fiftieth day after Passover, which celebrated God's gift of the land (see Deuteronomy 26:1–11). Perhaps Luke sees it as a fulfillment of Isaiah 66:15–20 and/or a reversal of the Tower of Babel story (Genesis 11:1–9). These references give Pentecost two notable settings: the Exodus liberation and the new creation envisoned by Isaiah. The Spirit comes from heaven with a good deal of noise, drama and color. The event empowers the church for a universal mission, allowing it to cross all language, ethnic and geographical barriers.

John's account is very different. It occurs in the evening of Easter Day during an appearance of the risen one. Pierced hands and a wounded side verify that the risen one is the same person as the crucified one. His greeting is "Peace." He came to the community in turmoil once before (6:16–21), and his presence calmed their fear. Now, these same disciples are commissioned, sent as Jesus was sent by the Father. And the intimacy of Lord and disciple in the Holy Spirit is captured in the image of the Spirit as the very breath of Jesus himself. They are new creations now. John recollects the original creation stories and the spirit of God hovering over the waters of fearsome chaos when the breath of God brought order, life and intimacy between creature and creator. So now the fractured intimacy of sinful humanity is renewed, healed by the breath of life itself.

1. Read Deuteronomy 16:1–11; Isaiah 66:15–20 and Genesis 15:1–9. What similarities do you detect between these Hebrew scriptures and Luke's account of Pentecost? Then read Genesis 2:4b–9 and Ezekiel 37:1–14. What similarities do you detect between the Eden story—garden, tree and breath—and John's passion account; and between the giving of new breath in a renewed land in Ezekiel and John's "Pentecost?"

2. In both Luke and John, it's clear that the Holy Spirit is a gift to a community, enabling it to breathe new life into the world. How does your community do this? What are the signs of new life?

Practice of **FAITH**

PENTECOST. The great 50 days come to a climax with the celebration of the coming of the Holy Spirit. Wind and flame are the signs God gives us to know the divine presence. Relax and rejoice today: Fly kites. Hang a wind chime to catch the sound of breezes. Play the flute or penny whistle if you can. Buy seven candles for the dinner table. End this holy season as it began eight weeks ago: a festive meal with family and friends, and evening prayer prayed at sunset. (See page 12.) Don't forget to sing the Easter Alleluia one last time. And what would Pentecost be without a chorus of "Come, Holy Ghost"?

Practice of **HOPE**

THE MANIFESTATION OF THE SPIRIT FOR THE COMMON GOOD. Fr. Elias Chacour is a Melkite priest from the village of Ba'ram in northern Galilee. As a child, he witnessed the Israeli government's destruction of his village.

Fr. Chacour has devoted his life to the founding of community centers, libraries, and kindergartens for Palestinian children—and to reconciliation in a badly divided land. "You can take our lands, you can take our houses, you can kill us," Chacour said, referring to the Israelis. "But you cannot take our hearts with violence. Impossible! . . . We have to tame each other. There is no alternative if we are to survive. We go on killing until there is no one left—or we choose to survive together."

Practice of **CHARITY**

EVEN SO I SEND YOU. The Vincent Pallotti Center for Apostolic Development taps into the desire of Christians to volunteer by matching their gifts with programs that could best use them. So the Center publishes *Connections*, a directory of lay volunteer service opportunities. This directory is free, and is updated annually. For a copy, write or call: St. Vincent Pallotti Center, Box 893–Cardinal Station, Washington DC 20064; 202-529-3330.

Weekday Reading
1 Peter, chapters 1–4

Summer Ordinary Time

You crown the year
 with riches.
All you touch is fertile.

Praise is yours,
God in Zion.
Now is the moment
to keep our vow.

You soak the furrows
and level the ridges.
With softening rain
you bless the land with growth.

You crown the year with riches.
All you touch is fertile.
Lands not tilled produce,
hills dress up in joy.

Pastures are clothed with flocks.
Valleys wrap themselves in grain.
They shout for joy.
They break into song.

—Psalm 65:2, 11–14

God who called each day's creation good,
all we have for our food
and shelter and clothing
are the crust and air, the light and water
    of this planet.
Give us care like yours for this earth:
to share its bounty
with generations to come
and with all alike in this generation,
to savor its beauty and respect its power,
to heal what greed and war and foolishness
have done to your earth and to us.
Bring us finally to give thanks,
always and everywhere.

—*Prayer of the Season*

MAY 29, 1994
THE HOLY TRINITY

READING I *Deuteronomy 4:32–34, 39–40*

[Moses said to the people,]

"Ask now of the days that are past, which were before you, since the day that God created humankind upon the earth, and ask from one end of heaven to the other, whether such a great thing as this has ever happened or was ever heard of. Did any people ever hear the voice of a god speaking out of the midst of the fire, as you have heard, and still live? Or has any god ever attempted to go and claim a nation from the midst of another nation, by trials, by signs, by wonders, and by war, by a mighty hand and an outstretched arm, and by great terrors, according to all that the LORD your God did for you in Egypt before your eyes? Know therefore this day, and lay it to your heart, that the LORD is God in heaven above and on the earth beneath; there is no other. Therefore you shall keep the statutes and the commandments of the LORD, which I command you this day, that it may go well with you, and with your children after you, and that you may prolong your days in the land which the LORD your God gives you for ever."

READING II *Romans 8:14–17*

For all who are led by the Spirit of God are children of God. For you did not receive the spirit of slavery to fall back into fear, but you have received the spirit of adoption. When we cry, "Abba! Father!" it is that very Spirit bearing witness with our spirit that we are children of God, and if children, then heirs, heirs of God and joint heirs with Christ, provided we suffer with Christ in order that we may also be glorified with Christ.

GOSPEL *Matthew 28:16–20*

Now the eleven disciples went to Galilee, to the mountain to which Jesus had directed them. And when they saw Jesus they worshiped him; but some doubted. And Jesus came and said to them, "All authority in heaven and on earth has been given to me. Go therefore and make disciples of all nations, baptizing them in the name of the Father and of the Son and of the Holy Spirit, teaching them to observe all that I have commanded you; and lo, I am with you always, to the close of the age."

REFLECTION

Today's readings from Deuteronomy, Romans and Matthew all share a common message: Because of what God has already done, we have a life stretching before us and filled with promise.

Deuteronomy rehearses the past actions of God for a people chosen out of love. The personal and communal response to such love is love, shown in the keeping of God's statutes and commandments. These are given not to inhibit or control but to allow the freedom found only in a loving relationship. Every relationship has "statutes and commandments" that protect involved parties from the kinds of abuse that issue from lost freedom. Their purpose is "to prolong your days in the land"—to allow people to live long, happy and productive communal lives. The understanding of God as a Trinity—a community of three persons—is the basis for this.

The passage from Romans sees the believer as a debtor of God for the past gift of the Holy Spirit—the spirit of adoption. Calling out, "Abba, Father," we are adopted children of a passionately loving God. In Paul's day, to be adopted meant to come into a position of inheriting everything without question or argument. Heirs receive everything to the full! As co-heirs (with Christ), believers must also expect the suffering that comes in any relationship, whether it be the opposition of others or simply the pains of growing in holiness.

Finally, the passage from the Gospel of Matthew shows that the fruits of the Trinity that Christians inherit—eternal life and love that knows no bounds —are not meant for an elite but for all. The evangelical commission to go to all nations and baptize those who come to believe means: "Bring everyone into this relationship of love, the love given to sons and daughters by a passionate God."

1. The Trinity is a doctrine about a communal God. If the one true God is communal in nature, what does that suggest about the value of our independent, rugged individualism?

2. How has the gift of the Spirit transformed your relationships, and your behaviors and attitudes within those relationships? What freedoms do you enjoy that may be found only in observing the rules of relationship? What are those rules? Of what did you have to let go?

Practice of FAITH

THE VISITATION. Think of someone who would be happy to see you. Can you arrange to make a visit this week? Tuesday we remember when Mary, young and pregnant, went to visit Elizabeth, old and about to give birth. The first stanza of the prayer we call the "Hail Mary" is the greeting that the angel Gabriel spoke to Mary at the annunciation (celebrated March 25); the second stanza is the words of Elizabeth on the occasion of the visit we celebrate May 31: "Blessed are you among women and blessed is the fruit of your womb!"

Because Elizabeth was elderly, it would be appropriate this week to visit someone who is older, someone who may not receive many visitors any more. If you make your visit out of love, you are practicing your faith.

Practice of HOPE

CHILDREN OF GOD, LED BY THE SPIRIT For more than a decade, Louie Vitale, OFM, and others have kept vigils of protest at the Nevada nuclear weapons test site near Las Vegas. After dark on Good Friday 1989, Vitale and ten others headed across the desert for the nuclear research laboratory that was once a chapel. They found the door unexpectedly open, commenting that perhaps the spot had been visited by the same angel that rolled the stone away from Jesus' tomb. (This "angel" was a carpet cleaner who had neglected to lock the door!)

They prayed in the former chapel, located on Trinity Avenue, named for the first nuclear bomb test. They blessed and renamed the building "Holy Trinity Chapel." "The monstrous weapons of destruction to protect our empire cannot stand in the sight of God," says Vitale. "In the end, God wins. But part of bringing about the new creation is our effort; God gives us a part."

Practice of CHARITY

ABBA! FATHER! For us to cry out "Abba" is for us to recognize that all of us are God's children: whites, blacks, Asians and Latinos; gays, lesbians, bisexuals and heterosexuals; rich and poor. The practice of charity is the practice of striving for good relationships. The model relationship that we Christians pattern ourselves after is that of the Trinity. This week, identify someone you come into contact with on a daily basis who belongs to a social or ethnic group you find difficult to accept. What can you do to promote mutual understanding? Think of a specific action, and then resolve to do it.

Weekday Reading
2 Timothy, chapter 1–4

JUNE 5, 1994
THE BODY AND BLOOD OF CHRIST

READING I *Exodus 24:3–8*

Moses came and told the people all the words of the LORD and all the ordinances; and all the people answered with one voice, and said, "All the words which the LORD has spoken we will do." And Moses wrote all the words of the LORD. And he rose early in the morning, and built an altar at the foot of the mountain, and twelve pillars, according to the twelve tribes of Israel. And Moses sent youths of the people of Israel, who offered burnt offerings and sacrificed peace offerings of oxen to the LORD. And Moses took half of the blood and put it in basins, and half of the blood he threw against the altar. Then he took the book of the covenant, and read it in the hearing of the people; and they said, "All that the LORD has spoken we will do, and we will be obedient." And Moses took the blood and threw it upon the people, and said, "Behold the blood of the covenant which the LORD has made with you in accordance with all these words."

READING II *Hebrews 9:11–15*

When Christ appeared as a high priest of the good things that have come, then through the greater and more perfect tent (not made with hands, that is, not of this creation) he entered once for all into the Holy Place, taking not the blood of goats and calves but his own blood, thus securing an eternal redemption. For if the sprinkling of defiled persons with the blood of goats and bulls and with the ashes of a heifer sanctifies for the purification of the flesh, how much more shall the blood of Christ, who through the eternal Spirit offered himself without blemish to God, purify your conscience from dead works to serve the living God.

Therefore Christ is the mediator of a new covenant, so that those who are called may receive the promised eternal inheritance, since a death has occurred which redeems them from the transgressions under the first covenant.

GOSPEL *Mark 14:12–16, 22–26*

On the first day of Unleavened Bread, when they sacrificed the passover lamb, Jesus' disciples said to him, "Where will you have us go and prepare for you to eat the passover?" And Jesus sent two of his disciples, and said to them, "Go into the city, and someone carrying a jar of water will meet you; follow him, and wherever he enters, say to the householder, 'The Teacher says, Where is my guest room, where I am to eat the passover with my disciples?' The householder will show you a large upper room furnished and ready; there prepare for us." And the disciples set out and went to the city, and found it as Jesus had told them; and they prepared the passover.

And as they were eating, Jesus took bread, and blessed, and broke it, and gave it to them, and said, "Take; this is my body." And he took a cup, and having given thanks he gave it to them, and they all drank of it. And he said to them, "This is my blood of the covenant, which is poured out for many. Truly, I say to you, I shall not drink again of the fruit of the vine until that day when I drink it new in the dominion of God."

And when they had sung a hymn, they went out to the Mount of Olives.

The Sacred Heart of Jesus
Friday, June 10, 1994

Hosea 11:1, 3–4, 8–9   My heart is overwhelmed with compassion.
Ephesians 3:8–12, 14–19   May Christ dwell in your hearts.
John 19:31–37   The soldier pierced Jesus' side with a lance.

Today is an echo of Good Friday, a reminder that every Friday is kept with renewed efforts to understand and to share the compassion of God. If Christ lives in our hearts, we bear the love of God in our own bodies.

REFLECTION

The past and the future are brought into the present at Jesus' last supper with his disciples. It is the eve of his death and his words interpret the coming Friday events and institute the eucharist as our real participation in his passion and resurrection. He shares broken bread as an anticipation of his body to be broken on the morrow—and thereafter it is the sacrament of his abiding presence. Prayer and thanksgiving over the cup of wine changes it into the cup of Jesus' blood; spilled on the altar of the cross, his blood inaugurates the new and everlasting covenant between God and humanity.

Moses ratified the covenant between God and the people by sprinkling them with blood from sacrificed animals (see Exodus 24:8 and 1 Corinthians 11:25). An ancient view held that spilling blood in a careful ritual allowed communication between human and divine beings. A covenant is a pact or agreement between two parties. Today's first reading illustrates the Mosaic covenant's requirement: "All that the Lord has spoken we will do, and will be obedient." Mark's portrait of Jesus is as the obedient Son. Now those who celebrate the eucharist are his siblings in obedience and self-sacrifice.

Covenant blood is "poured out for many." On Good Friday we read Isaiah's fourth servant song. The last verse (Isaiah 53:12) refers to the servant as the one who, "poured out himself to death and was numbered among transgressors." This is Jesus whose death, Mark shows us, is to be the perfect sacrifice.

Jesus' words about not drinking wine until the dominion of heaven gives the whole scene its future and messianic angle. The past ministry of Jesus is brought into the present of his passion and death and thereafter handed on to his disciples.

1. Connected with Mark's version of the Last Supper are other scenes of "table-fellowship": Read these passages: Mark 2:13–20, 23–28; 6:30–44; 8:1–10, 14–21; 11:35–40. What do they add to your perception of the eucharist? What are their implications for ministry?

2. How do you understand your participation in the eucharist as a commitment to mission and evangelization?

Practice of FAITH

AS THEY WERE EATING. Because Christ gave us the eucharist as an everlasting memorial of his dying and rising, every meal we eat with others echoes the eucharist's joy. In our day, with processed foods and tight schedules, we often eat hurriedly, with little enjoyment. Begin to take small steps so that at least one day a week—maybe Sunday—you share a meal with others at a leisurely pace, with attention to details like a tablecloth, candles and flowers. If you live alone, invite someone over. Renew the habit of praying before eating. Today, in honor of the feast and as an echo of the eucharist, search out or bake a whole loaf of bread to share. Make sangria (the Spanish word for "blood") by adding slices of oranges, lemons, pineapples and strawberries to red wine.

Practice of HOPE

CHRIST IS MEDIATOR OF A NEW COVENANT. A minister was showing off his fancy church to Clarence Jordan. He pointed to a huge, elaborate cross and said, "That cross alone cost us ten thousand dollars." Jordan looked at him and said, "You got cheated. Times were when Christians could get them for free."

Clarence Jordan, known as a "theologian in overalls," was well known for his "cotton patch" translation of the Bible, putting the gospels in the language and metaphor of his beloved South. He knew what it meant to bear a cross. He founded the Koinonia community in Georgia in 1942. The community ran a farm, built houses for needy neighbors, and shared meals around the table, black and white together. That brought out the Ku Klux Klan and gunfire in the night. The courageous community survived and thrived, and today celebrates more than five decades of faithfulness.

Practice of CHARITY

ALL THE PEOPLE ANSWERED WITH ONE VOICE. The work of evangelization —bringing Christ to all peoples— is a vital act of charity. All of the baptized are challenged to give witness to Christ in their daily lives. Such witness is complemented by the Catholic Communications Network. In addition, diocesan newspapers and communications offices, and national Catholic magazines are tremendous resources for nurturing and enlivening faith. In our age the secular media has a tendency to distort religious groups or ignore them. Because of this, it is more important than ever to make sure that the message of Jesus doesn't get lost. Make a donation this Sunday to the Communication Media Collection. Or this week, give a gift subscription for a Catholic magazine to someone who has fallen away from the church.

Weekday Reading
1 Kings, chapters 17–21

JUNE 12, 1994
ELEVENTH SUNDAY IN ORDINARY TIME

READING I   *Ezekiel 17:22–24*

Thus says the Lord GOD: "I myself will take a sprig from the lofty top of the cedar, and will set it out; I will break off from the topmost of its young twigs a tender one, and I myself will plant it upon a high and lofty mountain; on the mountain height of Israel will I plant it, that it may bring forth boughs and bear fruit, and become a noble cedar; and under it will dwell all kinds of beasts; in the shade of its branches birds of every sort will nest. And all the trees of the field shall know that I the LORD bring low the high tree, and make high the low tree, dry up the green tree, and make the dry tree flourish. I the LORD have spoken, and I will do it."

READING II   *2 Corinthians 5:6–10*

So we are always of good courage; we know that while we are at home in the body we are away from the Lord, for we walk by faith, not by sight. We are of good courage, and we would rather be away from the body and at home with the Lord. So whether we are at home or away, we make it our aim to please the Lord. For we must all appear before the judgment seat of Christ, so that each one may receive good or evil, according to what was done in the body.

GOSPEL   *Mark 4:26–34*

Jesus said, "The dominion of God is as if someone should scatter seed upon the ground, and should sleep and rise night and day, and the seed should sprout and grow, the sower knows not how. The earth produces of itself, first the blade, then the ear, then the full grain in the ear. But when the grain is ripe, at once the sower puts in the sickle, because the harvest has come."

And Jesus said, "With what can we compare the dominion of God, or what parable shall we use for it? It is like a grain of mustard seed, which, when sown upon the ground, is the smallest of all the seeds on earth; yet when it is sown it grows up and becomes the greatest of all shrubs, and puts forth large branches, so that the birds of the air can make nests in its shade."

With many such parables Jesus spoke the word to them, as they were able to hear it; he did not speak to them without a parable, but privately to his own disciples Jesus explained everything.

REFLECTION

The fourth chapter in the Gospel of Mark is the "parables chapter"—illustrations using everyday images of the dawning dominion of heaven. Both parables today show God's dominion in two aspects: its secret, unseen germination, then its breaking through, its bearing fruit for all creation.

The seed of God's dominion may germinate in the darkness of a person struggling for life. It may be sickness, addiction, confusion or a sense of broken hopelessness that forms the darkness. When the seed is planted and vigilantly tended, growth will come.

Whatever the variety of seed, to reach the light of day it has to struggle through much darkness. Paul touches on this in the second reading: ". . . while we are still in this tent [this earthly body], we sigh with anxiety." Believers know they are incomplete. Fullness awaits. But the seed is planted in our earthly setting. We may not grasp whether or how there is growth, but Jesus assures those who truly hear that it is happening and that fruit will appear.

So far in Mark, Jesus has announced the intention of his mission: "The time is fulfilled and the dominion of God is near; repent and believe in the good news" (Mark 1:15). He has begun selecting disciples—the first ones in whom the seed is planted. They are an illustration of these two parables in action. Their growth in faith is long and often occurs in the dark. They have to learn how truly available forgiveness is; how Jesus does not condemn them, even when they abandon him out of fear; even when they fail, sometimes miserably, to understand exactly who he is; even when they are more interested in self-aggrandizement than the mission.

The disciples' biggest obstacle—Jesus' ignoble death—becomes the focal point of their evangelization, as new life breaks out of death.

1. Read all of Mark 4. What facets of the dominion of heaven do you see in Jesus' images? What do they imply about your own spiritual growth?

2. Individually and as a member of a community, how do you cultivate the seed of God's dominion? How do you help others through the dark time of germination?

Practice of
FAITH

THE SEED SHOULD SPROUT AND GROW. The rogation days were once celebrated before Ascension each year to ask God's blessing on farms and gardens. Christians gathered and processed around the farm singing the Litany of the Saints. Now that seeds are already sown, you, too, can ask God to bless your "crops," even if it's only a window box of petunias. Use this prayer from *Catholic Household Blessings and Prayers*:

O God,
from the very beginning of time
you commanded the earth to bring forth vegetation
and fruit of every kind.
You provide the sower with seed and give bread to eat.
Grant, we pray, that this land,
enriched by your bounty and cultivated by human hands,
may be fertile with abundant crops.
Then your people, enriched by the gifts of your goodness,
will praise you unceasingly now and for ages unending.
Grant this through Christ our Lord.

Practice of
HOPE

SO WE ARE ALWAYS OF GOOD COURAGE. Friends active in the Southern Columbia Heights Tenants Union took suitcases downtown and marched in on a city council debate over rent control. They were making the point that if rent control didn't pass in Washington, D.C., many of them would be packing their bags, forced out of their inner-city apartments by high rents.

They lost that round of the battle. Afterward, I asked a few of them about how they felt. "We'll get it next time," one elderly woman said with confidence. And another added, "You know, it says in the Bible, 'It came to pass.' It doesn't say, 'It came to stay.'"

Practice of
CHARITY

SCATTER SEED UPON THE GROUND. Pick your favorite seed and plant it. All summer, water it, nurture it, and watch it grow. The growth of the seed reminds us that we must attend to our personal growth, too. A publication like *Just for Today* from Pax Christi, USA, can help us grow as Christians. It reminds us to perform the small, and not so small, acts of kindness that deepen our awareness of God's mercy. For a copy of *Just for Today*, write or call Pax Christi, 348 East Tenth Street, Erie PA 16503; 814-453-4955.

Weekday Reading
2 Kings, chapters 1–11

JUNE 19, 1994
TWELFTH SUNDAY IN ORDINARY TIME

READING I   *Job 38:1, 8–11*

The LORD answered Job out of the whirlwind:
"Who shut in the sea with doors,
    when it burst forth from the womb;
when I made clouds its garment,
    and thick darkness its swaddling band,
and prescribed bounds for it,
    and set bars and doors,
and said, Thus far shall you come, and no farther,
    and here shall your proud waves be stayed?"

READING II   *2 Corinthians 5:14–17*

The love of Christ controls us, because we are convinced that one has died for all; therefore all have died. And he died for all, that those who live might live no longer for themselves but for the one who for their sake died and was raised.

From now on, therefore, we regard no one from a human point of view; even though we once regarded Christ from a human point of view, we regard him thus no longer. Therefore, anyone being in Christ is a new creation; the old has passed away, behold, the new has come.

GOSPEL   *Mark 4:35–41*

On that day, when evening had come, Jesus said to the disciples, "Let us go across to the other side." And leaving the crowd, they took him with them in the boat, just as he was. And other boats were with him. And a great storm of wind arose, and the waves beat into the boat, so that the boat was already filling. But Jesus was in the stern, asleep on the cushion; and they woke him and said to him, "Teacher, do you not care if we perish?" And Jesus awoke and rebuked the wind, and said to the sea, "Peace! Be still!" And the wind ceased, and there was a great calm. Jesus said to them, "Why are you afraid? Have you no faith?" And they were filled with awe, and said to one another, "Who then is this, that even wind and sea obey him?"

The Birth of John the Baptist
Friday, June 24, 1994

VIGIL

Jeremiah 1:4–10   Before I formed you in the womb, I knew you.
1 Peter 1:8–12   Rejoice with inexpressible joy.
Luke 1:5–17   Many will rejoice at John's birth.

DAY

Isaiah 49:1–6   From my mother's womb I am given my name.
Acts 13:22–26   John's message is for all children of Abraham.
Luke 1:57–66, 80   What will the child be?

John said, I must decrease if Christ is to increase. Today the daytime begins to decrease. It is the midsummer nativity. John is born to be the best man of the Bridegroom, the lamp of the Light and the voice of the Word. Rejoice in John's birth!

REFLECTION

We last heard from the Book of Job on February 6. Job was complaining about the way God was treating him. Today's reading from Job is from part of God's final response to all of Job's questioning and challenging. God says, "Who are you, Job, to question me? Are you responsible for anything you benefit by in creation —including your own life?"

The ancient Hebrew concept of the world was of a flat disc with waters on it, below it and above it. As the reading says, because God keeps these waters apart, people survive and prosper. In the first creation account in the Book of Genesis, on the second day God made a dome separating "the waters from the waters" (1:6–10). All creation would have been totally destroyed had not God graciously kept the waters apart and allowed new life to blossom.

With this background, Mark retells the story of Jesus calming a storm. This act gives the disciples occasion to wonder, "Who is this, that even the wind and sea obey him?"

The story works on several levels. The disciples are faced with the issue of Jesus' true identity: Who is he? He's doing what the Hebrews believed only God could do! Mark places the story at this point to deepen the mystery about Jesus' persona. Disciples have to struggle through their own darkness ("Have you no faith?"), but in the presence of Jesus. They are learning to see differently, to break the ground of a faith-filled response to Jesus and so grow into a new kind of community. This is the disciples' first awestruck encounter with the one Mark calls Jesus Christ, the Son of God.

1. Read the concluding chapters of Job, 38–42. Then read the other versions of the gospel story in Matthew 8:18, 23–27 and Luke 8:22–25. What light do these scriptures shed on the ones read today? Specifically, what differences do you detect in the gospel stories and what is the significance of these differences?

2. Our conception of the world is very different from the ancient Hebrew view in Genesis and Job. With all our knowledge and experience of creation and the vastness of our universe, do we feel "in control," or does science inspire a new depth of awe? Do we have more answers or more questions?

Practice of FAITH

MIDSUMMER NATIVITY. Because John the Baptist said that he must decrease in order that Christ may increase, the birthday of the great forerunner is celebrated on June 24, once thought to be the day when daylight hours began to shrink. (The birth of Christ is celebrated on December 25, once thought to be the day when daylight hours began to lengthen.)

The midsummer nativity of John the Baptist has traditionally been a day of fire and water—a day for bonfires at the beach. Even if your "bonfire" is in a barbecue grill, use this prayer to bless God:

O God almighty, unfailing ray and source of all light, sanctify this fire that we have kindled in joy at the birth of John, the herald of your Son and great forerunner of the Way. Grant that after the darkness of this life, we may come to you who are light eternal. We ask this through Christ the Lord.

Practice of HOPE

THE OLD HAS PASSED AWAY; THE NEW HAS COME. Thirty years ago, Pamela Montgomery lived in a world of silence and isolation. A deaf child with cerebral palsy, she was declared mentally retarded and institutionalized at the age of 6. For six years, she was unable to communicate, and no effort was made to teach her. Then a seminarian discovered her, and she was released to join the Christian Family Community in Washington, D.C. She pursued training in housekeeping, and overcame vast obstacles of insensitivity on the part of employers to get a job and eventually her own apartment.

In 1987, Pamela Montgomery stood next to Washington, D.C.'s mayor as 1,500 people gave her a standing ovation. She had just received the city's "Handicapped Individual of the Year" award. Her broad smile exuded pride and triumph. Her upraised hand formed the American Sign Language sign for "I love you."

Practice of CHARITY

AND THEY WERE FILLED WITH AWE. As we build upon the relationships that result from our acts of charity, we begin to see new opportunities to glimpse the face of God. It is awesome to know that those whom we encounter on our daily journey are not strangers, but brothers and sisters in Christ. This week, resolve to pay attention to the strangers that you encounter in your daily routine. Notice their faces, look into their eyes when you pass by. When you pray at dinner or before going to bed, remember one or two of the people you passed by and pray for them.

Weekday Reading
2 Kings, chapters 17–24

JUNE 26, 1994
THIRTEENTH SUNDAY IN ORDINARY TIME

READING I *Wisdom 1:13–15, 2:23–24*

God did not make death,
and does not delight in the death of the living.
For God created all things that they might exist,
and the generative forces of the world are wholesome,
and there is no destructive poison in them;
and the dominion of Hades is not on earth.
For righteousness is immortal.
For God created humankind for incorruption,
and made human beings in the image of God's
    own eternity,
but through the devil's envy death entered the world,
and those who belong to the devil's party
    experience it.

READING II *2 Corinthians 8:7, 9, 13–15*

Now as you excel in everything—in faith, in utterance, in knowledge, in all earnestness, and in your love for us—see that you excel in this gracious work also.

For you know the grace of our Lord Jesus Christ, that though he was rich, yet for your sake he became poor, so that by his poverty you might become rich. I do not mean that others should be eased and you burdened, but that as a matter of equality your abundance at the present time should supply their want, so that their abundance may supply your want, that there may be equality. As it is written, "One who gathered much had nothing over, and one who gathered little had no lack."

GOSPEL *Mark 5:21–24, 35–43*

When Jesus had crossed again in the boat to the other side, a great crowd gathered about him; and he was beside the sea. Then came one of the rulers of the synagogue, Jairus by name; and seeing Jesus, he fell at his feet, and besought him, saying, "My little daughter is at the point of death. Come and lay your hands on her, so that she may be made well, and live." And Jesus went with him.

And a great crowd followed him and thronged about him.

There came from the ruler's house some who said, "Your daughter is dead. Why trouble the Teacher any further?" But ignoring what they said, Jesus said to the ruler of the synagogue, "Do not fear, only believe." And Jesus allowed no one to follow him except Peter and James and John the brother of James. When they came to the house of the ruler of the synagogue, Jesus saw a tumult, and people weeping and wailing loudly. And when he had entered, he said to them, "Why do you make a tumult and weep? The child is not dead but sleeping." And they laughed at him. But he put them all outside, and took the child's father and mother and those who were with him, and went in where the child was. Taking her by the hand Jesus said to her, "Talitha cumi"; which means, "Little girl, I say to you, arise." And immediately the girl got up and walked (she was twelve years of age), and they were immediately overcome with amazement. And Jesus strictly charged them that no one should know this, and told them to give her something to eat.

[Complete reading: Mark 5:21–43]

Peter and Paul
Wednesday, June 29, 1994

VIGIL
Acts 3:1–10 Peter cried, "Look at us!"
Galatians 1:11–20 God chose to reveal Christ to me.
John 21:15–19 Simon Peter, do you love me?

DAY
Acts 12:1–11 The chains dropped from Peter's wrists.
2 Timothy 4:6–8, 17–18 I have kept the faith.
Matthew 16:13–19 I entrust to you the keys of the kingdom.

This season is the beginning of the grain harvest. So today we keep a festival in honor of the two apostles who began the harvest of God's reign. They preached from Jerusalem to Rome, keeping the Easter commandment to bring good news to the ends of the earth.

REFLECTION

Death is *the* human certainty! The Book of Wisdom has some very realistic things to say about common attitudes toward this reality.

Mark gives us a scene of Jesus confronting death, not yet his own, but that of a twelve-year-old girl with a rather special father. From the beginning of the Gospel of Mark we already know that the local authorities have a plot to "destroy" Jesus. Jairus comes from that class and rank. He is "a ruler of the synagogue," an influential, well-respected man. Look what he does! "He fell at his feet, and besought him" What impression would that have made on the milling crowds? Their perception of Jesus must have shifted very quickly. As in the story of the calming of the storm, Mark depicts Jesus as one with unprecedented power and authority and, on this occasion, power over that final, fearful human mystery—death.

Jairus is respectful, showing major trust in Jesus; people at the house are making the traditional mourning noise. They laugh at Jesus' remark that the girl is sleeping. But Mark ends the scene with one of his favorite words, doubled up here in the Greek: "they were amazed with a huge amazement!" (He uses *ekstasis*, from which we get "ecstasy.") Mark uses the same word when Jesus' family says "He's gone out of his mind!" (3:21). In an awesome way, Jesus has disrupted the normal course of events. Death, as Mark's gospel ultimately will show us, has no finality in the presence of Jesus. He has the victory.

Strangely, perhaps, Jesus commands all to silence. Only the disciples, the child and her parents are aware of what has happened. Why the secrecy? Again it is a device Mark uses to delay full understanding of who Jesus is until all the facts are in. It is Jesus' death that will confuse, perplex and finally clarify, in faith, exactly who he is. When he rises from the dead, the disciples' first response is fear (see Mark 16:8). In this story, Jesus tells Jairus not to fall victim to fear.

1. Be sure to read Wisdom 1:12—2:9. In what way do people today still hold these attitudes toward death?

2. Read Mark 5:21–43. It's one of Mark's sandwiches! In the middle of the Jairus story is another about a woman with a hemorrhage. Fear and faith are important in both. How are the stories related? How are fear and faith related?

Practice of FAITH

PETER AND PAUL. On Wednesday we remember Peter and Paul, the founders of the church at Rome. Peter struggled with change. Specifically, he wasn't sure how to welcome the Gentiles into the church. Paul tried to welcome the Gentiles into the church by dispensing with some old customs: circumcision and kosher dietary laws.

This led to a conflict between the two leaders. Peter thought that circumcision and kosher dietary laws were necessary for being Christian. In Galatians 2:11, Paul tells us that he went to Peter "and opposed him to his face because he was wrong." Peter changed his mind and the church grew stronger. Sometimes being faithful means speaking up to church leaders when their policies hinder rather than help spread the gospel. Do you know of policies in your parish or in the universal church that are wrong? Pray to Peter and Paul for the inspiration to speak up.

Practice of HOPE

THAT THERE MAY BE EQUALITY. A backbone of apartheid in South Africa has been the "pass system," that required black men to carry a pass at all times. The government made a mistake in 1910 when it tried to extend the system to include women. Sometimes burning passes in public protest, women staved off the carrying of passes for more than 40 years. By the mid-1950s though, passes were mandated for women.

On August 9, 1956, 20,000 women from all over South Africa converged on the prime minister's office in Pretoria. They deposited masses of written protests on his doorstep, stood in silent protest for 30 minutes, and then sang the defiant chant that has become a cornerstone of the South African women's movement: "You have struck the women, you have struck the rock."

Practice of CHARITY

YOUR ABUNDANCE SHOULD SUPPLY THEIR WANT. On college campuses, hundreds of thousands of young adults with unlimited energy live and study. In a time when social services are limited and community needs continue to grow, thousands of these students are pitching in to help. Many of them volunteer through Campus Outreach Opportunity League (COOL). They work as tutors, lend a hand with environmental clean-up projects and help the hungry, the homeless and the elderly in various ways. If you would like to help COOL in some way or start a chapter, write or call: Campus Outreach Opportunity League, 386 McNeal Hall, University of Minnesota, St. Paul MN 55108-9932; 612-624-3018.

Weekday Reading
Amos—entire book

JULY 3, 1994
FOURTEENTH SUNDAY IN ORDINARY TIME

READING I *Ezekiel 2:2–5*

And when the LORD spoke to me, the Spirit entered into me and set me upon my feet; and I heard the LORD speaking to me, saying, "O human one, I send you to the people of Israel, to a nation of rebels, who have rebelled against me; they and their forebears have transgressed against me to this very day. The people also are impudent and stubborn: I send you to them; and you shall say to them, 'Thus says the Lord GOD.' And whether they hear or refuse to hear (for they are a rebellious house) they will know that there has been a prophet among them."

READING II *2 Corinthians 12:7–10*

And to keep me from being too elated by the abundance of revelations, a thorn was given me in the flesh, a messenger of Satan, to harass me, to keep me from being too elated. Three times I besought the Lord about this, that it should leave me; but the Lord said to me, "My grace is sufficient for you, for my power is made perfect in weakness." I will all the more gladly boast of my weaknesses, that the power of Christ may rest upon me. For the sake of Christ, then, I am content with weaknesses, insults, hardships, persecutions, and calamities; for when I am weak, then I am strong.

GOSPEL *Mark 6:1–6*

Jesus went away from there and came to his own country; and his disciples followed him. And on the sabbath he began to teach in the synagogue; and many who heard him were astonished, saying, "From where did these things come to him? What is the wisdom given to him? What mighty works are wrought by his hands! Is not this the carpenter, the son of Mary and brother of James and Joses and Judas and Simon, and are not his sisters here with us?" And they took offense at him. And Jesus said to them, "Prophets are not without honor, except in their own country, and among their own kin, and in their own house." And Jesus could do no mighty work there, except that he laid his hands upon a few sick people and healed them. And he marveled because of their unbelief.

And he went about among the villages teaching.

REFLECTION

Prophets in ancient times got a raw deal. One who knew this well was Jeremiah. Ezekiel, too. In today's first reading Ezekiel describes the people to whom he is to go. The worst part is that they are his own people!

Similarly, in the gospel, Jesus goes home to extend his mission to those he grew up among and who know him. So far, Mark has given us information about Jesus and his family. In 3:19b–20 they try to "restrain" him. They are clearly embarrassed by him and declare, "He has gone out of his mind" (3:21). A little later (1:31–35), he is approached by his mother and brothers —that occasions Jesus' declaration about who truly constitutes his family—"whoever does the will of God." When he goes home again (in today's gospel) the neighbors seem, at first, genuinely astonished, questioning where he could acquire such wisdom. (There also may be sarcasm intended here!) They want Jesus back on their level where he would be easier to control and less of a threat.

They "took offense" at him. Mark's word is *eskandalizonto*—scandalized, the same word used to describe Jesus' crucifixion. The "scandal" that the people in Jesus' hometown felt was their stumbling block. The townsfolk couldn't or didn't want to get beyond Jesus as the neighbor boy trying to make a name for himself. This time, Mark says, it was Jesus who was amazed.

Jesus' first overt rejection at home causes a change of pace and plan in Mark's story. Missionary outreach is how Jesus responds. So the disciples get their first "hands on" experience of ministry in a hostile world. They join the ranks of the prophets—Isaiah, Jeremiah, Ezekiel and Jesus—preaching the good news, but at high risk to their personal safety.

1. Read about how the people treat Jeremiah and how he complains: Jeremiah 11:18–20; 12:1–6; 15:10–21; 17:14–18; 18:18–23, 20:1–6 and 37:1–21. Why do prophets make us so uncomfortable? Why do they bring out so much violence in people?

2. God pointed out the problems that Ezekiel would have to face in his prophesying. In your communal task of evangelization, what are the things that scare you most? What forms do opposition to your prophesying take in your world?

Practice of **FAITH**

INDEPENDENCE DAY. Use this prayer from *Catholic Household Blessings and Prayers* to pray for the United States tomorrow:
God, source of all freedom,
this day is bright with the memory
of those that declared that life and liberty
are your gift to every human being.
Help us to continue a good work begun long ago.
Make our vision clear and our will strong:
that only in human solidarity will we find liberty,
and justice only in the honor that belongs
to every life on earth.
Turn our hearts toward the family of nations:
to understand the ways of others,
to offer friendship,
and to find safety only in the common good of all.
We ask this through Christ our Lord.

Practice of **HOPE**

MADE PERFECT IN WEAKNESS. "Amazing Grace" drifted from the ranks of the picket line outside the mines of the Pittston Coal Group in southwest Virginia. Miners—many of them disabled from crippling accidents or the disease known as "black lung"—and their families were protesting Pittston's callous cutoff of medical benefits and the expiration of their union contract.

Their struggle went on for months. "Whenever I feel that this cause may have a slim chance of winning," said Avis Sutherland, "I go back to the 34th psalm; God says he'll keep us in our time of need—it's a promise." United Mine Workers President Richard Trumka proclaimed that the weapons of the powerful "are powerless in the face of a community unified in nonviolent resistance." Courage and persistence paid off, as the Pittston company was forced to negotiate a contract.

Practice of **CHARITY**

WHEN I AM WEAK, THEN I AM STRONG. These are strange words spoken on the eve of our country's celebration of independence. The United States is a country that has been shaped by its wars. Generations are designated by the war they fought. "Peace through strength" has often been our rallying cry. Where is the dependence on God in those words? Where is the realization of our own brokenness? Is God invoked only to guarantee military success? It is time for us Christians, to reflect on how much we give over to God and how much we leave to the military machine to solve. It is in living the paradox of today's second reading that we come to let go of our illusions about the necessity of military might. This Fourth of July, let us pray for the kind of justice that brings lasting peace.

Weekday Reading
Hosea—entire book

JULY 10, 1994
FIFTEENTH SUNDAY IN ORDINARY TIME

READING I *Amos 7:12–15*

And Amaziah said to Amos, "O seer, go, flee away to the land of Judah, and eat bread there, and prophesy there; but never again prophesy at Bethel, for it is the king's sanctuary, and it is a temple of the kingdom."

Then Amos answered Amaziah, "I am no prophet, nor a prophet's son; but I am a shepherd, and a dresser of sycamore trees, and the LORD took me from following the flock, and the LORD said to me, 'Go, prophesy to my people Israel.'"

READING II *Ephesians 1:3–14*

Blessed by the God and Father of our Lord Jesus Christ, who has blessed us in Christ with every spiritual blessing in the heavenly places, even as God chose us in Christ before the foundation of the world, that before God we should be holy and blameless. God destined us in love for adoption through Jesus Christ: this was God's good pleasure and will, to the praise of God's glorious grace freely bestowed on us in the Beloved, in whom we have redemption through his blood, the forgiveness of our trespasses, according to the riches of God's grace lavished upon us. For God has made known to us in all wisdom and insight the mystery of the divine will, according to God's purpose set forth in Christ as a plan for the fullness of time, to unite all things in Christ, things in heaven and things on earth.

In Christ, according to the purpose of the one who accomplishes all things according to the counsel of divine will, we who first hoped in Christ have been destined and appointed to live for the praise of God's glory. In Christ you also, who have heard the word of truth, the gospel of your salvation, and have believed him, were sealed with the promised Holy Spirit, which is the guarantee of our inheritance until we acquire possession of it, to the praise of God's glory.

GOSPEL *Mark 6:7–13*

Jesus summoned the twelve, and began to send them out two by two, and gave them authority over the unclean spirits. He charged them to take nothing for their journey except a staff; no bread, no bag, no money in their belts; but to wear sandals and not put on two tunics. And Jesus said to them, "Where you enter a house, stay there until you leave the place. And if any place will not receive you and they refuse to hear you, when you leave, shake off the dust that is on your feet for a testimony against them." So they went out and preached that people should repent. And they cast out many demons, and anointed with oil many that were sick and healed them.

REFLECTION

The disciples get a very mixed review in the Gospel of Mark. Though they are hand-picked by Jesus, usually after intense prayer, their coming to genuine faith is a long, slow process. At one time they seem to have grasped who Jesus is; at another time they seem not to understand him at all.

However, Mark makes clear that their task remains to extend the mission of Jesus. Today's reading recounts the first occasion on which the disciples were commissioned. They have all they need from Jesus—the message, his authority and his commission. Other needs will be met by those who welcome them.

Their activity is threefold: preaching repentance, exorcising demons and anointing the sick with healing oil—the same work that Jesus does. And this charismatic band headed by Jesus, himself anointed with the Spirit, resembles Amos the prophet.

Amaziah, the priest, the representative of official religion and Amos' dramatic foil, is similar to those who eventually succeeded in condemning Jesus and scattering his followers. Amos' message was obviously an affront to King Jeroboam—political dynamite. We can almost sense Amaziah's panic at the threat, not only to king and country but to his own lofty position of religious power—and by a shepherd who says he was snatched from obscurity to prophesy to Israel.

Jesus and the disciples, in their mission, certainly rocked the religious boat. They went directly to the people, not through official channels. In comforting the afflicted, like Amos, they managed to afflict the comfortable. Like Amos, they paid for it. Truth that undermines people in power unleashes violence in one form or another. The rest of the Gospel of Mark demonstrates the deepening plot to silence Jesus and his followers.

1. Amos was the first in a series of strong charismatic prophets. He appeared, from Judah, when Israel was expanding, prosperous and powerful. His words were, therefore, all the less welcome. Read the book of Amos—aloud—to grasp the power and drama of his message. What does he say to our world?

2. Why is official religion so suspicious of independent prophets and preachers? To what extent is this justified?

Practice of FAITH

KATERI TEKAKWITHA. This Thursday, U.S. Catholics celebrate the memory of Blessed Kateri Tekakwitha. A Native American of the Algonquin tribe, Kateri was born to Christian parents in Osserneon, the present-day Auriesville, New York, the same place where Isaac Jogues and Jean Lalande were martyred ten years earlier. She was later captured by Iroquois warriors and married to a Mohawk chief. Her Catholicism was not accepted by her new people. She endured persecution for her beliefs, but eventually fled. Although her eyesight was impaired from smallpox, a disease unknown to Native Americans until Europeans brought it to North America, Kateri lived her life caring for others. She died in Canada on April 17, 1680.

The National Tekakwitha Conference (PO Box 6759, Great Falls MT 59401) is held each summer to explore the connections between native heritage and the Catholic tradition.

Practice of HOPE

PEACE FROM GOD. Warren McCleskey found Jesus on death row in a Georgia prison. "Warren taught me about a level of faith that I have not seen anywhere else," said Rev. Murphy Davis. McCleskey's case went through several appeals, including one before the Supreme Court based on overwhelming evidence that the death penalty is applied in a racially discriminatory way. But on September 25, 1991, Warren McCleskey was put to death. His final statement, asking for forgiveness and encouraging his brothers on death row, showed no bitterness. "The gift that Warren gave all of us was his dignity and inner peace," said Davis. "He had a conviction that if he had to die, some good would come of it—that his death would contribute to ending the death penalty."

Practice of CHARITY

GOD DESTINED US IN LOVE FOR ADOPTION. Children are our greatest treasure. The love that bore them into this world is a sign of the creative and dynamic love of God. Too many children, however, are abandoned or abused. Others have special needs that their biological parents are unable to satisfy. All these children long to be part of a family. In a society where the safety net is stretched thin, having loving families willing to care for them is a grace from God. Foster parents and adoptive parents are in especially short supply for children who have special needs. To adopt a child, or for information on how you can help in other ways, contact your diocesan Catholic Charities office.

Weekday Reading
Isaiah 1:10–17; 7:1–9; 10:5–7; 26:7–9, 12, 16–19; 38:1–6, 21–22

JULY 17, 1994
SIXTEENTH SUNDAY IN ORDINARY TIME

READING I *Jeremiah 23:1–6*

"Woe to the shepherds who destroy and scatter the sheep of my pasture!" says the LORD. Therefore thus says the LORD, the God of Israel, concerning the shepherds who care for my people: "You have scattered my flock, and have driven them away, and you have not attended to them. Behold, I will attend to you for your evil doings, says the LORD. Then I will gather the remnant of my flock out of all the countries where I have driven them, and I will bring them back to their fold, and they shall be fruitful and multiply. I will set shepherds over them who will care for them, and they shall fear no more, nor be dismayed, neither shall any be missing, says the LORD.

"Behold, the days are coming, says the LORD, when I will raise up for David a righteous Branch, who shall reign as king and deal wisely, and shall execute justice and righteousness in the land. In his days Judah will be saved, and Israel will dwell securely. And this is the name by which he will be called: 'The LORD is our righteousness.'"

READING II *Ephesians 2:13–18*

But now in Christ Jesus you who once were far off have been brought near in the blood of Christ. For Christ is our peace, who had made us both one, and has broken down the dividing wall of hostility, by abolishing in his flesh the law of commandments and ordinances, in order to create in himself one new human being in place of the two, so making peace, and [who] might reconcile us both to God in one body through the cross, thereby bringing the hostility to an end. And he came and preached peace to you who were far off and peace to those who were near; for through him we both have access in one Spirit to the Father.

GOSPEL *Mark 6:30–34*

The apostles returned to Jesus, and told him all that they had done and taught. And he said to them, "Come away by yourselves to a lonely place, and rest a while." For many were coming and going, and they had no leisure even to eat. And they went away in the boat to a lonely place by themselves. Now many saw them going, and knew them, and they ran there on foot from all the towns, and got there ahead of them. Going ashore, Jesus saw a great throng, and had compassion on them, because they were like sheep without a shepherd; and he began to teach them many things.

Mary Magdalene
Friday, July 22, 1994

Song of Songs 3:1–4   I found him whom my heart loves.
2 Corinthians 5:14–17   Anyone in Christ is a new creation.
John 20:1–2, 11–18   I have seen the Lord!

The church's memory is fuzzy: Exactly who is Mary Magdalene? Some confuse her with other women in scripture; some think her portrayal in the gospels is a composite of a number of faithful disciples. One thing is clear: This loving woman of the Fourth Gospel was faithful to Jesus to his death and was the first messenger of his resurrection. She went to the tomb weeping, carrying myrrh. She left the tomb rejoicing, carrying good news. (Her icon shows her holding a jar in one hand and a red Easter egg in the other.) She is the apostle to the apostles, running to the eleven to proclaim Christ risen.

REFLECTION

Jeremiah criticized the official "shepherds" and that included the king. What was expected of a king is expressed in the messianic prophecy of verses 5 and 6: one who will "deal wisely (like Solomon), and shall execute justice and righteousness in the land." The promised one will be of David's lineage and be a real shepherd.

Mark picks up the shepherd themes in his introduction to the feeding of the five thousand. To this miracle he attaches his description of Jesus' feelings of compassion toward them "because they were like sheep without a shepherd." Mark often deals with more than one aspect of Jesus at a time. Here he describes two aspects: Jesus' deep feelings for the needs of the people and his own role of shepherd-king. They have already been fed with his teaching (word); now he feeds their physical hunger (deed). This foreshadows the eucharist.

The action of Jesus is described in terms of the eucharistic liturgy that Mark probably knew. The sequence is still familiar to us: he looked up to heaven . . . blessed . . . broke the bread . . . gave it to the disciples for the people. The wandering sheep were "satisfied." Mark is also describing ministry in his church; those who minister do so with the commission of Jesus. In this feeding story, unlike John's later gospel (which we'll hear next week for five weeks), the disciples act on Jesus' behalf, once he has blessed and broken the bread. And they collect the leftovers. Disciples had been sent in twos on a preaching and teaching mission (last week) and returned successful. Here, Jesus shows them this extension of their ministry. They are to be shepherds of the flock, feeding and protecting them, reassuring the sheep of Jesus' continued presence by way of word and deed.

The next time that we will hear from Mark—in six weeks—the "official" shepherds of the people are on the attack, and the plot to destroy Jesus thickens.

1. Ezekiel also rails against unreliable shepherds of the people: 34:1–10, and presents God as *the* good shepherd: 34:11–16. Read Ezekiel 34. It includes a prophecy similar to Jeremiah's. What qualities should a true shepherd display?

2. How is the mission of word and deed carried on in your community? How do you evangelize and welcome inquirers? How do you explain eucharist and mission?

Practice of FAITH

MAGDALENE. On Thursday we remember Mary Magdalene, the first person to see the risen Lord. In *The Ongoing Journey: Women and the Bible,* Sharon Neufer Emswiler writes:

"Why was Mary Magdalene chosen? We do not know. But in that choice Jesus announced that in the new order women were to have a place and a role unlike any they had known before. Because of the role given to Mary Magdalene, women are entitled to take their place alongside their brothers in Christ's church. Unfortunately, the church has not yet in all quarters allowed women their rightful place, and Mary's experience often goes unrecognized. The church has pushed her to the sidelines and has devalued this very significant witness to the role that women can and should play in the church."

Discuss this with a few people you know this week. And don't forget to celebrate Thursday.

Practice of HOPE

BREAKING DOWN THE WALL. In the early 1980s, the U.S. government organized and funded the *contras* in Nicaragua. Then came reports of massacres, rapes, and torture by the *contras*. In October 1983, U.S. citizens launched Witness for Peace, a permanent, nonviolent, prayerful presence in Nicaragua's areas of hostility. Over the years, thousands of U.S. citizens have gone at their own expense to participate in this peace effort, holding prayer vigils and documenting the situation in an effort to provide some protection for the people of Nicaragua. In recent years, Witness for Peace has expanded its witness to include El Salvador, Guatemala, the Israeli-occupied territories of the Middle East, and South Africa.

Practice of CHARITY

THE DIVIDING WALL OF HOSTILITY. When the wall that separated East and West Berlin came down, we looked eagerly for a new world order. Lately in Germany though, we have seen a rise in ethnic hatred, unemployment and disillusionment. The dismantling of the wall was merely the beginning.

The same is true closer to home. In our own cities and towns we were compelled to tear down the walls of segregation and ignorance in the 60s, and yet that was only a beginning. Thirty years later we realize that the work of racial and economic equality has just begun. *Urban Family* is a quarterly magazine dedicated to helping people in urban communities deal with issues of racial reconciliation. To subscribe to this magazine, write or call *Urban Family*, 1581 Navarro Avenue, Pasadena CA 91103; 1-800-URBAN22. The cost is $10 per year.

Weekday Reading
Micah, chapters 6–7; Jeremiah, chapters 1–7

JULY 24, 1994

SEVENTEENTH SUNDAY IN ORDINARY TIME

READING I   *2 Kings 4:42–44*

A certain man came from Baal-shalishah, bringing Elisha, the man of God, bread of the first fruits, twenty loaves of barley, and fresh ears of grain in his sack. And Elisha said, "Give to the people, that they may eat." But his servant said, "How am I to set this before a hundred men?" So Elisha repeated, "Give them to the people, that they may eat, for thus says the LORD, 'They shall eat and have some left.'" So he set it before them. And they ate, and had some left, according to the word of the LORD.

READING II   *Ephesians 4:1–6*

I therefore, a prisoner for the Lord, beg you to lead a life worthy of the calling to which you have been called, with all lowliness and meekness, with patience, forbearing one another in love, eager to maintain the unity of the Spirit in the bond of peace. There is one body and one Spirit, just as you were called to the one hope that belongs to your call, one Lord, one faith, one baptism, one God and Father of us all, who is above all and through all and in all.

GOSPEL   *John 6:1–15*

Jesus went to the other side of the Sea of Galilee, which is the Sea of Tiberias. And a multitude followed him, because they saw the signs which he did on those who were diseased. Jesus went up on the mountain, and there sat down with his disciples. Now the Passover, the feast of the Jewish people, was at hand. Lifting up his eyes, then, and seeing that a multitude was coming to him, Jesus said to Philip, "How are we to buy bread, so that these people may eat?" This Jesus said to test Philip, for he himself knew what he would do. Philip answered him, "Two hundred denarii would not buy enough bread for each of them to get a little." One of Jesus' disciples, Andrew, Simon Peter's brother, said to Jesus, "There is a child here who has five barley loaves and two fish; but what are they among so many?" Jesus said, "Make the people sit down." Now there was much grass in the place; so they sat down, the men numbering about five thousand. Jesus then took the loaves, and having given thanks, he distributed them to those who were seated; so also the fish, as much as they wanted. And when they had eaten their fill, Jesus told his disciples, "Gather up the fragments left over, that nothing may be lost." So they gathered them up and filled twelve baskets with fragments from the five barley loaves, left by those who had eaten. When the people saw the sign which Jesus had done, they said, "This is indeed the prophet who is to come into the world!"

Perceiving then that they were about to come and take him by force to make him king, Jesus withdrew again to the mountain by himself.

REFLECTION

The last passage we heard from Mark contained a foreshadowing of the eucharist, so the passages we will now hear from John will explore this great gift further.

In the Gospel of John, the great teaching about Jesus and the eucharist is found in chapter six. For five weeks now we will hear most of that chapter. It's a dramatic chapter: Much is said and a lot happens. At the start, the crowds want to make Jesus king; at the end they want to kill him.

The feeding of 5,000 people—today's reading—opens the chapter. Jesus is enthusiastically followed by a crowd "because they had seen the signs which he did on the diseased." It's Passover, and the scene is a mountain area. Jesus is seated. Unlike the other gospels, it is Jesus who opens the dialogue with the disciples: "How are we to buy bread, so that people may eat?" This is a test of the disciples' faith. Jesus says that the people need to be fed, even though there is no mention of hunger from the crowd. The disciples' role is to present to Jesus the loaves and fishes offered by a child. Jesus then personally distributes the miraculous food. The disciples' next job is to pick up the pieces. The crumbs fill twelve baskets—more than they had when they started!

This is one of John's "signs" of who Jesus is. As the story is told, heavy hints are dropped: mountains, Passover, a miraculous feeding, the number twelve, a multitude following a wonder-worker. All these are reminders of Moses, Exodus, manna in the desert; all come up as chapter six proceeds. Jesus is identified by the people as "the prophet who is to come into the world."

1. Read the story of Israel in the desert: Exodus 15 and Numbers 33. Look at 2 Kings 4:42–44 and the parallels in Matthew 14:13–21; 15:32–38; Mark 6:32–44 and Luke 9:10–17. Taken together with today's gospel, what light do these scriptures shed on each other?

2. Instead of a eucharistic last supper of bread and wine, the Gospel of John tells the story of the washing of the feet. It reserves its description of the eucharist for after the resurrection—13:1–20. What does this suggest about the connection between eucharist and mission?

Practice of FAITH

A PRISONER FOR THE LORD. The apostle Paul often went to prison because his ministry disrupted everyday business and irritated authorities. Prisons in the United States and Canada are filled to overflowing today, and not everyone is incarcerated for noble reasons like Paul. But visiting those in prison—regardless of the reasons for their imprisonment—is a traditional act of mercy.

If your parish or diocese has a jail or prison ministry, find out if you can help. Otherwise, get hold of a copy of *Sojourners,* a Christian social justice magazine. *Sojourners* regularly publishes the names and addresses of those in prison who wish to correspond with people outside. Ask for *Sojourners* at your library or write 1321 Otis Street NE, Box 29272, Washington DC 20017. Your kindness may help bring a prisoner to the Lord!

Practice of HOPE

IN THE BOND OF PEACE. Twenty thousand young people worldwide are members of Young & Teen Peacemakers. The organization "encourages young people to recognize and begin to act on their own potential to make positive changes in their communities and in their own hearts." They meet in local chapters to discuss issues such as nonviolence, sexism, and racism; carry out projects including food pantries and recycling efforts; and hold marches for peace. "Being in Teen Peacemakers has exposed me to different ideas and allowed me to get to know people on a fundamental level, seeing them as they really are," said high school senior Emily Wilson. "That, I believe, is the foundation of peacemaking."

Practice of CHARITY

GIVE TO THE PEOPLE, THAT THEY MAY EAT. The number of people who are malnourished is staggering. It's estimated to be in the hundreds of millions. That's why it's important to donate money or canned goods to the local food pantry and to contribute to collections for the hungry at Mass. It's also important to help with the long-term needs of malnourished people, to give them the means to break the cycle of malnourishment. A sun-powered oven called the Solar Box Cooker, now being marketed in the Caribbean and Central America, may be one way of helping to break this cycle. It's easy to use and can be built from materials that are available in most communities. It requires no trees to be cut down, nor does it create any pollution. For more information, write or call Solar Box Cookers International, 1724 Eleventh Street, Sacramento CA 95814; 916-444-6616.

Weekday Reading
Jeremiah, chapters 14–26

JULY 31, 1994
EIGHTEENTH SUNDAY IN ORDINARY TIME

READING I *Exodus 16:2–4, 12–15*

The whole congregation of the people of Israel murmured against Moses and Aaron in the wilderness, and said to them, "Would that we had died by the hand of the LORD in the land of Egypt, when we sat by the pots filled with meat and ate bread to the full; for you have brought us out into this wilderness to kill this whole assembly with hunger."

Then the LORD said to Moses, "Behold, I will rain bread from heaven for you; and the people shall go out and gather a day's portion every day that I may prove them, whether they will walk in my law or not.

"I have heard the murmurings of the people of Israel; say to them, 'At twilight you shall eat meat, and in the morning you shall be filled with bread; then you shall know that I am the LORD your God.'"

In the evening quails came up and covered the camp; and in the morning dew lay round about the camp. And when the dew had gone up, there was on the face of the wilderness a fine, flake-like thing, fine as hoarfrost on the ground. When the people of Israel saw it, they said to one another, "What is it?" For they did not know what it was. And Moses said to them, "It is the bread which the LORD has given you to eat."

READING II *Ephesians 4:17, 20–24*

This I affirm and testify in the Lord, that you must no longer live as the Gentiles do, in the futility of their minds. You did not so learn Christ!—assuming that you have heard about him and were taught in him, as the truth is in Jesus. Put off your old nature which belongs to your former manner of life and is corrupt through deceitful lusts, and be renewed in the spirit of your minds, and put on the new nature, created after the likeness of God in true righteousness and holiness.

GOSPEL *John 6:24–35*

When the people saw that Jesus was not there, nor his disciples, they themselves got into the boats and went to Capernaum, seeking Jesus.

When they found him on the other side of the sea, they said to him, "Rabbi, when did you come here?" Jesus answered them, "Truly, truly, I say to you, you seek me, not because you saw signs, but because you ate your fill of the loaves. Do not labor for the food which perishes, but for the food which endures to eternal life, which the Man of Heaven will give to you; for on him God, the Father, has set the seal." Then they said to him, "What must we do, to be doing the works of God?" Jesus answered them, "This is the work of God, that you believe in the one whom God has sent." So they said to him, "Then what sign do you do, that we may see, and believe you? What work do you perform? Our forebears ate the manna in the wilderness; as it is written, 'He gave them bread from heaven to eat.'" Jesus then said to them, "Truly, truly, I say to you, it was not Moses who gave you the bread from heaven; my Father gives you the true bread from heaven. For the bread of God is that which comes down from heaven, and gives life to the world." They said to him, "Lord, give us this bread always."

Jesus said to them, "I am the bread of life; they who come to me shall not hunger, and they who believe in me shall never thirst."

The Transfiguration of the Lord
Saturday, August 6, 1994

Daniel 7:9–10, 13–14   I saw the son of man on the clouds.
2 Peter 1:16–19   We are eyewitnesses to God's glory.
Mark 9:2–10   How good it is to be here!

At the peak of the glory of summer, the Lord shines on the holy mountain. With the law and the prophets, we gaze face to face on God. Yet which mountain is it, Calvary or Tabor? Perhaps they are one and the same.

REFLECTION

We jump from John 6:15 (last week) to John 6:24. What happened in between? The disciples, while tossing about in a Lake Tiberius squall, are approached by Jesus. To their amazement, he is walking on the water. The seemingly absent Lord is really present. He calms their terrors and helps them reach the safety of the shore. The disciples now know much more about Jesus than the pursuing crowds!

On the previous day the crowd called Jesus "prophet." Today they call him "rabbi." Their perception of him has changed somewhat. Jesus casts the bait as he tells them the real reason for their seeking him out again: They had seen a crowd-pleasing miracle, not witnessed a sign. They had received free food, not "grace and truth" (1:17). So Jesus begins to distinguish between earthly food and heavenly bread. The key to perceiving the difference, Jesus says, is belief "in him whom God has sent." Faith in the whole Christ changes ordinary "seeing" into Spirit-filled vision.

In what sounds like a dialogue of controversy between synagogue and church in John's day, the crowd raises the issue of Moses and manna in the desert. Now Jesus sets the stage for his first shocking statement in this heretofore pleasant chapter. It was God who gave the bread, he explains. Moses was merely the minister. True bread, life-giving bread, comes from heaven. Then, like the woman at the well who wants the living water, so the crowd now wants the living bread. They now call Jesus, "Lord."

But Jesus drops the first bombshell: "I am the bread of life. . . ." Eating of heavenly bread means dining on Jesus—accepting the whole Christ—faith-feeding. Bread is sent from heaven by God; Jesus is sent by the Father. He is food and drink, sight and light, life and obedience. He is not the minister of anything other than himself: "I am the bread of life."

1. Read the section of chapter six so far omitted: verses 16 through 23. Compare them with Matthew 14:22–27 and Mark 6:45–51. This was a private "sign" for the disciples. What did it signify? How does it help you and your community? What other ways do you know of Jesus' abiding and protective presence?

2. When have you ever felt—like some of the crowd in John 6—that "This is too much!" when confronted with Jesus' words and actions via present day disciples? Tell about it.

Practice of FAITH

TRANSFIGURATION. When Jesus stood with Elijah and Moses and shone brighter than the sun, the apostles Peter, James and John saw him for who he is: Light from Light, true God. Long ago, when iconographers—artists who paint icons, that is holy pictures—began their career, the first subject they painted in brilliant gold was the Transfiguration. Gazing at icons is a spiritual practice that opens the heart to see Christ for who he is. This week, make a pilgrimage to an Eastern rite church to pray before an icon of the Transfiguration or some other icon. Take your time. Let the icon help you deepen your prayer.

In a perverse irony, Transfiguration day is also the anniversary of the day in 1945 when the first atomic bomb was dropped. In a flash of blinding light, the bomb destroyed Hiroshima and killed many thousands of its people. Thousands more died later or suffered permanent disabilities. Christians in the United States may want to fast as an act of penance this day.

Practice of HOPE

PUT ON THE NEW NATURE. George Zabelka served as Catholic chaplain to the crews that dropped the atomic bombs on Hiroshima and Nagasaki, Japan, on August 6 and 9, 1945. After the bombing, he walked through the ruins where Nagasaki's Urakami Cathedral had stood, and picked up a piece of a censer. "When I look at it today," he said, "I pray God forgives us for how we have distorted Christ's teaching and destroyed his world." Zabelka said that "to fail to speak to the utter moral corruption of the mass destruction of civilians was to fail as a Christian and a priest." Zabelka devoted the remaining years of his life to teaching nonviolence in parishes. "Jesus authorized none of his followers to substitute violence for love," he taught. "Christians the world over should be taught that Christ's teaching to love their enemies is not optional."

Practice of CHARITY

CREATED AFTER THE LIKENESS OF GOD. Jesus showed us who God is. His becoming human shows us the potential we have to share God's divinity, to be true reflections of God. Charity is the way we do this, living in right relationship with God, others and our own selves. If we believe that the human person is a reflection of God, then it means our stance towards ourselves and our neighbors must embody our belief. This week identify someone or some group of people that do not appear to you as a reflection of God. It may not be a single person, but a whole race of people, or gender, or nation. Do one thing towards making amends with them. If it's in your tradition, celebrate the Sacrament of Reconciliation.

Weekday Reading
Jeremiah, chapters 28–31

AUGUST 7, 1994
NINETEENTH SUNDAY IN ORDINARY TIME

READING I   *1 Kings 19:4–8*

Elijah went a day's journey into the wilderness, and came and sat down under a broom tree; and he asked that he might die, saying, "It is enough; now, O LORD, take away my life; for I am no better than my forebears." And he lay down and slept under a broom tree; and behold, an angel touched him, and said to him, "Arise and eat." And Elijah looked, and behold, there was at his head a cake baked on hot stones and a jar of water. And he ate and drank, and lay down again. And the angel of the LORD came again a second time, and touched him, and said, "Arise and eat, else the journey will be too great for you." And Elijah arose, and ate and drank, and went in the strength of that food forty days and forty nights to Horeb the mount of God.

READING II   *Ephesians 4:30 — 5:2*

Do not grieve the Holy Spirit of God, in whom you were sealed for the day of redemption. Let all bitterness and wrath and anger and clamor and slander be put away from you, with all malice, and be kind to one another, tenderhearted, forgiving one another, as God in Christ forgave you.

Therefore be imitators of God, as beloved children. And walk in love, as Christ loved us and gave himself up for us, a fragrant offering and sacrifice to God.

GOSPEL   *John 6:41–51*

The Jewish people then murmured at [Jesus], because he said, "I am the bread which came down from heaven." They said, "Is not this Jesus, the son of Joseph, whose father and mother we know? How does he now say, 'I have come down from heaven'?" Jesus answered them, "Do not murmur among yourselves. It is not possible for people to come to me unless the Father who sent me draws them; and I will raise them up at the last day. It is written in the prophets, 'And they shall all be taught by God.' Everyone who has heard and learned from the Father comes to me. No one has seen the Father except the one who is from God; this one has seen the Father. Truly, truly, I say to you, those who believe have eternal life. I am the bread of life. Your forebears ate the manna in the wilderness, and they died. This is the bread which comes down from heaven, that one may eat of it and not die. I am the living bread which came down from heaven; anyone who eats of this bread will live for ever; and the bread which I shall give for the life of the world is my flesh."

REFLECTION

The murmuring of Israel against Moses in the desert (see Exodus 16:1–12) is reenacted by the complaining crowd in today's portion from John 6. How can this man make such outrageous claims for himself: bread from heaven, indeed! No more hunger, no more thirst? They cease calling him "Lord," as they did after the miraculous feeding with the loaves and fishes, and begin to wonder: "Is not this Jesus, the son of Joseph?"

The controversy deepens when Jesus says, in effect, that some will never understand. In what might very well reflect the tension between the early church and the synagogue out of which it was born, the Gospel of John has Jesus saying that those who truly understand the scriptures have no difficulty recognizing him as the Messiah. The first shocking statement that Jesus made — that he is the bread from heaven — is now followed by a second, even more inflammatory remark: "Your ancestors ate manna in the desert and died."

The inference is shocking. The ancestors heard God's word, but they did not learn from it. They did not recognize in the signs they witnessed the love of their life-giving, liberating God. They saw the spectacle, but missed the sign. As when the 5,000 were fed, the act itself is popular but its meaning is missed.

Maybe the meaning is missed because it is too hard to swallow. Jesus compounds the difficulty for his hearers with his final statement in today's passage: "The bread which I shall give . . . is my flesh." It is not yet given. What they have witnessed thus far is a sign, an indication of a truth, the depths of which are yet to be disclosed fully in Jesus' dying and rising. This is too much for the crowd that wanted spectacle and not harsh reality, distraction and not discipleship.

1. When God's loving and caring are made so plain, why do people reject it? Is it too demanding? Too good to be true? Does it require too much change? How?

2. What is the simplest sign of God's abiding love and care for you and your community? What is the most challenging sign?

Practice of FAITH

DEACON LAWRENCE. Lawrence was tortured and martyred in 258. Years later, Augustine preached: "At the church at Rome, Lawrence ministered the sacred blood of Christ; there for the sake of Christ's name he poured out his own blood. St. John the apostle was teaching us about the Lord's supper when he wrote: 'Just as Christ laid down his life for us, so we ought to lay down our lives for others.' Lawrence understood this and, understanding, he acted on it. In his life he loved Christ; in his death he followed in his footsteps."

On Wednesday, pray for Christians around the world who suffer for the gospel. Use this prayer from the breviary: "Blessed Lawrence cried out: I worship my God and serve only the Lord. So I do not fear your torture. God is my rock; I take refuge in the Lord. So I do not fear your torture."

Practice of HOPE

WALK IN LOVE. Athol Gill introduced himself to the imposing chief of El Salvador's national police as a Bible professor from Australia. He had come to find out why the police had imprisoned and tortured a local Salvadoran Baptist pastor. "Tell me," Gill asked, "is it always a crime to serve the poor in El Salvador?"

A couple of hours before, Gill and a companion prayed for strength to face the colonel's arrogance. Their only strategy: "We will make the road as we walk it," said Gill. In their presence, the colonel signed a declaration that the Salvadoran Baptist community could continue its ministry with the poor without fear of reprisal.

Practice of CHARITY

ARISE AND EAT, ELSE THE JOURNEY WILL BE TOO GREAT FOR YOU. The horror of nuclear war is brought again into our consciousness by the anniversaries of the bombings of Hiroshima (August 6) and Nagasaki (August 9). Yet, this year the doomsday clock's hand continues to be pulled back from midnight. The fear of nuclear war is receding. Still, it is no time for complacency. To further reduce the threat of nuclear war, we must raise future generations of peacemakers. If you have children or grandchildren, you might help point them in this direction by getting hold of a copy of *Starting Out Right: Nurturing Young Children as Peacemakers* by Kathleen McGinnis and Barbara Oehlberg. It tells how to help youngsters develop social relationships and self-esteem, and how they are affected by violence, consumerism, racism and sexism. The book, published by Meyer-Stone Books in 1988 at $9.95, includes a good bibliography and specific activities.

Weekday Reading
Ezra, chapters 1–16

AUGUST 14, 1994
TWENTIETH SUNDAY IN ORDINARY TIME

READING I *Proverbs 9:1–6*

Wisdom has built her house,
 she has set up her seven pillars.
She has slaughtered her beasts, she has mixed her wine,
 she has also set her table.
She has sent out her maids to call
 from the highest places in the town,
"Let the simple turn in here!"
 To whomever is without sense she says,
"Come, eat of my bread
 and drink of the wine I have mixed.
Leave simpleness, and live,
 and walk in the way of insight."

READING II *Ephesians 5:15–20*

Look carefully how you walk, not as unwise but as wise, making the most of the time, because the days are evil. Therefore do not be foolish, but understand what the will of the Lord is. And do not get drunk with wine, for that is debauchery; but be filled with the Spirit, addressing one another in psalms and hymns and spiritual songs, singing and making melody to the Lord with all your heart, always and for everything giving thanks in the name of our Lord Jesus Christ to God, the Father.

GOSPEL *John 6:51–58*

[At that time Jesus said,]

"I am the living bread which came down from heaven; any who eat of this bread will live for ever; and the bread which I shall give for the life of the world is my flesh."

The Jewish people then disputed among themselves, saying, "How can this man give us his flesh to eat?" So Jesus said to them, "Truly, truly, I say to you, unless you eat the flesh of the Man of Heaven, and drink his blood, you have no life in you; they who eat my flesh and drink my blood have eternal life, and I will raise them up at the last day. For my flesh is food indeed, and my blood is drink indeed. They who eat my flesh and drink my blood abide in me, and I in them. As the living Father sent me, and I live because of the Father, so they who eat me will live because of me. This is the bread which came down from heaven, not such as the forebears ate and died; they who eat this bread will live for ever."

The Assumption of Mary
Monday, August 15, 1994

VIGIL

1 Chronicles 15:3–4, 15–16; 16:1–2 David rejoiced before the ark.
1 Corinthians 15:54–57 God gave us victory over death.
Luke 11:27–28 Blessed is the womb that bore you!

DAY

Revelation 11:19; 12:1–6, 10 I saw a woman clothed in the sun.
1 Corinthians 15:20–26 Christ is the firstfruits of the dead.
Luke 1:39–56 He has raised the lowly to the heights.

August gardens overflow with abundance. As each plant comes to fruit, it is harvested in proper order. So now, in proper order, we keep the festival of Mary's passover, of her harvesting into heaven. Christ is the firstfruits of the dead. In time each one of us will be gathered into the reign of God, shining like the sun, with the moon at our feet.

REFLECTION

Last week the people "murmured." This week they "complained" among themselves. The word John uses here for "complained" is closely related to the Greek word for "battle." Perhaps this is a hint of the threatened violence that ends chapter six (verse 71) and eventually befalls Jesus. There can be no discussion about the eucharist without a reference to Jesus' passion.

There is no doubt that Jesus' words so far have shocked his hearers. Their growing distrust of him deepens now as they hear not only about eating flesh but also about drinking blood. The law given by Moses absolutely forbade the drinking of any blood (Leviticus 17:10–14). But John loves irony! The law, while forbidding the "eating" of blood, also justifies Jesus' words: "for, as life, it is the blood that makes atonement" (Leviticus 17:11). And it is in John's theology and story that the one already identified as "lamb of God," should also be the one sacrificed for the good of the people (note also the irony of who says this—John 11:45–53). Jesus' blood will be shed for the life of the world. By eating his flesh and blood, believers become part of his atoning self-sacrifice: They experience "at-one-ment" with God.

According to the Law, blood is life. The gospel, unlike the Law, distinguishes between flesh and blood to emphasize an important point: Jesus speaks of eating flesh and drinking blood to emphasize that he is the source of life for the believer. Flesh and blood, bread and wine, are signs of the fact that the community of believers abides in Christ.

1. How are eucharist and the cross connected?

2. Eucharist establishes and maintains a believer's "abiding" in Jesus (John 15:1–12). What responsibilities and commitments does sharing in the eucharist bring in terms of evangelization and mission for you and your community?

Practice of FAITH

ASSUMPTION JOY. Celebrating Mary's assumption into heaven strengthens our belief that the human body is sacred and destined for glory. Just as Christ was raised from the dead bodily—nail prints and all—so we rejoice that when she fell asleep in death, Mary's body was raised to heaven, too. And we celebrate this when Mother Earth is ripe with fruits and flowers—when life is abundant everywhere.

Cut flowers from your garden or window box and take them to church to leave at Mary's shrine tomorrow. Do something nice for your own body: go swimming, take an extra long bath, enjoy a massage. Do something nice for someone whose body is giving out or broken: take someone in a wheelchair for a ride, or bring a gift of body lotion to someone in a nursing home. Pray the *Regina caeli* found on page 95.

Practice of HOPE

IN PSALMS AND HYMNS. In 1921 Simon Kimbangu of Zaire (then the Belgian Congo) began preaching that Africans are the equals of Europeans, which got him 30 years in prison. His legacy is the Kimbanguist Church, the largest indigenous expression of Christianity in Africa.

The church embraces nonviolence, the equality of women, and communal life. Every evening about sundown in the Kimbanguist compound in Kinshasa, Zaire, just after the heavens open with a brief torrent of rain, the singing begins. Rich harmonies reflect the influence of both traditional hymns and African rhythms. But the greatest influence, according to church members, is the Holy Spirit. These beautiful melodies—now numbering more than a thousand—have been bestowed on members of the church who share them with the others.

Practice of CHARITY

WISDOM HAS BUILT HER HOUSE. The nations of North, Central and South America comprise a large household. True wisdom will be born when the nations begin to learn from each other and live together in harmony. This Sunday the U.S. bishops ask us to be generous to the people of Latin America, many of whom still live shackled by oppression, illiteracy, hunger, unemployment and inadequate health care. Your gift to this collection helps our sister churches to continue their mission among the poor and the oppressed in our own hemisphere.

Weekday Reading
Ezra, chapters 28–43

AUGUST 21, 1994
TWENTY-FIRST SUNDAY IN ORDINARY TIME

READING I *Joshua 24:1–2, 15–17, 18*

Joshua gathered all the tribes of Israel to Shechem, and summoned the elders, the heads, the judges, and the officers of Israel; and they presented themselves before God. And Joshua said to all the people, "Thus says the LORD, the God of Israel:

"And if you be unwilling to serve the LORD, choose this day whom you will serve, whether the gods your forebears served in the region beyond the River, or the gods of the Amorites in whose land you dwell; but as for me and my house, we will serve the LORD."

Then the people answered, "Far be it from us that we should forsake the LORD, to serve other gods; for it is the LORD our God who brought us and our forebears up from the land of Egypt, out of the house of bondage, and who did those great signs in our sight, and preserved us in all the way that we went, and among all the peoples through whom we passed; therefore we also will serve the LORD, for the LORD is our God."

READING II *Ephesians 5:21–32*

Be subject to one another out of reverence for Christ. Wives are subject to their husbands, as to the Lord. For the husband is the head of the wife as Christ is the head of the church, the body, and is its Savior. As the church is subject to Christ, so let wives also be subject in everything to their husbands. Husbands, love your wives, as Christ loved the church and gave himself up for it, that he might sanctify it, having cleansed it by the washing of water with the word, that he might present the church to himself in splendor, without spot or wrinkle or any such thing, that it might be holy and without blemish. Even so husbands should love their wives as their own bodies. He who loves his wife loves himself. People do not hate their own bodies, but nourish and cherish them, as Christ does the church, because we are parts of his body. "For this reason a man shall leave his father and mother and be joined to his wife, and the two shall become one flesh." This mystery is a profound one, and I am saying that it refers to Christ and the church.

GOSPEL *John 6:60–69*

Many of Jesus' disciples, when they heard his words, said, "This is a hard saying; who can listen to it?" But Jesus, knowing in himself that his disciples murmured at it, said to them, "Do you take offense at this? Then what if you were to see the Man of Heaven ascending where he was before? It is the spirit that gives life, the flesh is of no avail; the words that I have spoken to you are spirit and life. But there are some of you that do not believe." For Jesus knew from the first who those were that did not believe, and who it was that would betray him. And he said, "This is why I told you that people are not able to come to me unless it is granted them by the Father."

After this many of his disciples drew back and no longer went about with him. Jesus said to the twelve, "Do you also wish to go away?" Simon Peter answered him, "Lord, to whom shall we go? You have the words of eternal life; and we have believed, and have come to know, that you are the Holy One of God."

REFLECTION

Jesus has managed to alienate a once enthusiastic crowd and now, since the talk of drinking blood (last week's gospel), it seems that even his chosen disciples are having second thoughts. Many "drew back and no longer went about with him." Some of the disciples, like the crowds, murmured at what he said. If they found his words thus far offensive, what will they think of Jesus' ascension to heaven? John's is not a reference to Luke's image of Jesus disappearing into heaven in a cloud after the resurrection. In the Gospel of John, "ascending to where he was before" refers to Jesus' return to the Father, his exaltation through death and resurrection. Such a claim is as much a *skandalon* as his sayings about flesh and blood.

So now, to the Twelve, all is revealed. A messiah, hanging on a cross, however dignified John's description of it might be, is a scandal. What plain sight and hearing convey is pain, suffering, humiliation and contradiction. What the Spirit succeeds in achieving is a different seeing, a different hearing. It's called believing, and it allows one who believes to see beyond an agony-racked human body dying on a cross to the Son of God dying for love of the world, returning to whence he came. The world does its worst to him but this, ironically, is his glory.

1. What happened to turn the enthusiasm of the crowds at the beginning of John 6 into hostility at the end? We don't often think of the eucharist as divisive. Is it? How? Why?

2. The word *skandalon*—scandal—arises in relation to both cross and eucharist. How are the cross and the eucharist a scandal? To whom?

Practice of **FAITH**

MONICA AND AUGUSTINE. Saturday we remember Monica. Her son Augustine's feast day is the next day, but we don't celebrate it this year because it falls on the Lord's Day. These two Africans are firm foundations of the early church. Augustine's understanding of faith, preserved in his writings, continues to shape our theology today. We have nothing of Monica's writings, but we know that Augustine would have never come to Christ if not for her faith, her gentle persuasion and her love. (He tells us so!)

Find a copy of Augustine's *Confessions* and begin reading it this week. (It's widely available at bookstores and libraries.) As you read the story of this saint's conversion—and his holy mother's role—begin to keep a notebook. Jot down the events and people in your life that have led or are leading you to the Lord.

Practice of **HOPE**

WE WILL SERVE THE LORD. In South Africa, in the black township of Duncan Village, the security police escorted us and our young guide Jam Jam to a military tower for interrogation. We were taken there at gunpoint. Jam Jam had just been released from ten months in detention, during which he had been kept in a cold cell, fed cornmeal infested with worms, and tortured.

When the security police officer threatened him with a return to detention, Jam Jam's only response was to reach calmly into his back pocket, remove his pocket New Testament, put it in front of the officer's face, and say simply, "I am a Christian." A brief moment of silence descended as the arrogance of evil met the quiet power of the gospel.

With determination written on his face, Jam Jam told us after we were let go, "We are going forward. It's not the time to be afraid."

Practice of **CHARITY**

HUSBANDS SHOULD LOVE THEIR WIVES. In our efforts to be charitable to all those outside of our home we sometimes neglect the people in our own homes. Married couples: Do something positive for your relationship this week, even something as simple as sharing an evening together. Reaffirm your covenant with one another and recommit yourselves as partners for your whole life. Single people: Do something to reaffirm the importance of a primary relationship you share with another. Or cook a meal that you and a few other single people can enjoy together.

Weekday Reading
2 Thessalonians—entire book

AUGUST 28, 1994
TWENTY-SECOND SUNDAY IN ORDINARY TIME

READING I *Deuteronomy 4:1–2, 6–8*

[Moses said to the people,]

"And now, O Israel, give heed to the statutes and the ordinances which I teach you, and do them; that you may live, and go in and take possession of the land which the LORD, the God of your forebears, gives you. You shall not add to the word which I command you, nor take from it; that you may keep the commandments of the LORD your God which I command you. Keep them and do them; for that will be your wisdom and your understanding in the sight of the peoples, who, when they hear all these statutes, will say, 'Surely this great nation is a wise and understanding people.' For what great nation is there that has a god so near to it as the LORD our God is to us, whenever we cry out? And what great nation is there, that has statutes and ordinances so righteous as all this law which I set before you this day?"

READING II *James 1:17–18, 21–22, 27*

Every good endowment and every perfect gift is from above, coming down from the Father of lights with whom there is no variation or shadow due to change. Out of divine will God brought us forth by the word of truth that we should be a kind of first fruits of God's creatures.

Receive with meekness the implanted word, which is able to save your souls. But be doers of the word, and not hearers only, deceiving yourselves. Religion that is pure and undefiled before God and the Father is this: to visit orphans and widows in their affliction, and to keep oneself unstained from the world.

GOSPEL *Mark 7:1–8, 14–15, 21–23*

When the Pharisees gathered together with Jesus, with some of the scribes, who had come from Jerusalem, they saw that some of his disciples ate with hands defiled, that is, unwashed. (For the Pharisees, and all the Jewish people, do not eat unless they wash their hands, observing the tradition of the elders; and when they come from the marketplace, they do not eat unless they purify themselves; and there are many other traditions which they observe, the washing of cups and pots and vessels of bronze.) And the Pharisees and the scribes asked Jesus, "Why do your disciples not live according to the tradition of the elders, but eat with hands defiled?" And he said to them, "Well did Isaiah prophesy of you hypocrites, as it is written,

'This people honors me with their lips,
but their heart is far from me;
in vain do they worship me,
teaching human precepts as doctrines.'

You leave the commandment of God, and hold fast to human tradition."

And Jesus called the people to him again, and said to them, "Hear me, all of you, and understand: nothing which goes into a person from the outside is defiling; but the things which come out are what defile a human being. For from within, out of the human heart, come evil thoughts, fornication, theft, murder, adultery, coveting, wickedness, deceit, licentiousness, envy, slander, pride, foolishness. All these evil things come from within, and they defile a human being."

REFLECTION

Having completed John 6, we now return to Mark's gospel for the rest of the year—until Christ the King Sunday—November 20.

When we left Jesus and the disciples in the Gospel of Mark, the issue of who the genuine shepherds of the people are and what God expects of them was being raised. In Jesus' day the Pharisees would certainly have been counted among the official shepherds of the people. These officials are critical of the disciples—"free-lance" shepherds—for not observing the rules of ritual cleansing at meals. Jesus responds with scripture (Isaiah 29:13), accusing the official shepherds of substituting, in effect, human tradition for the commands and precepts of God. In its context, the Isaiah quote attacks the superficiality of religious practices when God's counsel is ignored.

Jesus directly warns the people about hypocrisy. He suddenly is usurping the jealously guarded position of authority that religious officials believed they occupied. Jesus has gone to the heart of the issue. Evil, in all its forms, is not like a disease, accidentally caught and curable by external treatments, however complex, impressive or self-gratifying these may be. It is a human indulgence in which truly good things, given freely by God, are twisted to achieve selfish ends and usually at the expense of others and oneself. These are the things that defile a human being. Only God has the cure.

1. Read Isaiah 29:13–21 where a new union with God is prophesied. What kind of human "wisdom" gets us into most trouble?

2. How do you become aware of the need for internal or spiritual cleansing? What helps accomplish such a cleansing?

Practice of **FAITH**

DOERS OF THE WORD. Try this. As you study the scriptures in this book each week, ask yourself this question: "What are these scriptures asking me to do?" Pray to the Holy Spirit for help in answering the question, and jot down your answer in the blank space. It may be a big thing; it may be a small thing. It may be something new; it may be something that you already do. The Spirit will help you figure it out.

When you accomplish what you jotted down, cross it off the page. Try this until the end of the year if it helps you live by God's word. When you accomplish what you wrote down, offer it to God in a prayer. Say something like, "I offer to you, O God, this act of my faith in your word, this act of my love for you."

Practice of **HOPE**

NOT HEARERS ONLY. An ancient Greek philosopher was once asked, "When will justice come?" His answer was, "Justice will come when those of us who are not injured are as indignant as those who are." One person who shared the indignation was Ammon Hennacy, a pioneer in the peace and justice movement. One day he was carrying a protest sign for peace in the street. Someone called to him, "Hey, Mister! Do you think that you are going to change society by carrying around that sign?" Hennacy's quick reply: "I don't know if I'll be able to change society, but I'm determined that society is not going to change me."

Practice of **CHARITY**

VISIT ORPHANS AND WIDOWS IN THEIR AFFLICTION. Millions of people in our country cannot afford health insurance. At the same time, the cost of health care continues to spiral upward. While our political leaders continue to struggle with this problem, one organization has taken steps to solve it. Called Access to Care, it serves those who make too much to be eligible for Medicaid or Medicare, but too little to afford medical insurance. Access patients pay $5 for each office visit to doctors who have also signed on with Access. This puts the cost of an office visit within the reach of practically everyone. The result: Access members with routine illnesses are much more likely to see a doctor. That in turn results in early diagnosis and treatment before the routine problems become major (and much more costly) problems. Though this system can't solve the health-care crisis all by itself, it's a step in the right direction. For more information, write or call: Access to Care, 2235 Enterprise Drive, Suite 3501, Westchester IL 60154; 708-531-0680.

Weekday Reading
1 Corinthians, chapters 1–4

SEPTEMBER 4, 1994
TWENTY-THIRD SUNDAY IN ORDINARY TIME

READING I   *Isaiah 35:4–7*

Say to those who are of a fearful heart,
  "Be strong, fear not!
Behold, your God
  will come with vengeance,
with the recompense of God.
  God will come and save you."
Then the eyes of the blind shall be opened,
  and the ears of the deaf unstopped;
then shall the lame leap like a hart,
  and the tongue of the dumb sing for joy.
For the waters shall break forth in the wilderness,
  and streams in the desert;
the burning sand shall become a pool,
  and the thirsty ground springs of water.

READING II   *James 2:1–5*

My dear people, show no partiality as you hold the faith of our Lord Jesus Christ, the Lord of glory. For if a person with gold rings and in fine clothing comes into your assembly, and a poor person in shabby clothing also comes in, and you pay attention to the one who wears the fine clothing and say, "Have a seat here, please," while you say to the poor person, "Stand there," or "Sit at my feet," have you not made distinctions among yourselves, and become judges with evil thoughts? Listen, my beloved ones. Has not God chosen those who are poor in the world to be rich in faith and heirs of the dominion promised to those who love God?

GOSPEL   *Mark 7:31–37*

Jesus returned from the region of Tyre, and went through Sidon to the Sea of Galilee, through the region of the Decapolis. And they brought to him someone who was deaf and had a speech impediment; and they besought Jesus to lay his hand upon him. And taking him aside from the multitude privately, Jesus put his fingers into the man's ears, and spat and touched the man's tongue; and looking up to heaven, he sighed, and said to him, "Ephphatha," that is, "Be opened." And the man's ears were opened, his tongue was released, and he spoke plainly. And Jesus charged them to tell no one; but the more he charged them, the more zealously they proclaimed it. And they were astonished beyond measure, saying, "He has done all things well; he even makes those who are deaf to hear and those who are dumb to speak."

The Birth of Mary
Thursday, September 8, 1994

Micah 5:1–4   She who is to give birth is born!
Romans 8:28–30   We share the image of Christ.
Matthew 1:1–16, 18–23   Of her Jesus was born.

The words mother, *mater,* and material things, *matter,* are one and the same. In September, Mother Earth gives forth in fruitful abundance our material sustenance. Mother Mary is born, who knit together in her own fruitful body earth and heaven.

REFLECTION

Unreliable shepherds and helpless sheep have been a focus of these recent lectionary passages from the Gospel of Mark.

Between the controversy with the Pharisees and today's miraculous healing, Jesus had met "the Syro-Phoenician woman" (Mark 7:24–30), and he had healed her little daughter. He had left the territory under the control of the official leaders of his religion and had entered foreign parts. The religious officials of Jesus' day would not have spoken to such a woman nor have been caught in her territory. Yet Jesus brings hope to the woman and life to her daughter—despite their nationality, religious affiliation and social standing as women in a patriarchal world. Scandalous!

Jesus turns to another individual in the misled flock. He is deaf and consequently is unable to speak clearly. He's almost a symbol of the poorly shepherded people: They've stopped listening because what is preached at them makes life harder not easier. And, of course, they have no voice. Who listens to the ordinary people, anyway? So Jesus gives this one man what is needed by all: ears to hear and a voice to make himself heard.

And yet they are told to keep it all quiet! Jesus is aware of officialdom and its uncompromising methods of disposing of dangerous people like him (Mark 3:6; 6:14–29). The joy of the man and the amazement of the crowd are too great to stifle. Now that they have a voice, they're going to use it.

This is a miracle of liberation. As one man is set free to hear and proclaim (a process the disciples are also going through) the whole crowd feels renewed energy to listen to this mysterious shepherd who teaches with authority—not like their leaders (Mark 1:22). They will also proclaim what they have witnessed: They assume leadership roles now, too.

1. Jesus healed people and each gospel uses the occasions to instruct us. Read these healing miracles: John 9:1–41—what kind of blindness and seeing is it about? Luke 7:1–10—what kinds of people and faith is this about? Matthew 9:27–38—what kind of health does Jesus give?

2. Is it true that good people don't speak out because they're deaf to the cries of the poor, the homeless, the persecuted and the outcasts? What do you think causes such deafness? How is it healed?

Practice of FAITH

LABOR DAY. Pray this prayer from *Catholic Household Blessings and Prayers* as you rest from work tomorrow:

God our creator,
we are the work of your hands.
Guide us in our work,
that we may do it, not for self alone,
but for the common good.
Make us alert to injustice,
ready to stand in solidarity,
that there may be dignity for all
in labor and labor's reward.
Grant this through Christ our Lord. Amen.
Joseph, patron of laborers, pray for us.

If you belong to a union, resolve to be a more active participant in its activities. Show equal respect to people regardless of their station—be as polite to a janitor as you are to the corporation president. Remember the unemployed in your prayers, and if there is something more that you can do to alleviate their plight, do it as an act of faith.

Practice of HOPE

GOD HAS CHOSEN THE POOR TO BE RICH IN FAITH. For two centuries, descendants of African slaves have lived on South Carolina's Sea Islands, where their unique culture known as Gullah flourished. Oyster harvesting, basket weaving, and baptisms by the shore marked their way of life. "Everybody was like one big family," said Yvonne Wilson of Daufuskie Island. "If you had, I had." "We didn't consider we were poor," added Billie Burn. "We considered we were blessed."

But developers have taken over the island's beaches and cut acres of natural forest for golf courses. Daufuskie natives are fighting for their way of life. "It may be a losing battle," said 72-year-old Louise Wilson, "but you gotta show some people you're not scared. You got to fight back and let them know you was here when they came."

Practice of CHARITY

THE TONGUES OF THE DUMB SING FOR JOY. The ability to articulate our feelings and thoughts clearly is a gift. We admire great orators who can take ordinary language and transform it into poetry. And yet, there are more than three million people in the U.S. who stutter. For fear of embarrassment, many of them are reluctant to speak, thereby severely limiting their ability to enter into relationships and to express their feelings. There are no answers to the causes of stuttering. However, the Stuttering Foundation of America provides the best information about the prevention of stuttering in children and the best treatment of stuttering available for teenagers and adults. Among the resources of the foundation are books, videos, educational conferences. For more information, write or call: Stuttering Foundation of America, PO Box 11749, Memphis TN 38111-0749; 800-992-9392.

Weekday Reading
1 Corinthians, chapters 5–10

SEPTEMBER 11, 1994
TWENTY-FOURTH SUNDAY IN ORDINARY TIME

READING I *Isaiah 50:5–9*

The Lord GOD has opened my ear,
　and I was not rebellious,
　　I turned not backward.
I gave my back to the smiters,
　and my cheeks to those who pulled out the beard;
I hid not my face
　from shame and spitting.
For the Lord GOD helps me;
　therefore I have not been confounded;
therefore I have set my face like a flint,
　and I know that I shall not be put to shame;
　　the one who vindicates me is near.
Who will contend with me?
　Let us stand up together.
Who is my adversary?
　Let my adversary come near to me.
Behold, the Lord GOD helps me;
　who will declare me guilty?

READING II *James 2:14–18*

What does it profit, my dear people, if someone claims to have faith but has not works? Is faith able to save? If a brother or sister is ill-clad and in lack of daily food, and one of you says to them, "Go in peace, be warmed and filled," without giving them the things needed for the body, what does it profit? So faith by itself, if it has no works, is dead.

But someone will say, "You have faith and I have works." Show me your faith apart from your works, and I by my works will show you my faith.

GOSPEL *Mark 8:27–35*

Jesus went on with his disciples to the villages of Caesarea Philippi; and on the way he asked his disciples, "Who do people say that I am?" And they told him, "John the Baptist; and others say, Elijah; and others one of the prophets." And Jesus asked them, "But who do you say that I am?" Peter answered him, "You are the Christ." And he charged them to tell no one about him.

And Jesus began to teach them that the Man of Heaven must suffer many things, and be rejected by the elders and the chief priests and the scribes, and be killed, and after three days rise again. And Jesus said this plainly. And Peter took him, and began to rebuke him. But turning and seeing his disciples, Jesus rebuked Peter, and said, "Get behind me, Satan! For you are thinking in human terms, and not in those of God."

And Jesus called to him the multitude with his disciples, and said to them, "Those who would come after me, let them deny themselves and take up their cross and follow me. For those who would save their life will lose it; and those who lose their life for my sake and the gospel's will save it."

The Triumph of the Cross
Wednesday, September 14, 1994

Numbers 21:4–9　Whoever gazed on the serpent received life.
Philippians 2:6–11　He accepted death on a cross.
John 3:13–17　God so loved the world. . . .

As the darkness of another autumn lowers around us, we lift high the shining cross. The means of the execution of a criminal has become the means of entering into eternal life. The wood of the cross is the ark that rescues us and the tree that feeds us.

REFLECTION

Today's gospel is often called "Peter's confession," and because it is a major event in the Gospel of Mark, it is placed almost exactly in the middle. The drama is passionate, as Jesus and his disciples face one another in a moment of revelation. Mark's account is terse, with none of the embellishments of Matthew (16:13–23) or (Luke 9:18–22). But the terseness adds to its impact. Jesus' heart must have leaped when Peter said the Twelve really did recognize him as "the Christ." (The "you" in "who do *you* say that I am," is plural: Jesus is asking the question of all of the disciples.)

Conversely Jesus' heart must have sunk at Peter's next reaction. Taking hold of Jesus, Peter began to "rebuke" him. This provokes Jesus to attack the disciples, but his attack is aimed at Peter: "Satan!" There has to be a recollection of his time of temptation after baptism (1:12–13). Here, within his own circle, after a major revelation, Jesus detects the hand of the one who would turn him aside from what he "must" do.

The disciples had seen "the Christ," but were unaware of what it meant for Jesus to be the Messiah. His first mention of an inevitably violent death at the hands of the religious officials is the plan of God. The disciples cannot yet see this, and it will take a long time for them to grasp that if God decides to approach and address the world in the person of this human Son, the world is going to react violently.

The awful truth is that any claimant to true discipleship needs to be prepared for similar treatment. Disciples had to be dislodged from their false sense of security. Their message of reconciliation to a loving God strikes at the very roots of the world's violent worship of itself. Its common language is violence and death.

1. The first reading is the third servant song from Isaiah (50:4–11). Read it as a probable meditation for Jesus himself. He would have known that a life of preaching could end violently. As a disciple of the 1990s, how do you face the antagonism toward the gospel message?

2. In Mark, Jesus predicts his passion three times: Read these three predictions in 8:31; 9:31 and 10:33. Note their location in the text. What happens before each prediction and after each one? What occasions Jesus' foreboding words and what is the reaction of the disciples?

Practice of FAITH

THE HOLY CROSS. Holy legend says that on September 14, St. Helena found the cross upon which Jesus died. The church celebrates the 14th by lifting high the sign of our salvation, that instrument of torture and death that brought us eternal life. A few generations after the resurrection, Christians began to use the cross for prayer. At first, they drew a simple cross on the east wall of their rooms to show the direction to face when praying for Christ's return. Later, the beautiful gesture of tracing the cross on one's body developed.

If you don't have a cross in your home, make or buy one. For Wednesday, decorate it with flowers and burn candles in front of it. Carefully make the sign of the cross on yourself. With your thumb make it on the foreheads of your children and spouse before they leave the house or go to sleep.

Practice of HOPE

FAITH WITHOUT WORKS IS DEAD. In the 1930s, at the height of the Great Depression, Dorothy Day was transformed by the suffering she saw around her. She founded a radical Catholic newspaper, started bread lines for the hungry, and opened up houses of hospitality for the homeless. Six decades later, the Catholic Worker movement still thrives, with houses in most of the country's major cities. Wrote Dorothy Day of its humble beginnings: "We were just sitting there talking when lines of people began to form, saying, 'We need bread.' We could not say, 'Go, be thou filled.' If there were six small loaves and a few fishes, we had to divide them."

Practice of CHARITY

WHO DO YOU SAY THAT I AM? The question Jesus asked his disciples nearly 2,000 years ago is the same question that is asked of each of us today. Our response to this question sheds light not only on who Jesus is, but also on who the church is. If Jesus is servant, then we, too, must be servants. If Jesus is Son of God, we, too, must be sons and daughters of God.

Take some time to answer the question this week. Peter's response is obviously our response as Christians. But what does it mean for Jesus to be the Christ, the Messiah? Jesus showed us the way. The cross is a reminder of what it means for us Christians to proclaim Jesus as the Messiah. We, too, are called to give of ourselves to those in need. This week, pick up and carry someone else's cross. Help the elderly person whose body is giving out. Visit someone who is sick. Speak up on behalf of someone who is unjustly treated. Give a kind word to someone who seems dejected.

Weekday Reading
1 Corinthians, chapters 11–15

SEPTEMBER 18, 1994
TWENTY-FIFTH SUNDAY IN ORDINARY TIME

READING I *Wisdom 2:12, 17–20*

Let us lie in wait for the righteous man,
because he is inconvenient to us and opposes
 our actions;
he reproaches us for sins against the law,
and accuses us of sins against our training.
Let us see if his words are true,
and let us test what will happen at the end of his life;
for if the righteous man is God's son, God will
 help him,
and will deliver him from the hand of his adversaries.
Let us test him with insult and torture,
that we may find out how gentle he is,
and make trial of his forbearance.
Let us condemn the righteous man to a
 shameful death,
for, according to what he says, he will be protected.

READING II *James 3:16 — 4:3*

Where jealousy and selfish ambition exist, there will be disorder and every vile practice. But the wisdom from above is first pure, then peaceable, gentle, open to reason, full of mercy and good fruits, without uncertainty or insincerity. And the harvest of righteousness is sown in peace by those who make peace.

What causes wars, and what causes fightings among you? Is it not your passions that are at war in your bodies? You desire and do not have; so you kill. And you covet and cannot obtain; so you fight and wage war. You do not have, because you do not ask. You ask and do not receive, because you ask wrongly, to spend it on your passions.

GOSPEL *Mark 9:30–37*

Jesus and his disciples went on from [the mountain] and passed through Galilee. And he would not have anyone know it; for he was teaching his disciples, saying to them, "The Man of Heaven will be delivered into human hands, and they will kill him; and when he is killed, after three days he will rise." But they did not understand the saying, and they were afraid to ask him.

And they came to Capernaum; and when he was in the house he asked them, "What were you discussing on the way?" But they were silent; for on the way they had discussed with one another who was the greatest. And Jesus sat down and called the twelve, and said to them, "Anyone who would be first must be last of all and servant of all." And Jesus took a child, and put it in the midst of them; and taking the child in his arms, he said to them, "Whoever receives one such child in my name receives me; and whoever receives me, receives not me but the one who sent me."

REFLECTION

Between Peter's confession of faith (last week's gospel) and the second passion prediction (this week's gospel), Mark has arranged important information for us that might explain the disciple's lack of understanding and fear.

Jesus has been transfigured (9:2–8), has mentioned "rising from the dead," (9:9–13) and has healed an epileptic child after the disciples had been unable to (9:14–29). They are then taken aside, privately, for more instruction. When the disciples failed to heal the child, Jesus reacts angrily: "faithless generation . . . how much longer do I have to be with you? . . . how long must I put up with you?"

Despite what Jesus has been trying to teach them, the disciples are still trying to fit Jesus and his mission into existing social and religious structures. Thus, the silly debate over who will sit where—that is, who is more important than whom in the reign of God. The disciples are "thinking in human terms, and not in those of God," (8:33). In human terms there has to be rank: the powerful and the powerless; slave and free; rich and poor, etc. The disciples assume that there must be rank in God's dominion. Wrong! A child in its trusting simplicity is the example of how things are reversed in the dominion of heaven. It is the one who serves (*diakonos*), the "slave," who becomes the ideal example. Jesus is the servant. The disciples are servants also, and this best describes their mission.

1. Why do you think the disciples have such a hard time figuring out who Jesus is and what he's really about?

2. What are the essential differences between the dominion of God and human power structures? How does your community reflect the standards and demands of God's rule? How do those demands come into conflict with civic duty and allegiance?

Practice of
FAITH

FAITH ON CAMPUS. Now that school is well underway, pray for students, especially those who have left home for college. Most Christian churches provide a ministry to students on college campuses; the Catholic campus ministry is often called a Newman Center. In 1883, Mrs. John C. Melvin invited some Catholic students from the University of Wisconsin to her home for dinner. The students wanted to grow in faith, so she suggested they form a club. They did. Later, one student formed another such club at the University of Pennsylvania. He named it the Newman Club, after Cardinal John Henry Newman, an English intellectual.

Today, 1,200 Catholic campus ministries serve 3,500 institutes of higher education in the United States. To help, write the Catholic Campus Ministry Association, 300 College Park, Dayton OH 45469. Or do as Mrs. Melvin did: Invite some hungry college kids over for a home-cooked meal!

Practice of
HOPE

THE HARVEST OF RIGHTEOUSNESS. Randy Kehler and Betsy Corner have been arrested, sent to jail, evicted from their home, and have had it sold out from under them—all because they believe that paying their federal taxes is "collaboration in crimes against humanity." Instead of sending money to the IRS that they know will fund nuclear weapons and wars, they donate their taxes to human service groups. Their convictions created a vast "community of conscience" that maintained a rotating vigil on their behalf outside their Massachusetts home and prompted many other people of faith to consider war-tax resistance. While in jail, Kehler found comfort in these words of former Czechoslovakian president Vaclav Havel: "Even a purely moral act that has no hope of any immediate and visible effect can gradually and indirectly, over time, gain in political significance."

Practice of
CHARITY

HIS DISCIPLES WENT ON FROM THERE. As the days shorten and the weather cools, we begin longing for the warmth of southern lands. Travel agents' phones are busy reserving airline tickets and hotel rooms in the Carribean and Mexico for the holidays, helping to make tourism the world's largest industry. Now is a good time for us to reflect on what it means to be responsible travelers. For one thing, it means being sensitive to the people who live in the countries we visit. The Center for Responsible Tourism is an organization that helps people develop this kind of sensitivity. Its Alliance on Responsible Travel provides members with information on how the people in host countries are affected by tourism. The Center also publishes a quarterly newsletter containing travel suggestions, background reports on specific places and their cultures, and suggested reading materials. For information write or call: North American Coordinating Center for Responsible Tourism, PO Box 827, San Anselmo CA 94979; 415-258-6594.

Weekday Reading
Proverbs, chapters 3 and 21; Ecclesiastes, chapters 1, 3 and 11

Autumn Ordinary Time

Behold! The harvest!

God brings us back to Zion;
we are like dreamers,
laughing, dancing,
with songs on our lips.

Other nations say:
"A new world of wonders!
The Lord is with them."
Yes, God works wonders.
Rejoice! Be glad!

Lord, bring us back
as water to thirsty land.
Those sowing in tears
reap, singing and laughing.

They left weeping, weeping,
casting the seed.
They come back singing, singing,
"Behold! The harvest!"

—*Psalm 126*

What tears you cry,
sower God, over us all.
But how you laugh in amazement
and what songs you sing
when there is some harvest.
Your saints from Adam and Eve,
from Moses and Miriam,
from Mary and Joseph,
until our own grandparents and parents,
and we too,
need your tears
and long to hear your laughter.
Harvest us home to sing your praise
forever and ever.
—*Prayer of the Season*

SEPTEMBER 25, 1994
TWENTY-SIXTH SUNDAY IN ORDINARY TIME

READING I *Numbers 11:25–29*

Then the LORD came down in the cloud and spoke to Moses, and took some of the spirit that was upon him and put it upon the seventy elders; and when the spirit rested upon them, they prophesied. But they did so no more.

Now two men remained in the camp, one named Eldad, and the other named Medad, and the spirit rested upon them; they were among those registered, but they had not gone out to the tent, and so they prophesied in the camp. And a youth ran and told Moses, "Eldad and Medad are prophesying in the camp." And Joshua the son of Nun, the minister of Moses, one of his chosen ones, said, "My lord Moses, forbid them." But Moses said to him, "Are you jealous for my sake? Would that all the LORD's people were prophets, that the LORD's Spirit would be given to them all!"

READING II *James 5:1–6*

Come now, you rich, weep and howl for the miseries that are coming upon you. Your riches have rotted and your garments are motheaten. Your gold and silver have rusted, and their rust will be evidence against you and will eat your flesh like fire. You have laid up treasures for the last days. Behold, the wages of the laborers who mowed your fields, which you kept back by fraud, cry out; and the cries of the harvesters have reached the ears of the Lord of hosts. You have lived on the earth in luxury and in pleasure; you have fattened your hearts in a day of slaughter. You have condemned, you have killed the righteous one, who does not resist you.

GOSPEL *Mark 9:38–43, 45, 47–48*

John said to Jesus, "Teacher, we saw someone casting out demons in your name, whom we forbade, because he was not following us." But Jesus said, "Do not forbid him; for no one who does a mighty work in my name will be able soon after to speak evil of me. For whoever is not against us is for us. For truly, I say to you, those who give you a cup of water to drink because you bear the name of Christ, will by no means lose their reward.

"Those who cause one of these little ones who believe in me to sin, it would be better for them if a great millstone were hung round their neck and they were thrown into the sea. And if your hand causes you to sin, cut it off; it is better for you to enter life maimed than with two hands to go to hell, to the unquenchable fire. And if your foot causes you to sin, cut it off; it is better for you to enter life lame than with two feet to be thrown into hell. And if your eye causes you to sin, pluck it out; it is better for you to enter the dominion of God with one eye than with two eyes to be thrown into hell, where their worm does not die, and the fire is not quenched."

Archangels Michael, Gabriel and Raphael
Thursday, September 29, 1994

Daniel 7:9–10, 13–14 A thousand thousand wait upon God.
Revelation 12:7–12 The warrior Michael defeated the dragon.
John 1:47–51 You will see heaven open, and angels descend.

The passage from summer to autumn represents the battle of sin and death against the kingdom of heaven. Jesus himself uses this mythological language to describe the reality of his battle against evil. And Christ conquers: Michael defeats the dragon, Gabriel announces the kingdom, Raphael heals the wounded.

REFLECTION

Moses is angry at God! Since Egypt, the Bible's premier prophet has had a whining people arouind his neck like a millstone. They would rather exchange their freedom for their former slavery and good square meals. Numbers 11:10–15 contains Moses' tirade against God, whose solution is to appoint seventy elders to share the work of Moses and ease his burden. Moses then cools off. Eldad and Medad also receive the spirit, though they did not follow the instructions that God gave the seventy. Those instructions were to meet at the tabernacle outside the camp. Some, including Joshua, object: Eldad and Medad did not follow the rules.

The disciples present Jesus with a similar situation. They resent others doing their commissioned job. Whoever was casting out demons in Jesus' name obviously knew of and believed in the power of his name. Like Moses, Jesus has to explain that God's spirit is not their private possession. John puts it well: "The wind blows where it chooses, and you hear the sound of it, but you do not know where it comes from or where it goes" (3:8). The one who uses the name of Jesus will soon appreciate the overpowering force of that name and person. To the ancient Hebrews, one's name was the totality of a person. One who knows a name has power. That's why the evil spirits are terrified of Jesus: He knows their names. He has power. The Spirit is given, not as a personal asset, but to allow God the freedom to be among people in ways they understand: in word and deed.

So the consequences of blocking the work of the Spirit are grave and are broached in the concluding verses of today's gospel. This is an instruction to the community of believers in very colorful language about how members should treat one another. The "little ones" are not children but plain, ordinary believers in the care of appointed shepherds. Nothing must come between them and God.

1. Read all of Numbers 11 for the full context of today's first reading. How do you feel about people, not of your community or church, who preach effectively in Jesus' name?

2. If we give our demons a name, we can begin to assert our power over them. What are your demons? Do you have the courage to name them?

Practice of
FAITH

HOLY ARCHANGELS. Three archangels are mentioned by name in the scriptures. Michael—whose name means "Who is like God?"—battles Lucifer. Look up Daniel 10:13 and 12:1, Jude 9 and Revelation 12:7. Gabriel, "the power of God," is mentioned in four episodes where God's might is displayed. Look up Daniel 8:16-26 and 9:21-27, Luke 1:11-20 and 1:26-38. Raphael, meaning "God has healed," is mentioned in the book of Tobit. Read chapters 5-12.

This Thursday we remember Michael, Gabriel and Raphael. As the days become shorter, and in many places colder, pray these words from Psalm 91: "For God will command the angels to guard you in all your ways. On their hands they will bear you up, so that you will not dash your foot against a stone."

Practice of
HOPE

THE WAGES OF THE LABORERS CRY OUT. Hilton Head Island, South Carolina, is a premier playground for the wealthy, with miles of golf courses, marinas, exclusive tennis clubs, and upscale shops and restaurants. But Doris Grant knows none of these things. She lives in a trailer at the end of an unpaved road. The minimum wage for maids, waitresses and groundskeepers is $4.85, and much of the work is seasonal. "People work two-and-a-half jobs," says Grant. "One to pay the bills, one for the children, and a little for yourself. It's like a slave market.

"I couldn't take it. You fight over a 15-cent raise—and then they spend $18,000 on a picture for the wall," she says, referring to a multi-million-dollar renovation at the Hyatt resort. But she and a group of friends have begun meeting in her front yard to confront the island's apartheid system. They call themselves a modern "underground railroad."

Practice of
CHARITY

BE AT PEACE WITH ONE ANOTHER. The history of the encounter of Europeans with Native American Indians is marked by broken promises, oppression, disease and betrayal. The descendants of the victims of this encounter, today's Native Americans, are the poorest of the poor in "our" country. They have the poorest general health and the shortest life expectancy of any Americans. They suffer the worst housing conditions, the highest unemployment and the lowest per capita income. Their struggle for justice continues. The Native American Rights Fund is dedicated to legal cases of major importance to Native peoples. It has had success in helping Native Americans regain their tribal sovereignty, their historic land and water rights, and the basic human rights that can help them regain their dignity. If you would like to help them in their struggle for justice, write Native American Rights Fund, 1506 Broadway, Boulder CO 80302.

Weekday Reading
Job—entire book

OCTOBER 2, 1994
TWENTY-SEVENTH SUNDAY IN ORDINARY TIME

READING I *Genesis 2:18–24*

The LORD God said, "It is not good that the man should be alone; I will make him a companion fit for him." So out of the ground the LORD God formed every beast of the field and every bird of the air, and brought them to the man to see what he would call them; and whatever the man called every living creature, that was its name. The man gave names to all cattle, and to the birds of the air, and to every beast of the field; but for the man there was not found a companion fit for him. So the LORD God caused a deep sleep to fall upon the man, and while he slept took one of his ribs and closed up its place with flesh; and the rib which the LORD God had taken from the man, the LORD God made into a woman and brought her to the man. Then the man said,

"This at last is bone of my bones
  and flesh of my flesh;
she shall be called a woman,
  because she was taken out of a man."

Therefore a man leaves his father and his mother and cleaves to his wife, and they become one flesh.

READING II *Hebrews 2:9–11*

We see Jesus, who for a little while was made lower than the angels, crowned with glory and honor because of the suffering of death, so that by the grace of God Jesus might taste death for everyone.

For it was fitting that God, for whom and by whom all things exist, in bringing many children to glory, should make the pioneer of their salvation perfect through suffering. For the one who sanctifies and those who are sanctified have all one origin. That is why he is not ashamed to call them brothers and sisters.

GOSPEL *Mark 10:2–16*

Pharisees came up and in order to test Jesus asked, "Is it lawful for a husband to divorce his wife?" Jesus answered them, "What did Moses command you?" They said, "Moses allowed a husband to write a certificate of divorce, and to put her away." But Jesus said to them, "For your hardness of heart Moses wrote you this commandment. But from the beginning of creation, 'God made them male and female.' 'For this reason a man shall leave his father and mother and be joined to his wife, and the two shall become one flesh.' So they are no longer two but one flesh. What therefore God has joined together, let no human being put asunder."

And in the house the disciples asked Jesus again about this matter. And he said to them, "Whatever man divorces his wife and marries another, commits adultery against her; and if she divorces her husband and marries another, she commits adultery."

And they were bringing children to him, that he might touch them, and his disciples rebuked them. But seeing it Jesus was indignant, and said to them, "Let the children come to me, do not hinder them; for to such belongs the dominion of God. Truly, I say to you, whoever does not receive the dominion of God like a child shall not enter it." And Jesus took them in his arms and blessed them, laying his hands upon them.

REFLECTION

Jesus is put to the test by the religious authorities about divorce. When questioned, Jesus frequently turns the tables, posing questions to those who would question him. Here, what begins as a legal question about divorce becomes Jesus' teaching about relationships—among human beings and between them and God.

In Jesus' time, divorce was all too often an irresponsible action of a husband against his wife, one that left the woman and children destitute. In criticizing divorce as his society practiced it, Jesus was criticizing a notion of marriage that regarded women and children as men's property. Instead, Jesus points out that human marriages must reflect the covenant that God has with Israel. Even though the law allowed divorce, Jesus is calling men to be responsible. There was no room for abandonment in that kind of marriage.

The creation account from Genesis provides the context in which to understand Jesus' thoughts on divorce. The covenant between God and humanity is in the very bones of human beings—a relationship of love that transcends social convention and mere law. Also, the fact that Eve is created from and set by Adam's side is an indication that she is an equal partner in marriage, not subservient.

God's relationship to humanity is a faithful partnership. Breaking faith is no small matter. Mark portrays Jesus as the embodiment of the faithful partnership between God and humanity, come what may. And Jesus reveals that in God's dominion, women and children are not the possessions of men but equal partners with them in humanity's covenant with God, with all the rights and responsibilities that such a covenant of faithfulness demands.

1. How does Jesus' teaching about faithfulness in marriage apply to other relationships that Christians have?

2. Like the Pharisees that Mark describes, certain members of the church today want to haggle over the tragedy of divorce and judge and punish divorced Christians. Jesus is not lenient on the issue of divorce in his teaching, but how do you think he would treat today's divorced people? What stops people in the church from doing the same?

Practice of FAITH

THERESA AND TERESA. In October we celebrate two saints with the same name spelled differently. Both were Carmelite nuns. The French Theresa of Lisieux (1873-97) loved life profoundly. She embodied goodness. Her autobiography, *The Story of a Soul,* was widely read in the early part of this century. A few years ago, a beautiful movie was made about her life. *Therese* is now available on video, too. Rent it and watch it this week.

The Spanish Teresa of Avila (1515-82) is a "doctor of the church"—the first woman so named. A great mystic, she wrote *Autobiography, The Way of Perfection,* and *Interior Castle*—books still studied today. She traveled all over Spain reforming convents, despite the opposition of many church officials.

Find out if a Carmelite monastery is near your home. If so, go pray with the nuns on October 15, Avila's feast day. (Lisieux's feast was yesterday.) Call for prayer times.

Practice of HOPE

SHE SHALL BE CALLED A WOMAN. The creation story in Genesis 2 has often been used as theological proof of the inferiority of women. The subjugation of women has led to an epidemic of sexual violence, an explosion in pornography, and a backlash against gains toward women's equality.

But the good news is that women have continued to proclaim equality and seek empowerment. There has been large growth in services and shelters for battered women, as well as healing centers for survivors of rape and incest. Many women and men exhibit an increased desire to understand the roots and effects of sexism, continuing the quest for economic justice for women and full participation in the church.

Practice of CHARITY

BY THE GRACE OF GOD. Pray the rosary this month as a way of committing yourself to respect life from womb to tomb. While meditating on the mysteries of the rosary, keep in mind the sacredness of life and intercede for those who suffer. Pray about a different life issue each week: abortion, capital punishment, homelessness and hunger, and militarism. As your fingers slip over the beads, may your prayer transform your heart and move you to action. When you are through praying, follow the Spirit in making a response. Your response may be as simple as writing a letter or as serious as nonviolent civil disobedience. But if you respond in love and from out of your prayer, your action will change at least one heart—yours—and maybe others, too.

Weekday Reading
Galatians, chapters 1–3

OCTOBER 9, 1994
TWENTY-EIGHTH SUNDAY IN ORDINARY TIME

READING I *Wisdom 7:7–11*

I prayed, and understanding was given me;
I called upon God, and the spirit of Wisdom
   came to me.
I preferred her to scepters and thrones,
and I accounted wealth as nothing in comparison
   with her.
Neither did I liken to her any priceless gem,
because all gold is but a little sand in her sight,
and silver will be accounted as clay before her.
I loved her more than health and beauty,
and I chose to have her rather than light,
because her radiance never ceases.
All good things came to me along with her,
and in her hands uncounted wealth.

READING II *Hebrews 4:12–13*

For the word of God is living and active, sharper than any two-edged sword, piercing to the division of soul and spirit, of joints and marrow, and discerning the thoughts and intentions of the heart. And before God no creature is hidden, but all are open and laid bare to the eyes of the one with whom [we have to reckon].

GOSPEL *Mark 10:17–30*

As Jesus was setting out on his journey, a man ran up and knelt before him, and asked him, "Good Teacher, what must I do to inherit eternal life?" And Jesus said to him, "Why do you call me good? No one is good but God alone. You know the commandments: 'Do not kill, Do not commit adultery, Do not steal, Do not bear false witness, Do not defraud, Honor your father and mother.'" And the man said to Jesus, "Teacher, all these I have observed from my youth." And Jesus looking upon him loved him, and said to him, "You lack one thing; go, sell what you have, and give to the poor, and you will have treasure in heaven; and come, follow me." At that saying his countenance fell, and he went away sorrowful; for he had great possessions.

And Jesus looked around and said to his disciples, "How hard it will be for those who have riches to enter the dominion of God!" And the disciples were amazed at his words. But Jesus said to them again, "Children, how hard it is to enter the dominion of God! It is easier for a camel to go through the eye of a needle than for the rich to enter the dominion of God." And they were exceedingly astonished, and said to him, "Then who can be saved?" Jesus looked at them and said, "With humankind it is impossible, but not with God; for all things are possible with God." Peter began to say to him, "Lo, we have left everything and followed you." Jesus said, "Truly, I say to you, there is no one who has left house or brothers or sisters or mother or father or children or lands, for my sake and for the gospel, who will not receive a hundredfold now in this time, houses and brothers and sisters and mothers and children and lands, with persecutions, and in the age to come eternal life."

REFLECTION

Wealth is a blessing. Certain books of the Bible are quite certain about that. The Book of Wisdom is one. However, today's first reading and gospel clarify this understanding.

"I accounted wealth as nothing in comparison to [Wisdom]." Wisdom is loved more than health and beauty. So, what—or who—is Wisdom? The scriptures contain a whole collection of books called "wisdom literature," or "the Writings." In these are recorded the wealth of experience and reflection on practical living which is truly conscious of the presence of God. When the one true God is daily acknowledged and thanked, nothing else can supplant that practical wisdom. But money and its attendants—power and influence—are God's closest rival for human hearts. It even figures in the temptations of Jesus!

So, when the young man, doubtless schooled in ancient wisdom, asks Jesus how his sanctity might be rounded out, the response cuts him to the quick. Jesus has no interest in condemning anyone—not even a wealthy man. But he is very interested in where this man's heart is truly invested: is it totally given to God, as he claims? Is his life really grounded in wisdom? Jesus' suggestion that he sell all provides an answer, not so much for Jesus who "loved him," but for the man whose life of strict observance had enabled him to leave unresolved the more fundamental issues of himself and God.

The man has his "self-image" shattered by Jesus, not maliciously, but to clear the ground for more profound radical growth. Sad as he may be, the man is now in a position to accept or reject, with his heart, a life of true wisdom. Elsewhere, change of heart or "repentance" might describe this scene. He had done nothing evil. He had simply failed to examine the real basis of his impressive personal claims.

1. Jesus says it will be difficult for the rich to enter the dominion of heaven. Did he mean impossible? If you are wealthy, personally or as a community, what questions does this gospel raise for you?

2. Who is first in your life: God or the bank account? Who is first in the life of your parish?

Practice of **FAITH**

HOLY WISDOM. Look again at the first reading. Do you notice how Holy Wisdom, an image for God in this scripture, is female? Although God does not have gender, our tradition is heavy on male images of God: Lord, King, Father. Today we are treated to one of the feminine images of God that the Bible has preserved for us from ancient times.

There are other feminine images of God in the Bible. It is important that our images of God never become too fixed—that is idolatry. By fixing solely on male images for God and ignoring the female ones, we run the risk of thinking we have God all figured out. We don't.

Get to know the feminine images of God. Virginia Ramey Mollenkott wrote a scholarly book titled *The Divine Feminine*. It was published in 1988 by The Crossroad Publishing Company, 370 Lexington Avenue, New York NY 10017.

Practice of **HOPE**

SELL WHAT YOU HAVE AND GIVE TO THE POOR. Dr. Janelle Goetcheus had a lucrative suburban medical practice. But in 1976 she abandoned it to move into one of Washington, D.C.'s, poorest neighborhoods. She lives among and heals the homeless poor, who suffer from infections, foot problems, AIDS, and a variety of other illnesses related to exposure to the elements and poor nutrition.

"I find that just being with them is a gift to my soul," said Goetcheus. "That doesn't mean I don't ache. My inner self just aches when I come out of a shelter. . . . But what gives me deepest joy is the sense that I'm trying to listen to God and be obedient to what God is asking."

Practice of **CHARITY**

THE WORD OF GOD IS LIVING AND ACTIVE. Most of us have access to religious education and Catholic literature in our parishes. This is not necessarily true for the people of western Alaska. The only link that many of these rural people have to any religious education is the radio. Station KNOM, founded by Father Jim Poole, SJ, is committed to providing religious education, spiritual inspiration and information over the air waves. This tremendous resource of Catholic evangelization is run by private donations and a full-time volunteer staff. In this mission land of the U.S. it is good to know that "the word of God is living and active" for the people in the 85 scattered villages of the region. KNOM welcomes donations. If you would like to make one, send your check or money order to Alaska Radio Mission–KNOM, Box 988, Nome AK 99762-9987.

Weekday Reading
Galatians, chapters 45; Ephesians, chapters 1–2

OCTOBER 16, 1994
TWENTY-NINTH SUNDAY IN ORDINARY TIME

READING I   *Isaiah 53:10–11*

Yet it was the will of the LORD to bruise this servant;
   the LORD has put him to grief;
making himself an offering for sin,
   the servant shall see offspring and shall
     prolong his days;
the will of the LORD shall prosper in the hand
   of the servant,
   who shall see the fruit of the travail of his soul
     and be satisfied;
by his knowledge shall the righteous one, my servant,
   make many to be accounted righteous;
   my servant shall bear their iniquities.

READING II   *Hebrews 4:14–16*

Since then we have a great high priest who has passed through the heavens, Jesus, the Son of God, let us hold fast our confession. For we have not a high priest who is unable to sympathize with our weaknesses, but one who in every respect has been tempted as we are, yet without sin. Let us then with confidence draw near to the throne of grace, that we may receive mercy and find grace to help in time of need.

GOSPEL   *Mark 10:35–45*

James and John, the sons of Zebedee, came forward to Jesus, saying, "Teacher, we want you to do for us whatever we ask of you." And Jesus said to them, "What do you want me to do for you?" And they said to him, "Grant us to sit, one at your right hand and one at your left, in your glory." But Jesus said to them, "You do not know what you are asking. Are you able to drink the cup that I drink, or to be baptized with the baptism with which I am baptized?" And they said to him, "We are able." And Jesus said to them, "The cup that I drink you will drink; and with the baptism with which I am baptized, you will be baptized; but to sit at my right hand or at my left is not mine to grant, but it is for those for whom it has been prepared." And when the ten heard it, they began to be indignant at James and John. And Jesus called them to him and said to them, "You know that those who are supposed to rule over the Gentiles are domineering, and their mighty ones exercise authority over them. But it shall not be so among you; but whoever would be great among you must be your servant, and whoever would be first among you must be slave of all. For the Man of Heaven also came not to be served but to serve, and to give his life as a ransom for many."

REFLECTION

Once again disciples are off on the wrong track. This time it's James and John. They want Jesus to decide some order of precedence for them within the community of the disciples and in relation to Jesus in his "glory." In some ways they resemble the rich man from last week. They are asking for more than they know, because there is a condition attached to what they seek and they are not yet aware of it. They will need to "drink the cup" and "be baptized with the baptism" of their leader.

We read this gospel today with the poetry of Isaiah's fourth servant song (the first reading) still reverberating. It's the song of the suffering servant who bears all persecution silently. It adds color to our image of Jesus in this liturgy and describes the contents of "the cup," and the nature of "the baptism" to which Jesus refers. To place themselves in the running for the exaltation they seek, the disciples will have to tread a strange path. It leads to the cross, not to the kind of glory envisioned in worldly terms. James and John create a disturbance among the rest with their concern. But Jesus uses the occasion to teach them all about one of the truly mysterious facts relating to the dominion of heaven. Those who seek "glory" must become *douloi*, slaves, the disenfranchised, powerless servants of whoever requires their ministrations.

1. The whole fourth servant song is Isaiah 52:13—53:12. Pick out the characteristics of the servant which best fit your understanding of Jesus. Which features characterize your discipleship most closely?

2. The cup and the baptism create a share in Jesus' ministry and that includes a cross. How does your baptism and participation in the eucharist manifest the passion of Jesus in your life and that of your community?

Practice of FAITH

WE HAVE A GREAT HIGH PRIEST. Episcopalians have a problem: They have many more priests than they have parishes. Catholics have a problem: They have many more parishes than they have priests. (Or, more accurately, some parishes have no full-time priest; other parishes fewer priests than they need.) All Christians have a solution: Jesus Christ is the High Priest, the head of every parish, present in every gathering of the baptized who belong to him. Strong faith in Christ and openness to the Holy Spirit will solve any of our leadership problems.

Invite your parish priest or minister over for dinner sometime this month. Or write a note of support. In addition to showing gratitude, don't forget to be honest about what you think or how you feel about important issues. Be candid, but be respectful. Remember that you can be respectful of a person's authority without being subservient to that person.

Practice of HOPE

THAT WE MAY RECEIVE MERCY AND FIND GRACE. Four years ago Leroy was in a coma; his doctors gave his family the choice of whether or not to keep him alive. They chose against sustaining him, but somehow Leroy went on living. "The head doctor, which is God," Leroy said later, "saw fit to override their decision and give me another chance at life."

Leroy's is just one of many "resurrection stories" at Joseph's House, a home in Washington, D.C., for HIV-positive homeless men. Compassion, forgiveness, and grace abound among people who before knew only isolation and fear.

Dr. David Hilfiker, the physician who lives at Joseph's House with his family, said, "AIDS destroys the fantasy of independence, which is a problem for all of us. When we get rid of the fantasy, it allows for community." Added Leroy, "We are all learning to be as one in this house".

Practice of CHARITY

GRACE TO HELP IN TIME OF NEED. As the winter months approach, it is a time to be mindful of the elderly and the poor who need help to winterize their homes. Become involved with a neighborhood or parish group who work with the poor, or organize a group through your parish to work on a Saturday at putting storm windows or panels in place, installing insulation or putting weather stripping around doors. If your area does not have a need, see if an inner-city parish does.

A group that works year round to provide the poor with housing is Habitat for Humanity. They rehab abandoned buildings or construct new ones. To see if Habitat has a project in your area, write: Habitat for Humanity, 121 Habitat Street, Americus GA 31709-3498.

Weekday Reading
Ephesians, chapters 3–4

OCTOBER 23, 1994
THIRTIETH SUNDAY IN ORDINARY TIME

READING I   *Jeremiah 31:7–9*

For thus says the LORD:
"Sing aloud with gladness for Jacob,
   and raise shouts for the chief of the nations;
proclaim, give praise, and say,
   'The LORD has saved the remnant of Israel,
    the people of the LORD.'
Behold, I will bring them from the north country,
   and gather them from the farthest parts
    of the earth,
among them the blind and the lame,
   the woman with child
    and her who is in labor, together;
   a great company, they shall return here.
With weeping they shall come,
   and with consolations I will lead them back,
I will make them walk by brooks of water,
   in a straight path in which they shall not stumble;
for I am as a father to Israel,
   and Ephraim is as my first-born."

READING II   *Hebrews 5:1–6*

Every high priest chosen from among the people is appointed to act on behalf of the people in relation to God, to offer gifts and sacrifices for sins. The high priest can deal gently with the ignorant and wayward, since he himself is beset with weakness. Because of this he is bound to offer sacrifice for his own sins as well as for those of the people. And one does not take the honor upon himself, but is called by God, just as Aaron was.

So also Christ did not exalt himself to be made a high priest, but was appointed by the one who said to him,

"You are my Son,
today I have begotten you";

as God says also in another place,

"You are a priest for ever,
after the order of Melchizedek."

GOSPEL   *Mark 10:46–52*

Jesus and his disciples came to Jericho; and as he was leaving Jericho with his disciples and a great multitude, Bartimaeus, a blind beggar, the son of Timaeus, was sitting by the roadside. And hearing that it was Jesus of Nazareth, he began to cry out and say, "Jesus, Son of David, have mercy on me!" And many rebuked him, telling him to be silent; but he cried out all the more, "Son of David, have mercy on me!" And Jesus stopped and said, "Call him." And they called the blind man, saying to him, "Take heart; rise, he is calling you." And throwing off his mantle he sprang up and came to Jesus. And Jesus said to him, "What do you want me to do for you?" And the blind man said to him, "Rabbi, let me receive my sight." And Jesus said to him, "Go your way; your faith has made you well." And immediately he received his sight and followed Jesus on the way.

REFLECTION

Death was to be the fate of Jeremiah (Jeremiah 26) because he prophesied the downfall of Jerusalem, the Temple, the king and the deportation of the people. Not a popular message—but it happened! Today's Jeremiah extract is from his promise of restoration from "The Book of Consolation" (Jeremiah 30:1—31:40). Among the restored exiles will be the blind and the lame. This is a prophecy about a new life that excludes no one.

So Jesus' final healing miracle in Mark is the giving of sight to Bartimaeus. Six of the 16 chapters of this gospel tell of the passion and resurrection of Jesus. The healing of this blind beggar is strategically placed immediately before the passion account. It infers a question: What are you going to see in this forthcoming tale of woe and apparent defeat? The question Jesus posed to his disciples, "Who do *you* say I am?" (8:29) is here rephrased in terms of blindness and sight about the passion. Your answer depends on what you see and how you see it. So the giving of sight to Bartimaeus at this juncture is more than *just* a miracle. It is also a literary device of Mark to prepare us to see the events that follow in their true light.

Look at Mark's closure to the story. Jesus had said, "What do you want from me?"—a question for all would-be disciples. Bartimaeus, not with physical sight —he's still blind—can at least recognize Jesus as "Rabbi." He wants to receive his sight. Then Jesus' words are interesting: "Go *your* way." The blind man's power of faith, in the presence of Jesus, bestows a faculty to see more than a rabbi. Bartimaeus did not go *his* way, he "followed Jesus on *the* way." He joined the party headed for Jerusalem and whatever awaited Jesus. His seeing makes a true disciple of him, and he joins the ranks of Jeremiah, Jesus, his original disciples and many followers since, all of whom have seen as God sees (Mark 8:31–33) and become caught up in God's burgeoning dominion.

1. Put yourself in Bartimaeus's place. What do you ask of Jesus?

2. In what areas of your life are you blind to God's working? In what areas of communal life is your parish blind to God's working?

Practice of FAITH

THE JESUS PRAYER. Bartimaeus's prayer, "Jesus, Son of David, have mercy on me!" has been used for centuries by Christians. Another version of it is: "Jesus Christ, Son of the living God, have mercy on me, a sinner." Repeating either of these phrases over and over again can lead you into a deep prayer.

Go someplace quiet. Sit comfortably. Pace the words with your breathing. Breathe in and hold your breath gently: "Jesus, Son of David," or "Jesus Christ, Son of the living God." Slowly breathe out: "have mercy on me," or "have mercy on me, a sinner."

If you want to try this kind of prayer with a group, get a copy of *Catholic Household Blessings and Prayers*. (You may order one by calling Liturgy Training Publications toll-free at 1-800-933-1800.) The Litany of the Holy Name on page 335 gives various names for Jesus. One person speaks the name and all answer, "Have mercy on us."

Practice of HOPE

JESUS, HAVE MERCY ON ME. South Africa's Archbishop Desmond Tutu spoke of "butterflies in my tummy" when he marched on the parliament to demand an end to apartheid. But, he said, his fear was overcome by the hope of his people.

Tutu recalled an evening he shared with the villagers of Mogopa, whose homes were going to be bulldozed by the government the following morning. Clinics, churches, and shops had already been demolished in the effort to convert the spot to a "white area," and the villagers were going to be moved out at gunpoint. While Tutu was praying with them, in the middle of the night, a humble man got up and prayed, "God, thank you for loving us."

Practice of CHARITY

LET ME RECEIVE MY SIGHT. Those who wear eye glasses know the importance of being able to see clearly. Some of our fondest memories of life include seeing breath-taking vistas or our baby's first step. The joy that comes from the gift of sight allows us to transcend the present moment. But there are many who can't afford new glasses or who don't have access to optometrists. The Christian Medical & Dental Society's Mission Group wants everyone to see clearly. They clean and repair old eye glasses and lenses and determine the prescription. Then they send the glasses and lenses to Mexico, the Caribbean and Central America. There, people who need glasses are given a free examination to determine the proper correction. They are then fitted with the donated glasses. If you're about to change your prescription or dispose of old glasses, consider giving them to CMDS for re-use by the poor in these Third World countries. Just send them to Mission Group/CMDS, 12281 SW 28th Street, Miami FL 33175. Or, if you are willing to organize a collection box, write or call Christian Medical & Dental Society, PO Box 830689, Richardson TX 75083-0689; 214-783-8384.

Weekday Reading
Ephesians, chapters 4–5

OCTOBER 30, 1994
THIRTY-FIRST SUNDAY IN ORDINARY TIME

READING I *Deuteronomy 6:2–6*

[Moses said to the people,]

"Fear the LORD your God, you and your children and your children's children, by keeping all the statutes and the commandments of the LORD, which I command you, all the days of your life, that your days may be prolonged. Hear therefore, O Israel, and be careful to do them; that it may go well with you, and that you may multiply greatly, as the LORD, the God of your forebears, has promised you, in a land flowing with milk and honey.

"Hear, O Israel: the LORD our God is one LORD; and you shall love the LORD your God with all your heart, and with all your soul, and with all your might. And these words which I command you this day shall be upon your heart."

READING II *Hebrews 7:23–28*

The former priests were many in number, because they were prevented by death from continuing in office; but Jesus holds his priesthood permanently, because he continues for ever. Consequently he is able for all time to save those who draw near to God through him, living always to make intercession for them.

For it was fitting that we should have such a high priest, holy, blameless, unstained, separated from sinners, exalted above the heavens, who has no need, like those high priests, to offer sacrifices daily, first for his own sins and then for those of the people; he did this once for all when he offered up himself. Indeed, the law appoints as high priests weak human beings, but the word of the oath, which came later than the law, appoints a Son who has been made perfect for ever.

GOSPEL *Mark 12:28–34*

One of the scribes came up to Jesus and asked him, "Which commandment is the first of all?" Jesus answered, "The first is, 'Hear, O Israel: The Lord our God, the Lord is one; and you shall love the Lord your God with all your heart, and with all your soul, and with all your mind, and with all your strength.' The second is this, 'You shall love your neighbor as yourself.' There is no other commandment greater than these." And the scribe said to Jesus, "You are right, Teacher; you have truly said that God is one, and there is no other but God; and to love God with all the heart, and with all the understanding, and with all the strength, and to love one's neighbor as oneself, is much more than all whole burnt offerings and sacrifices." And seeing that the scribe had answered wisely, Jesus said to him, "You are not far from the dominion of God." And after that no one dared to ask him any question.

All Saints' Day
Tuesday, November 1, 1994

Revelation 7:2–4, 9–14 The crowd stood before the Lamb.
1 John 3:1–3 We shall see God.
Matthew 5:1–12 How blest are the poor in spirit.

We welcome the winter with a harvest homecoming. All the people of God are gathered into the new Jerusalem to begin the supper of the Lamb. The poor, the mourning, the meek and the lowly remove their masks and see themselves as they truly are: the beloved children of God, the saints of heaven.

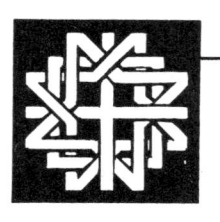

All Souls' Day
Wednesday, November 2, 1994

Daniel 12:1–3 The dead will rise to shine like stars.
Revelation 21:1–7 There will be no more death or sorrow.
Matthew 25:1–13 The bridegroom comes. Go out to meet him.

In the northern hemisphere, nature shows forth the awesome beauty of the harvest. Yesterday we rejoiced in the harvest of the saints. Today we reflect on what made this harvest possible: self-sacrifice, completed labors and death.

REFLECTION

Jesus has reached his journey's destination—Jerusalem. Today's gospel finds him in conversation with the Sadducees, who denied the resurrection of the dead and thus opposed the Pharisees. A trap has been set to catch Jesus teaching something unacceptable to the Law. But Jesus ends up preaching the Law in its totality, and with power.

It's an unusual scene in that the scribe is friendly, admiring the way Jesus handled the Sadducees. Perhaps the scribe was a Pharisee! Jesus is affirmed and supported by a member of a group that the gospels usually depict as "the bad guys." But not all scribes and Pharisees opposed Jesus and his message (see Acts 23:6–11).

Mark notes the effect of the exchange between Jesus and the scribe: "after that no one dared ask him any questions." The fact that even among the official religious leaders, usually identified as plotters against Jesus, there were people "not far from the dominion of God" shows how the gospel knows no bounds. Recall Nicodemus in John (3:1–10; 19:39), the Roman officer in Luke (7:1–10), and the tax collector in Matthew (9:9)—all people unlikely to be holy, but nonetheless singled out by Jesus as people who had faith. They heard the voice and message of Jesus and responded in action described here by the scribe: love of God, love of neighbor as self!

1. Jesus said, "those who are not against us are for us" (Mark 9:40). But for stories like today's story in Mark we might consign "scribes and Pharisees" to the category of "bad guys." This would be unjust. How do you identify those not of your community, perhaps not of your faith or style of believing who are, in fact, allies in loving God and their neighbor?

2. Jesus identifies a first and a second commandment: love of God, love of neighbor. But can you love God and not your neighbor? What actions proclaim these two aspects of the one love?

Practice of **FAITH**

SAINTS AND SOULS. After celebrating on November 1 the glory of the new Jerusalem, and the victory of those who have won the race by practicing faith, we turn our prayers to those we know who have died. From November 2 until Advent begins, we remember the dead. At church, you may have the opportunity to write the names of your deceased loved ones in the book of the names of the dead. At home, place their pictures or other mementos of them near your cross. Light a seven-day candle, too.

When you pray, say the names of your loved ones who have died, and then offer this prayer: "Eternal rest grant unto them, O Lord, and let the perpetual light shine upon them. May their souls, and all the souls of the faithful departed, through the mercy of God rest in peace. Amen."

Practice of **HOPE**

WITH ALL YOUR HEART. Black historian Vincent Harding likens the "cloud of witnesses" mentioned in Hebrews 11 and 12 to "a great cheering squad for us." He preaches:

"No excuse for drooping—at least not for long. No excuse for not running—or at least walking strong. 'Cause we are surrounded. So let's get down to some real long-distance walking and running—and maybe even some flying, like eagles, in due time. That's our tradition. That's our destiny. That's our hope. So go right on, sisters and brothers: walk in the light, run with the cloud, mount up on wings."

As we commemorate All Saints' Day this week, we remember that vast, encouraging "cloud of witnesses": all those who have gone before in the pursuit of justice, freedom and peace; loving God with all their heart.

Practice of **CHARITY**

YOU SHALL LOVE YOUR NEIGHBOR AS YOURSELF. We Christians have a powerful mandate, and it is not optional. It is the directive Jesus gave us to follow in our daily lives. We hear it at least once a year in the Sunday readings; we've heard it countless other times from parents and grandparents. It's the Golden Rule: Do unto others as you would have them do unto you." Loving others means ultimately laying down your life for them—either literally or metaphorically. But the spirit of self-sacrifice grows out of simple kindnesses that we practice daily.

For example, it is so easy to fall into the trap of talking negatively about another, perhaps destroying his or her reputation. Yet we may do this without thinking. This week, let us all be mindful about how we speak about others and walk away from any harmful gossip session we may encounter. Instead, let us repeat to ourselves the words of the Golden Rule as we heard them from our parents, our grandparents, and from Jesus himself.

Weekday Reading
Philippians, chapters 1–4

NOVEMBER 6, 1994
THIRTY-SECOND SUNDAY IN ORDINARY TIME

READING I *1 Kings 17:10–16*

So Elijah arose and went to Zarephath; and when he came to the gate of the city, behold, a widow was there gathering sticks; and he called to her and said, "Bring me a little water in a vessel, that I may drink." And as she was going to bring it, he called to her and said, "Bring me a morsel of bread in your hand." And she said, "As the LORD your God lives, I have nothing baked, only a handful of meal in a jar, and a little oil in a cruse; and now, I am gathering a couple of sticks, that I may go in and prepare it for myself and my son, that we may eat it, and die." And Elijah said to her, "Fear not; go and do as you have said; but first make me a little cake of it and bring it to me, and afterward make for yourself and your son. For thus says the LORD the God of Israel, 'The jar of meal shall not be spent, and the cruse of oil shall not fail, until the day that the LORD sends rain upon the earth.'" And she went and did as Elijah said; and she, and he, and her household ate for many days. The jar of meal was not spent, neither did the cruse of oil fail, according to the word of the LORD which the LORD spoke by Elijah.

READING II *Hebrews 9:24–28*

Christ has entered, not into a sanctuary made with hands, a copy of the true one, but into heaven itself, now to appear in the presence of God on our behalf. Nor was it to offer himself repeatedly, as the high priest enters the Holy Place yearly with blood not his own; for then he would have had to suffer repeatedly since the foundation of the world. But as it is, Christ has appeared once for all at the end of the age to put away sin by the sacrifice of himself. And just as it is appointed for human beings to die once, and after that comes judgment, so Christ, having been offered once to bear the sins of many, will appear a second time, not to deal with sin but to save those who are eagerly waiting for him.

GOSPEL *Mark 12:38–44*

In his teaching Jesus said, "Beware of the scribes, who like to go about in long robes, and to have salutations in the market places and the best seats in the synagogues and the places of honor at feasts, who devour widows' houses and for a pretense make long prayers. They will receive the greater condemnation."

And Jesus sat down opposite the treasury, and watched the multitude putting money into the treasury. Many rich people put in large sums. And a poor widow came, and put in two copper coins, which make a penny. And Jesus summoned his disciples, and said to them, "Truly, I say to you, this poor widow has put in more than all those who are contributing to the treasury. For they all contributed out of their abundance; but she out of her poverty has put in everything she had, her whole living."

The Dedication of St. John Lateran, the Cathedral of Rome
Wednesday, November 9, 1994

1 Kings 8:22–23, 27–30   Heaven cannot hold you.
Ephesians 2:19–22   You are God's temple.
John 4:19–24   Do not worship in buildings, but in Spirit.

The kingdom of the saints is a temple of the Spirit. Human flesh is God's dwelling place. In November, a season of ingathering, we assemble in the Spirit. Our own flesh and blood is becoming God's holy temple. All creation is becoming Jerusalem.

REFLECTION

Today's gospel draws attention to the difference between religion-for-religion's-sake and faith rooted in human dependence on God.

The scribe in last week's gospel agreed with Jesus and was portrayed in a positive light. The scribes in this week's gospel though are examples of self-indulgent illusion. God has no desire for such religion. Religious posturing is no substitute for a change of heart that turns one toward God.

Contrasted to the scribes is the widow. She knows she is dependent on God and that religion is a matter of relationship with God, not posturing. The reign of God has dawned in her life. Her worship is true. Out of her poverty, the widow gives "her whole living"— her very self symbolized in the copper coins.

In Jesus' day, widows—like divorced women and orphaned children—were outcasts. They lived in a man's world without a man. Although the religious tradition of Israel taught that widows and orphans were the responsibility of those who could afford to help them, the fact that such outcasts often did not behave in socially accepted ways was an excuse for many self-righteous religious people not to help them. But Jesus makes it clear that the simple trust of widows and orphans is more acceptable to God than all the learning of the scribes and the self-indulgence that this learning breeds.

1. Read about other widows and rich people: Luke 18:1–8, Luke 16:19–31; Luke 19:1–10. Who are the widows in our day?

2. What style of giving do you use to further the mission of Jesus? Do you give what's left over and will not be missed or is your commitment—personal and communal—from every level of your life?

Practice of FAITH

VISITING THE CEMETERY. Because we know that death is not the end of life, it is not morbid for Christians to visit the graves of their loved ones who have died. It is a good practice of faith to visit the cemetery in November, when the earth itself seems to be dying and light and warmth are in short supply.

In some countries in Europe, tombstones have little basins in them to hold holy water, and people burn seven-day candles in red glass containers anchored to the grave. The water and the fire are reminders that in baptism, we die with Christ, and so are to be raised up with Christ, too.

Remember Mary Magdalene and the other Marys going to visit Christ's tomb. Confident that what they found we will find, make pilgrimages to the graves of your loved ones this month.

Practice of HOPE

FEAR NOT. During the height of the civil rights movement, a Montgomery, Alabama, black Baptist youth choir was visiting at the Highlander Center in Tennessee, a place that has been a catalyst for justice for more than six decades. Whites—both deputies and people who had been deputized for a raid—came in with guns and demanded that the youths turn out the lights. The air grew tense as the young people refused to comply with what would have made them even more vulnerable than they already were. Suddenly, from a corner, one of the young people began quietly singing "We Shall Overcome." Others joined in, and soon the church was filled with their voices. A new verse was added to the song that night: "We are not afraid. . . . " The infuriated whites left, disarmed by the power of a song.

Practice of CHARITY

TWO COPPER COINS. What an amazing woman! The woman Jesus speaks about in today's gospel gave all that she had. She understood the gospel message. Modern day examples of people who have followed the gospel in this way are Dorothy Day, a founder of the Catholic Worker, and many sisters from religious communities. Such detachment from material goods brings with it a freedom that is hard to imagine.

We could practice that detachment in another way by tithing—giving ten percent or some other significant portion of our income to those less fortunate. Christian tithing is a stewardship of time, talent and treasure. Explore with your family what tithing would mean to your way of living. You may not be able to give the full ten percent, but perhaps you could work toward this goal. You may want to divide the total so that some goes to your parish, some to an agency that helps the poor and some to the poor directly. As you do so, the freedom of the poor widow will be yours.

Weekday Reading
Titus—entire book; Philomen—entire book

NOVEMBER 13, 1994
THIRTY-THIRD SUNDAY IN ORDINARY TIME

READING I   *Daniel 12:1–3*

At that time shall arise Michael, the great ruler who has charge of your people. And there shall be a time of trouble, such as never has been since there was a nation till that time; but at that time your people shall be delivered, everyone whose name shall be found written in the book. And many of those who sleep in the dust of the earth shall awake, some to everlasting life, and some to shame and everlasting contempt. And those who are wise shall shine like the brightness of the firmament; and those who turn many to righteousness, like the stars for ever and ever.

READING II   *Hebrews 10:11–14, 18*

And every priest stands at the daily service, offering repeatedly the same sacrifices, which can never take away sins. But when Christ had offered for all time a single sacrifice for sins, he sat down at the right hand of God, then to wait until his enemies should be made a stool for his feet. For by a single offering Christ has perfected for all time those who are sanctified. Where there is forgiveness of these, there is no longer any offering for sin.

GOSPEL   *Mark 13:24–32*

[At that time Jesus said,]

"In those days, after that tribulation, the sun will be darkened, and the moon will not give its light, and the stars will be falling from heaven, and the powers in the heavens will be shaken. And then they will see the Man of Heaven coming in clouds with great power and glory. And then he will send out the angels, and gather his elect from the four winds, from the ends of the earth to the ends of heaven.

"From the fig tree learn its lesson: as soon as its branch becomes tender and puts forth its leaves, you know that summer is near. So also, when you see these things taking place, you know that he is near, at the very gates. Truly, I say to you, this generation will not pass away before all these things take place. Heaven and earth will pass away, but my words will not pass away.

"But of that day or that hour no one knows, not even the angels in heaven, nor the Son, but only the Father."

REFLECTION

In Mark's "apocalyptic" chapter 13, Jesus describes in the language of parable how dramatic will be the effect of the final revelation of the Man of Heaven. The whole cosmos will be jolted by it.

For those who have heard and whole-heartedly responded to the word of Jesus and the dawning dominion of God, the question, "When?" naturally occurs. They have already relinquished old ways of seeing, hearing, believing and living; they have already undergone some shattering changes. Whole lives have been re-oriented because of Jesus' presence. Ultimately everything will be shaken at its roots. It will be as if the moon were to grow dark and the stars were to fall out of the sky.

This style of language made sense to those for whom the Gospel of Mark was first written. They witnessed growing tensions between Christians and Jews, as well as the destruction of the Temple by the Romans in the year 70. But the apocalyptic catastrophes recorded here are more cosmic and universal for a very important reason. The specific disasters that Mark's church experienced were translated into universal ones so that every age—including our own—would be encouraged to see in its own events that this world is passing and that the dominion of God is dawning.

The key to understanding the meaning of any catastrophe is the passion and resurrection of Jesus. That's why Mark's apocalyptic language could be read as a commentary on Christ's crucifixion—that original time when sun and moon darkened, although it was day, and when the earth was shaken to its foundations. That is the pivotal event that jolts us into a new way of living, and changes us forever.

1. How is your own ongoing conversion a parable of what God plans for the whole of creation?

2. How would you describe the upheaval in your own life caused by your vibrant faith? What's the major difference between your old life and your new life in Christ?

Practice of FAITH

WITH CLOUDS DESCENDING. Charles Wesley captured many of the images of the scriptures of these last weeks of the year in a beautiful hymn, "Lo, He Comes with Clouds Descending":

"Lo, he comes with clouds descending/once for favored sinners slain. Thousand, thousand saints attending/swell the triumph of his train. Alleluia! Alleluia! Alleluia! God appears on earth to reign.

"Yea, amen, let all adore thee/high on thine eternal throne. Savior, take the power and glory/claim the kingdom for thine own. Lord, come quickly! Lord, come quickly! Lord, come quickly! Everlasting God, come down!"

Have you ever written a poem or a song that expresses your faith? With the cold weather perhaps keeping you inside, this is a good time to try it.

Practice of HOPE

SHINE LIKE THE BRIGHTNESS OF THE FIRMAMENT. Brazilian archbishop Dom Helder Camara is one of God's gems. For decades, he has tirelessly advocated justice for the poor. In response, some of the country's rich and powerful citizens once hired a professional assassin to kill him. The killer walked through Camara's small flower garden and arrived at his simple home. When the humble and frail-looking archbishop himself answered the door, the killer became flustered. He stated his purpose, and Camara told him he should go ahead and carry out his mission. "No," said the man, astonished at the small man's courage. "You are one of the Lord's." And he left.

Practice of CHARITY

GOD WILL SEND OUT ANGELS. The readings speak of the hope that comes with the coming of the end. This hope of the world yet to come is what motivates us to minister in the world here around us. This weekend the collection for the Campaign for Human Development will be taken up. This is the anti-poverty, social justice program of the U.S. Catholic Bishops. Its goal is to address the root causes of poverty in America through promotion and support of community-controlled, self-help organizations, and through education. The key factors are the empowerment and the participation of the poor. Seventy-five percent of the collection goes to the national CHD office to fund projects throughout the country. The remaining 25% stays in the dioceses for local efforts. To get involved or for more information write: Campaign for Human Development, United States Catholic Conference, 3211 Fourth Street NE, Washington DC 20017-1194.

Weekday Reading
Revelation, chapters 1–11

NOVEMBER 20, 1994
THE LAST SUNDAY IN ORDINARY TIME: CHRIST THE KING

READING I *Daniel 7:13–14*

I saw in the night visions,
and behold, with the clouds of heaven
  there came one like a human being,
and he came before the Ancient of Days,
  before whom he was presented.
And to the human being, was given rule
  and glory and dominion,
that all peoples, nations, and languages
  should serve him;
the rule of this man of heaven is an everlasting rule,
  which shall not pass away,
and his dominion one
  that shall not be destroyed.

READING II *Revelation 1:5–8*

Jesus Christ is the faithful witness, the first-born of the dead, and the ruler of rulers on earth.

To the one who loves us and has freed us from our sins by his blood and made us a dominion, priests to his God and Father, to Jesus Christ be glory and dominion for ever and ever. Amen. Behold, he is coming with the clouds, and every eye will see him, everyone who pierced him; and all tribes of the earth will wail on account of him. Even so. Amen.

"I am the Alpha and the Omega," says the Lord God, who is and who was and who is to come, the Almighty.

GOSPEL *John 18:33–37*

Pilate said to Jesus, "Are you the King of the Jews?" Jesus answered, "Do you say this of your own accord, or did others say it to you about me?" Pilate answered, "Am I a Jew? Your own nation and the chief priests have handed you over to me; what have you done?" Jesus answered, "My kingship is not of this world; if my kingship were of this world, my servants would fight, that I might not be handed over to the Judeans; but my kingship is not from this world." Pilate said to him, "So you are a king?" Jesus answered, "You say that I am a king. For this I was born, and for this I have come into the world, to bear witness to the truth. Everyone who is of the truth hears my voice."

Thanksgiving Day
Monday, October 10, 1994
(CANADA)
Thursday, November 28, 1994
(U.S.A.)

Deuteronomy 8:7–18 When you eat, you must bless the Lord.
1 Timothy 6:6–11, 17–19 Be rich in good works.
Luke 12:15–21 There was a man who had a good harvest.

God has given us the earth to be our homeland, a land flowing with milk and honey. Yet along with this gift, we have been given the command to show our thankfulness by being wise and selfless stewards of the earth, by proclaiming God's peaceable dominion, and by sharing our own gifts with one another.

REFLECTION

The Emperor Tiberius (14–37 CE) was the only king Pontius Pilate knew or cared about. True, there was Herod (4 BCE–39 CE), but he was only a puppet of Rome and a flagrant scandal to his fellow Jews (Mark 6:14–29). So, when the powerful in Jesus' day heard "king," they thought, naturally, of Tiberius, and in terms of absolute power, wealth, armies, intrigue, death, extortion, scandal, slavery, war and so on.

That some barely known local called Jesus could be described to Pilate as "king of the Jews," would have perplexed if not amused the Procurator. Jesus of Nazareth did not resemble any king Pilate knew. Jesus knew this and said so: "My kingship is not of this world." That statement lifts all the issues involved out of Pilate's power, authority and comprehension. Pilate faces a dilemma. It is not, as he himself probably assumed, about Jesus the local trouble-maker who had succeeded in getting the Jerusalem clergy all over Pilate's back. No, Pilate is faced with the dilemma posed by the truth—not a priority in the corridors of human power. He is face to face with the one whom John tells us is the truth in the flesh. So, in a sense, Pilate is on trial here.

Pilate's main claim to historical fame is his association with Jesus of Nazareth. It was Christians, not the Roman authorities, who preserved his memory. Later, he was fired from his job governing the Jews for undue harshness and he "did the right thing" after his king, Tiberius, condemned him: He committed suicide, the acceptable way out for a Roman nobleman who had failed. But before that he faced another king whom he could not comprehend. Jesus did not condemn him. This king fearlessly offered life to a Roman procurator, a power greater than Pilate's power to crucify Jesus.

1. The whole of the Jesus and Pilate scene in John's passion account has to be read to understand its richness: 18:28—19:22. Why does the Fourth Gospel so elaborately expand a scene that the other gospels deal with so briefly? All the clues are in the text.

2. With Christ as king, truth reigns. How onerous are the demands of a disciples' commitment to the truth in all things? How does Jesus, the way, the truth and the life put you on trial?

Practice of FAITH

CROWN OF GLORY. The year of grace ends with the image of Christ crowned—first with thorns, then with the victor's laurel hat, the evergreen crown of glory. No wonder then that Christ the King Sunday gives way next week to the First Sunday of Advent. After you finish your traditional Thanksgiving dinner on Thursday, prepare your Advent wreath. Whether you make or buy the evergreen circle, see it as a promise of the glory that awaits you. On your baptism day the crown of your head was smeared with chrism, that royal oil that makes you another *Christos,* another *Anointed One.* You have the power to live faithfully and love fiercely. The crown of glory—Christ's very own—is promised you. On your baptism day you were given a candle lit from the paschal candle. As you light the first candle next Saturday night, know that Christ's light is in you.

Practice of HOPE

THE ALPHA AND THE OMEGA. Daniel Berrigan, SJ, has spent decades resisting war, serving the poor, and writing for peace. When asked by *Sojourners* magazine to write for a special issue on hope, he penned these words:

Christ, alpha, omega
avatar of hope
whose heart in spite of all
hopes on in spite of us
hopes on for us, in spite of us—
rain, rain on us
untamed, unconstrained
your wildfire storm of hope.

May this be our blessing: to carry a "wildfire storm of hope" into yet another year.

Practice of CHARITY

TO BEAR WITNESS TO THE TRUTH. In practicing charity, we "bear witness to the truth." The truth is that our world is being transformed by the power of God's love, born to us in Jesus Christ and lavished upon us by the Spirit. The relationship between the three persons of the Trinity is perfect charity. This year, through the suggestions offered here and in countless other ways that only you and God know about, you have grown in understanding that charity is not only a "doing for," not only a "giving to," but most importantly a "being with." The only way this world will know the perfect charity of the Trinity is by way of the imperfect charity that we practice. This week, look back at the practices suggested in these pages over the past year. Then repeat the one that moved you most. But this time, invite someone else to join you.

Weekday Reading
Revelation, chapters 12–21

Information On The License To Reprint From
AT HOME WITH THE WORD – 1994

The low bulk-rate prices of *At Home with the Word 1994* are intended to make quantities of the book affordable. A single copy is $6.00; 2–99 copies are $4.00 each; 100 or more copies are $2.50 each. We encourage parishes to buy quantities of this book.

However, Liturgy Training Publications makes a simple reprint license available to parishes that would find it more practical to reproduce some parts of this book. Reflections (and questions), Practices, Prayers of the Season, and/or the holy day boxes can be duplicated for the parish bulletin, or reproduced in other formats. These can be used every week or as often as the license holder chooses. The page size of *At Home with the Word 1994* is 8 x 10 inches.

The license granted is for the period beginning with the First Sunday of Advent—November 28, 1993—through the Solemnity of Christ the King—November 20, 1994.

Note also that the license does *not* cover the scriptures, psalms or morning, evening or night prayer texts. See the acknowledgments page at the beginning of this book for the names and addresses of these copyright owners. Directions for obtaining permission to use these texts are given there.

The materials reprinted under license from LTP may not be sold and may be used only among the members of the community obtaining the license. The license may not be purchased by a diocese for use in its parishes.

No reprinting may be done by the parish until the license is signed by both parties and the fee is paid. Copies of the license agreement will be sent on request. The fee varies with the number of copies to be reproduced on a regular basis:

Up to 100 copies: $100
101 to 500 copies: $300
501 to 1000 copies: $500
More than 1000 copies: $800

For further information, call the reprint permissions department at 312-486-8970 x38.

Sunday Morning

By Gail Ramshaw

A perfect gift for birthdays, baptisms, first communions and Christmas! A beautiful book for young children (and parents) that will help you explore the words and phrases used at Sunday worship. Full-color art and short explanations make this a wonderful, practical teaching tool.

$15.95

Fling Wide the Doors: An Advent and Christmastime Calendar

LTP's *Fling Wide the Doors!* was designed by St. Louis artist Steve Erspamer, SM. It's a three-dimensional tower designed to be part of the seasonal decorations and to draw children to open a door each day – sometimes even two or three! The opened doors allow light to pass through the art producing a stained-glass window effect. The text on the inside of each door is about the saint of the day or is a quotation from scripture. The calendar doesn't stop at Christmas! There are doors for every day from November 30 until the feast of the Baptism of the Lord in January. A booklet comes with the calendar to use each day when opening the doors and praying with the church during Advent.

Family size (12 inches high)	**$10**
Community size (18 inches high)	**$17**

A delight for children of every age!

We invite you to try other LTP resources and prayer books

LTP
1•800•933•1800

Catholic Household Blessings and Prayers

Prepared by the Bishops' Committee on the Liturgy. This beautiful book offers a wealth of prayers and sets a foundation for the Christian life. At the heart of this book are prayers for every day, the prayers to know by heart. Then come the prayers and blessings for the seasons: Advent wreath, Christmas tree, Easter food, feasts of saints and days of national importance. The third section offers blessings for ritual moments in life. The final pages contain the basic Catholic prayers, litanies, psalms and other texts that Christians should know. The calendar of saints is listed in an appendix, and an index is provided. The two-color art, the binding, the paper, large type, three ribbon bookmarks and a presentation bookplate make this a handsome gift to be treasured by you and by others.

Single copies:	**$18.95** each
10 – 99 copies:	**$14.95** each
100 or more copies:	**$12.95** each

At Home with the Word 1995

A new edition of *At Home with the Word* is published each year by Liturgy Training Publications. The 1995 edition will be ready after August 1, 1994. Its contents will begin with the First Sunday of Advent, November 27, 1994. Share *At Home with the Word* with your friends, your study group and those who cannot always be present for Sunday Mass. It is an inexpensive way to bring the scriptures into every household in the parish.

Single copies:	**$6.00** each
2 – 99 copies:	**$4.00** each
100 or more copies:	**$2.50** each

Order At Home with the Word for 1995!

popular anthologies for
PRAYER, STUDY AND MEDITATION

An Advent Sourcebook
edited by Thomas O'Gorman

A Christmas Sourcebook
edited by Mary Ann Simcoe

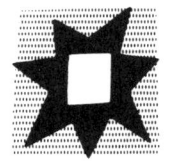

A Lent Sourcebook: The Forty Days
edited by J. Robert Baker, Evelyn Kaehler and Peter Mazar (2-volume set: $23.95)

Our *Sourcebooks* are designed to please body and soul! Wire-bound, they are designed to stay open for study or display. The distinctive art and fine papers show the respect we have for the treasury of hymns, prayers, poetry and wisdom found in these seasonal volumes.

Single copies: **$12.95** each

An Easter Sourcebook: The Fifty Days
edited by Gabe Huck, Gordon Lathrop and Gail Ramshaw

A Sourcebook about Christian Death
edited by Virginia Sloyan

A Baptism Sourcebook
edited by J. Robert Baker, Larry J. Nyberg and Victoria M. Tufano

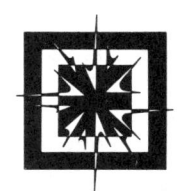

Pocket Prayer Books

Prayerbook for Engaged Couples
by Austin Fleming

A beautiful book for couples in the months before their wedding. This is not a "choose your readings and songs" book. It is, rather, a way to take the wedding liturgy itself as the central moment of many rituals, a way to invite the couple to reflect on and pray with the scriptures and other texts that will be heard at their wedding. Each person and couple has a way of praying. Here is an invitation to both the couple and the person charged with their preparation before marriage to join in prayer and spiritual growth.

$5.95

LTP's pocket-sized prayer book series (all 4 1/4 x 5, 48 pages) fills a need to have Christian prayers at hand when the occasion arises. These prayers are from our traditions, old and new — the treasures of poetry and prose we use in common prayer.

All Pocket Prayer Books:
Single copies: **$1.25** each
25 - 299 copies: **$1.00** each
300 or more copies: **$ .75** each

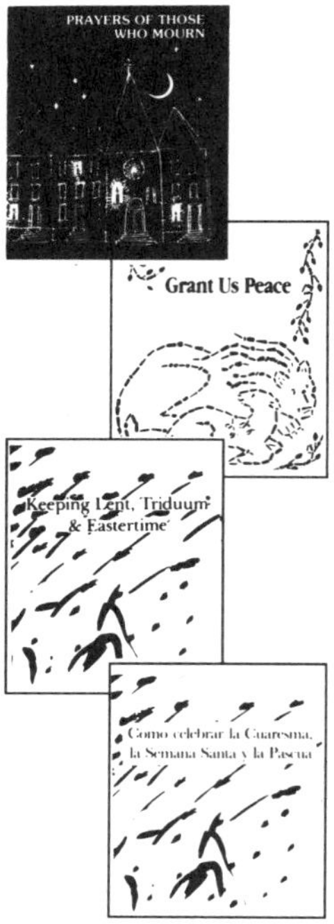

Scripture at Weddings: Choosing and Proclaiming the Word of God
By Graziano Marcheschi and Nancy Seitz Marcheschi.

This book will help the couple select the scriptures that will be heard at their wedding. Use it as a "workbook for lectors and gospel readers" to help prepare those who will proclaim the scriptures. All 28 readings from the lectionary are included with the usual directions for the reader and helpful commentaries.

$4.50

phone 1•800•933•1800   fax 1•800•933•7094

Liturgy Training Publications • 1800 North Hermitage Ave • Chicago IL 60622-1101

Prices subject to change without notice. If ordering from LTP, include 10% shipping and handling charge for shipping within the United States. Minimum $3.00.